Walk!

The

Alpujarras

with

Charles Davis

DISCOVERY WALKING GUIDES LTD

Walk! The Alpujarras
Second Edition - November 2012
Copyright © 2012

Published by
Discovery Walking Guides Ltd
10 Tennyson Close, Northampton NN5 7HJ,
England

Maps
Maps are adapted from **Alpujarras Tour & Trail
Map** published by **Discovery Walking Guides Ltd**.

Photographs
All photographs in this book were supplied by the
author.

Front Cover Photographs

Walk 27   Walk 16

Walk 2   Walk 10

ISBN 9781904946878

The author and publishers have tried to ensure that the information and maps in this publication are as accurate as possible. However, we accept no responsibility for any loss, injury or inconvenience sustained by anyone using this book.

Walk!
The Alpujarras

CONTENTS

WALKS BELOW 1500 METRES

ACKNOWLEDGEMENTS

My thanks to Jeannette who still, quite unaccountably, sustains an invincible readiness to follow me up remote mountains, and to Ros and David who, only marginally less mysteriously, remain happy to publish the results.

After twenty years travelling the world pretending to be a teacher, Charles Davis concluded that prancing about mountain tops was a more productive way of spending his time than standing in front of a classroom, a decision that has lead to over a dozen books for Discovery Walking Guides.

He is also the author of three published novels and several others that are lying in wait ready to pounce on an unwary publisher.

He is accompanied in his peregrinations by Jeannette (a refugee from the French education system) and assorted dogs that other people saw fit to dump in the local Rescue Centre, often for very good reasons.

For more information, see www.redroom.com/author/charles-davis

Charles Davis is also author of the following (Discovery Walking Guides Ltd):-

Walk! The Lake District South
ISBN 9781904946168

Walk! The Axarquia
ISBN 9781904946656

Walk! Dorset
ISBN 9781904946205

Walk! Brittany (North)
ISBN 9781904946359

GR221 Mallorca's Dry Stone Way
ISBN 9781904946489

Bumping About Brittany
ISBN 9781904946441

Walk! Mallorca North & Mountains
ISBN 9781904946496

Walk! La Gomera
ISBN 9781899554904

Walk! Mallorca West
ISBN 9781904946700

Walk! La Palma
ISBN 9781904946687

Walk! The Axarquia
ISBN 9781904946656

Walk! Andorra
ISBN 9781904946045

Walk! The Costa Blanca Mountains
ISBN 9781904946854

- and also

Walk On, Bright Boy	ISBN 9781579621537 (Permanent Press)
Walking The Dog	ISBN 9781579621674 (Permanent Press)
Costa del Sol Walks	ISBN 9788489954397 (Santana)
Costa Blanca Walks	ISBN 9788489954571 (Santana)
Standing At The Crossroads	ISBN9781579622138 (Permanent Press)

Blessed with high peaks, long ridges, deep valleys, clear mountain streams, idyllic aquifers, lovely woods, eye-popping vistas, and a host of picturesque villages, the High Alpujarras of **Granada**, traditionally the singular **Alpujarra Alta** or **Nevedense**, are the setting for some of the best hiking in Spain; for increasing numbers of discerning walkers, this privileged corner of Andalusia has become a place of pilgrimage to which they return year after year.

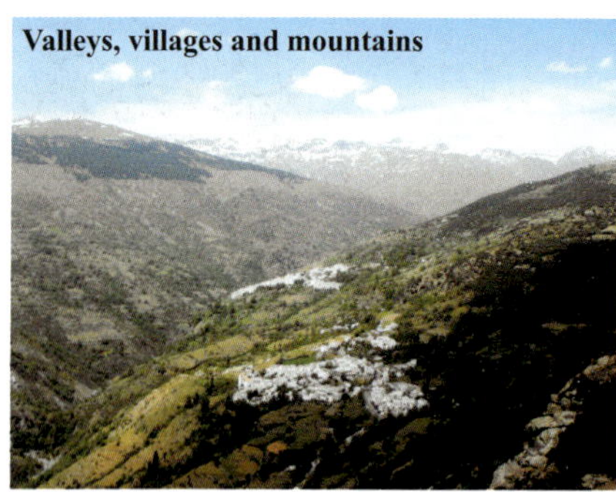

Valleys, villages and mountains

In this fully revised edition of Walk! The Alpujarras, we feature a selection of old favourites plus twenty new walks and new versions of established itineraries, aiming to provide both a perfect introduction for newcomers and sufficient novelty to tempt previous visitors back for another trip.

Ranging from relaxed strolls in the foothills to athletic excursions in the high mountains (including two of the three highest peaks of the **Sierra Nevada**, of which the Alpujarras form the southern flank), the itineraries detailed here will take you as far into the mountains as you want to go, and offer enough variety of landscape and altitude to guarantee good, year round walking.

To facilitate planning and selection, the walks have been reclassified according to altitude. As a rough guide, walks below 1500 metres are practical throughout the year, though they can be tough going at the height of the summer. Walks between 1500 and 2500 metres are best done between late spring and autumn. Realistically speaking, for most people, those above 2500 metres are summer/early autumn walks, though don't forget that even in summer the temperature at 3000 metres can drop to zero at night, and conditions can change suddenly and dramatically.

WHEN TO GO

Subject to the above stipulations about the seasonal feasibility/desirability of discrete walks, there are a number of considerations that may influence when you choose to visit the Alpujarras. For obvious reasons, spring is the best time for lovers of wildflowers and mountain torrents, though it's also the season when paths are most vulnerable to landslips and the rivers will be in spate, rendering some fords (even bridges) impassable.

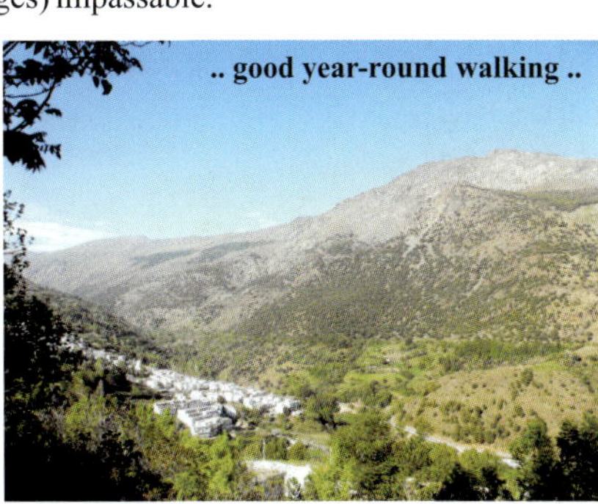

The chestnut forests are at their finest in autumn, bird watching is best outside the summer months, and the winter weather in the high mountains is most stable around February. If you're not keen on crowds, avoid Easter week and August.

WHAT TO EXPECT

The Alpujarras have been likened to the Alps, the Pyrenees and the Atlas mountains, and there is some justification for all these comparisons. However, they remain uniquely themselves and their distinctive character has proved a lure for individuals as diverse as Gerald Brenan, the Bloomsburyite who settled in the Alpujarras after the First World War and subsequently became a Spanish icon in his own right, celebrating his seven year sojourn in the classic 'South From Granada', and Chris Stewart, whose bestselling 'Driving Over Lemons' has done so much to popularize the region with the British.

Historically, the area is significant as the last bastion of the Moriscos, the Christianized Moors who populated the mountains until their expulsion in 1609, and whose culture continues to influence and even define Alpujarran toponymy, architecture, agriculture, and, to a lesser extent, cottage industries and cuisine. The very name 'Alpujarra' is of Arabic origin, various etymologies claiming it comes from words for 'grass land', 'turbulent', 'unvanquished', 'fortified', and 'white mountains', any one of which would do as a description of this snow capped rocky fastness whose aquifers fed some of the most fertile valleys in the country.

For many visitors, the principal attraction of the Alpujarras are the White Villages that lend an almost Berberesque aspect to the mountains. **Pampaneira**, **Bubíon**, and **Capileira** in the **Poqueira** valley are the most famous, and they all offer fine walking in the immediate vicinity as well as ready access to the high mountains

However, it's worth getting off the beaten track a little, for instance to the lovely hamlets of the **Tahá** (**Fondales**, **Mecina**, **Ferreirola**, and **Atalbéitar**), or the larger villages along its rim (**Pitres**, **Pórtugos**, **Busquistar**), or to **Trevélez** which, at 1486 metres, often claims (wrongly) to be the highest municipality in Spain, or to the horticultural and chestnut capitals of **Bérchules** and **Mecina-Bombarón**, or (in winter) to the sleepy, perfectly preserved settlements south of **Cádiar** (**Lobras**, **Nieles**, **Cástaras**, **Notáez**, and **Almegijar**).

Even the 'main' towns in the west, **Lanjarón** (famous for its mineral water, which is sold all over Spain) and **Órgiva** (home to the highest concentration of expats) are not without their charms. Wherever you go, though, the walking is the thing, and the walking is almost invariably good.

At lower altitudes, there are lovely cobbled mule trails winding between terraced fields, and though many of the fields have been abandoned due to the rigours of farming such steeply shelving terrain, the chances are that you will still see pannier laden mules transporting feedstuff and crops between hamlets.

Terracing above Lanjarón

The silk trade, which did so much to define the countryside, died out after the expulsion of the Moors, but the mulberry trees on which the silk worms fed are still abundant, and there's more than one hiker who has returned to their lodging streaked with the sticky and nigh on indelible evidence of their foraging. I know. I'm one of them.

Flora and insects flourish

Once abandoned, the fields tend to be reclaimed by more varieties of broom than I'd care to name let alone identify, though principal and most distinctive among them is retama with its long, spindly, splayed fronds speckled with yellow flowers. Alyssum, aloe, agave, caper, camomile, rosemary, thyme, saxifrage, and oregano grow wild, too.

Higher up come the great (and greatly vulnerable; don't even think of lighting a fire) chestnut, oak, and pine forests, laced with logging tracks, royal ways, drove trails, and transhumance paths leading to the high pasture and the bare, rocky wildness of the peak country, including **Mulhacén**, which at 3483 metres is the Iberian peninsula's highest summit. But by far the most distinctive features of the Alpujarran topography are the *acequias*.

Who first developed these irrigation channels tapping the aquifers of the high mountain is disputed, some crediting the Moors, others the Romans. Either way, it had become a Moorish 'art' by the time Felipe II expelled the remaining Moslems after the rebellion of 1568, as he made one family in each village stay behind to show the Christian settlers how the system worked, a situation sufficiently fraught with potential as to inspire my first novel, 'Walk On, Bright Boy'.

Some *acequias* were hacked into cliff faces by masons suspended over vertiginous drops (beware of exploring *acequias* without taking a close look at the contour lines on the map), but most follow gentler slopes and are more like ditches, dug into the hillside and reinforced by the skein of roots encouraged by filtration.

Occasionally you will see an 'improved' version lined with PVC or concrete to prevent leakage, but probably not for long as the ground tends to dry out, the supporting vegetation dies, the undergrowth rots, and the whole lot falls apart.

Acequia Almiar (Walk 17)

Walking along *acequias* is a delight - but remember, these are still working paths. You may see an *acequero* with an adze fishing rocks from the water, clearing obstructions, or rebuilding the wall. For him walking is a chore, not necessarily a pleasure. Recreational walkers should be careful not to exacerbate wear and tear.

Given the influx of tourists and the conflicting interests of leisure seekers and labourers, the people of the Alpujarras are remarkably welcoming, and are nearly always ready to help visitors with advice and directions. We still quote the occasion when, camping wild in the entrance to a field, we suddenly saw the field's owner approaching in a battered van, which he had just driven half way up the mountain on a rough dirt track with the express intention of inspecting his field. Scrabbling to make ourselves scarce, we apologised for any inconvenience caused and said we'd get out of the way pronto. The man wasn't having any of it. "¡Tranquilo! ¡Tranquilo!" He'd come back the next day. In the Alpujarras, 'Can I help you?' generally means 'Can I help you?', not 'What are you doing on my land?' The locals also do a nice line in wry observations on the eccentricities of tourists. One old boy saw me labouring up the mountains with a couple of unwilling dogs and told me I should walk with a goat instead of a dog, since at least a goat gave milk!

WAYMARKED PATHS

PR waymarking (Walk 29)

There were relatively few official waymarked paths when we first went to the Alpujarras, but nowadays it's hard to keep up with all the new PRs (Pequeño Recorridos or Short Walks identified by yellow and white blazes) and SLs (Senderos Locales or Local Paths with green and white blazes) being wayposted by the local authorities.

When these constitute a major part or the totality of a described itinerary, the SL/PR tag appears in the title. Otherwise, stretches of the official routes coinciding with our walks are mentioned in the text. There are also three long distance paths.

In previous editions of this book, the Alpujarran stretch of the **GR7** (Gran Recorrido, red and white waymarks), which runs from Andalusia to Andorra, featured as a series of linear itineraries linking the main villages on our map. We've opted to incorporate the best bits of the **GR7** into circular walks.

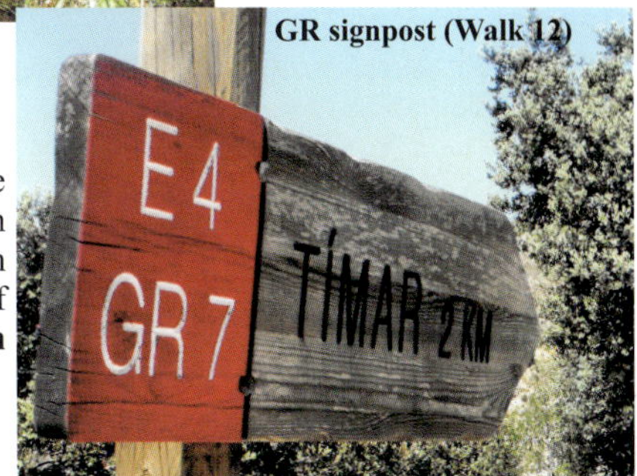

This is also the case for the **GR142**, dubbed 'Between Peaks & Valleys', a 144km route traversing the foothills of the Alpujarras from **Lanjarón** to **Fiñana** in **Almeria**.

The big innovation for long distance walking in the region since we first mapped the area is the **GR240 Sendero Sulayr**, named after the Moorish term for the *sierra*, Yabal Sulayr or 'Mountain of the Sun', a nineteen stage, 300 kilometre tour of the entire **Sierra Nevada**. At first glance, this seemed like a hugely exciting development, but look at it a little more closely and one discovers a couple of fairly fundamental flaws. Not only does the itinerary cleave a little too closely to dirt tracks, there are long stretches that imply carrying a tent and several days' worth of food, in which case you might as well head for the high ground rather than skirting its edges.

That said, it does bring to attention and protect some little known paths, at least two of which were completely new to me. Three of the more accessible and more desirable sections feature in our described itineraries, the full route falling within our area is marked on the map, and more information is available through the links in Appendix B.

Also worth mentioning here the **PR299 Ruta Medieval**, a long PR between **Juviles** and **Pitres**, piecing together some particularly fine and little-known paths, stretches of which feature in Walks 9, 10, 11, & 12.

A WORD ABOUT WORDS

In the descriptions, I've sought to avoid excessive detail. Nonetheless, tricky points are described minutely and I hope there's enough information to keep you on track and enhance the experience. The number of words does not correspond to distance covered. A paragraph may detail a hundred yards, a line half a mile. It all depends on the complexity of the terrain.

Although inevitably subjective, I have sought consistency by describing all climbs as 'steep', 'steady', or 'gentle' except on the rare occasions when I found something particularly onerous and was moved to reach for a metaphor rather than cluttering up the text with a lot of expletive symbols.

A dirt track is anything that might be used (albeit misguidedly in some cases) by a car. A trail is a broad path or a narrow track, often cobbled with rocks from the days when these were the principal thoroughfares between villages. A path is a path is a path, except when it's a goat track, which is a wilful sort of 'way' frequently disappearing and splintering into a confusing web calculated to baffle non-herbivorous bipeds.

Bear in mind that timings are all 'pure'. All the lounging about (and there's a lot of that in the Alpujarras) has been edited out. Only the superfit or frankly deranged will complete the walks in the stated time. Allow at least fifteen minutes on top of every hour for pathfinding, pleasure taking and breath catching.

GETTING THERE, GETTING ABOUT, GETTING A BED, AND GETTING FED

Despite a brief dalliance with Ryan Air, **Granada** has not really caught up with the no frills, low cost flight phenomenon, and **Málaga** remains the best destination for cheap flights. Once there, I'd recommend hiring a car and driving east along the coast to **Salobreña** (E15/N340 direction **Motril/Almería**) then following the **Valle Lecrín** (N323 direction Granada) north to the **Lanjarón** turning (A348), which takes about two hours. Otherwise, there's a daily coach to **Órgiva** from the central bus station (dep. 3.30pm, rtn. 8.15am) and more frequent services changing at **Motril** or **Granada**. There are two buses to **Granada** from **Málaga** airport (11.30am and 6.30pm), otherwise there are buses every thirty minutes from **Málaga**'s airport to its bus station, which has an hourly service to **Granada**.

Though a car makes life considerably easier, most walks are accessible by public transport. To get into and around the Alpujarras by bus, check out the Alsina Graells site www.alsa.es and tick the 'consulta sin fecha' box if you're making general plans and aren't sure which day you'll be travelling on. Although their site displays a flabbergasting degree of optimism (suggesting timetables are valid until 2099!), I prefer not to publish lots of information that may be outdated overnight (and I'm not suggesting this book will still be in print in 2099), so it's worth making preliminary plans on line before heading for Spain.

Accommodation in the Alpujarras is plentiful and cheap. Except for Christmas, Easter and sometimes August, you should have no trouble finding a room on the spot.

As with buses, in this digital age there is no point publishing information that might be superseded the moment we go to print, but a good starting point for booking accommodation is the link in Appendix B.

There are four campsites in the Alpujarras; two at **Órgiva**, one in **Pitres** and one in **Trevélez** (the last is far and away the best and the only one I can really recommend), and a designated camping area at **Puente Palo** above **Cáñar**. See Appendix B for a link to a survey of the unmanned refuges in the high mountains.

The Alpujarran diet is a meat (carne) and potatoes affair and generally very good (for the palate if not the arteries). *Charcuterie* is a specialty and hams hang from every ceiling. Classic local dishes include spiced and/or dried sausages (chorizo, longaniza, salchichón), black pudding (morcilla), broad beans fried with ham (habas con jamón), and any number of cuts of pork (cerdo), lamb (cordero), kid (choto), rabbit (conejo) and chicken (pollo), generally griddled (a la plancha), smothered in garlic (ajillo), or stewed in an earthenware casserole dish (cazuela). Beef is elderly veal (ternera) and not very exciting. *Lomo* is loin, usually pork, *chuletas* are chops, *bocadillos* are sandwiches, and *casero/a* indicates something home made.

Doubtless, vegetarians will be disheartened by this carnal catalogue, concluding they'd best bring their vitamin supplements with them . . . and rightly so. Traditionally in Spain, a 'vegetarian' dish was a plate of beans with a lump of dripping lard melting all over it, and anyone insisting on something purely vegetarian, would be faced with a sorry looking plate of peas and an even sorrier looking waiter. This is starting to change, but if you do find yourself stuck with a conventional menu, look for *revuelto* (eggs scrambled with vegetables), *tortilla de patatas* (Spanish omelette), *berenjenas fritas* (fried aubergine), *patatas a lo pobre* (potatoes fried with garlic and peppers), or *sopa de ajo* (garlic soup) . . . and hope the chef resists the temptation to embellish it with a little cured ham. *Ensaladas mixtas* are usually 'garnished' with half a tin of tuna.

Despite some trout fishing in local streams, the Alpujarras are not the obvious place for fish (pescado), though the ubiquitous salted cod (bacalao, as much the national dish as paella) is on most menus, and if you can't get to one of the restaurants on the coast, you might like to try boquerónes (fresh anchovies), *calamares* (squid rings) or, their babies, *chipirónes*.

The pudding is not an art the Spanish have perfected and often entails a glossy card listing the factory made ice creams on offer. However, most places will have rice pudding (arroz con leche), cottage cheese with honey (queso con miel), crème caramel (flan), and an assortment of fresh and dried fruit.

Breakfast (desayuno) is equally unimaginative and generally means toasted, baguette-style bread (tostadas) with *tomate* (crushed garlic and tomato), *aceite* (olive oil), *mermelada* (jam), or *mantequilla* (butter, which is never as good as the oil).

Tapas are sometimes still given free with a drink, rather than being a bought appetizer, which they have become in most of Spain. *Raciónes* are larger portions of *tapas*, *platos combinados* a full single course meal, and the *menu del dia* a cheap three course lunch.

Wine is cheap and generally cheerful. The locals drink *costa* which tastes like a bizarre blend of fortified wine and *retsina*. Some of it is vile (beware if someone offers you something they are pleased to call 'wine' and claim is 22° proof!), but at its best it goes down with dangerous ease.

Alhambra beer (cerveza) is not bad by Spanish standards, shorts are never short, *sol y sombra* is a kill or cure mixture of brandy and *anis* often deemed necessary early in the morning (this may explain why the rest of breakfast is so pedestrian), and *carajillo* is the name given to the endearing Spanish habit of brightening up their coffee with a tot of brandy.

'Nuff said. Go forth, enjoy. The world is your playground.

The highlands to the west of Mulhacén, as seen on Walk 33

 our rating for effort/exertion:- **1** very easy **2** easy **3** average **4** energetic **5** strenuous

 approximate **time** to complete a walk (compare your times against ours early in a walk) - does not include stopping time

 approximate walking **distance** in kilometres

 250m / 850m approximate **ascents/descents** in metres (N=negligible)

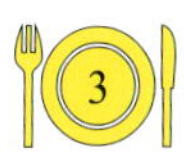 **circular** route

linear route

figure of eight route

risk of **vertigo**

refreshments (may be at start or end of a route only)

- Walk descriptions include:
- timing in minutes, shown as (40M)
- compass directions, shown as (NW)
- heights in metres, shown as (1355m)
- GPS waypoints, shown as (Wp.3)

Notes on the text

Place names are shown in **bold text**, except where we refer to a written sign, when they are enclosed in single quotation marks. Local or unusual words are shown in *italics*, and are explained in the accompanying text.

MAP NOTES

The map sections used in this book have been taken from **Alpujarras Tour & Trail Super-Durable Map** 3rd edition (ISBN 9781904946885) published by Discovery Walking Guides Ltd.

All map sections are aligned so that north is at the top of the page. In the interests of clarity waypoint positions and numbers refer to the walking route illustrated by the map section. Adjoining and inter-linking walking routes do not have any waypoints shown on those routes.

Alpujarras Tour & Trail Super-Durable Map 3rd edition is a 1:40,000 scale full colour map. For more information on DWG publications, visit:

www.walking.demon.co.uk   www.dwgwalking.co.uk

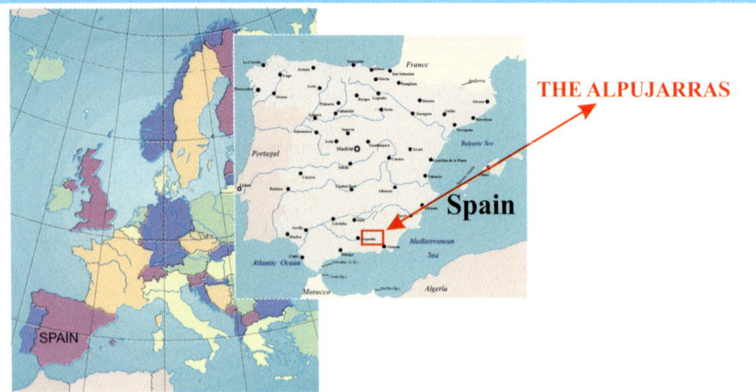
SPAIN
Spain
Portugal
France
Madrid
Mediterranean Sea
Atlantic Ocean
Morocco
Algeria
THE ALPUJARRAS

Mulhacen
32
Caballo
30
P. Alegas
20
19
21
31
16
18
23
Capileira
4
17
22
5 Pitres Por
Bubion
Pampaneira
3
6
Cañar
Mecina
7
Lanjaron
Carataunas
Fondales
2
8
1
Orgiva
Los Tablones
T

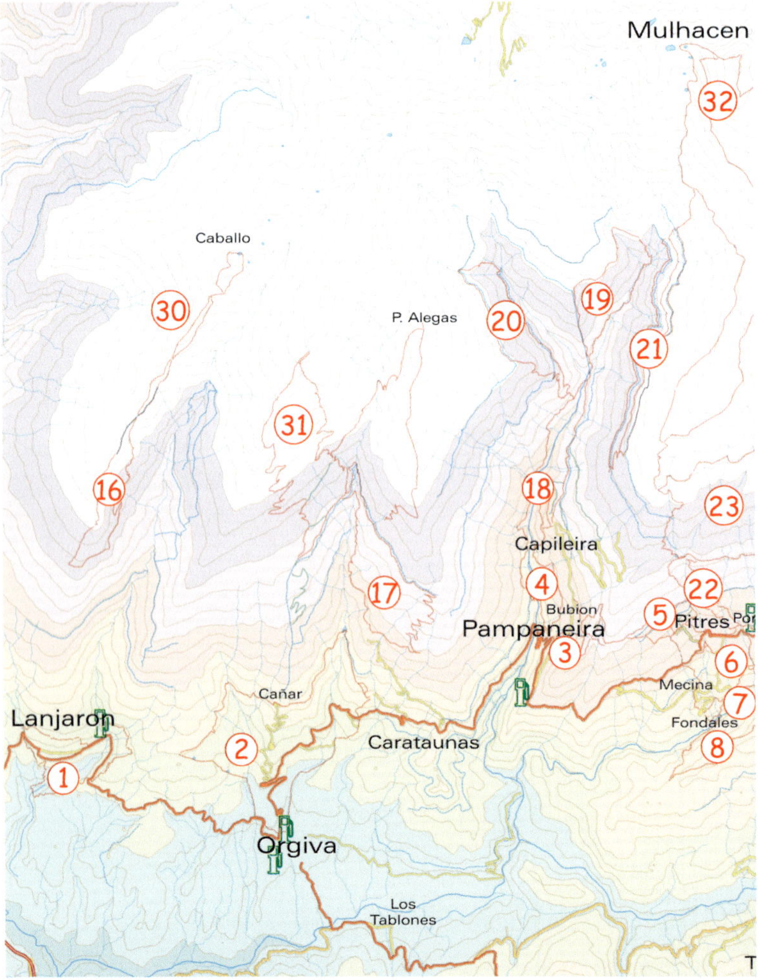

This locator map and the maps
accompanying the walk descriptions
are adapted from
Alpujarras Tour & Trail Super-
Durable Map
(ISBN 9781904946885)
published by Discovery Walking
Guides Ltd.

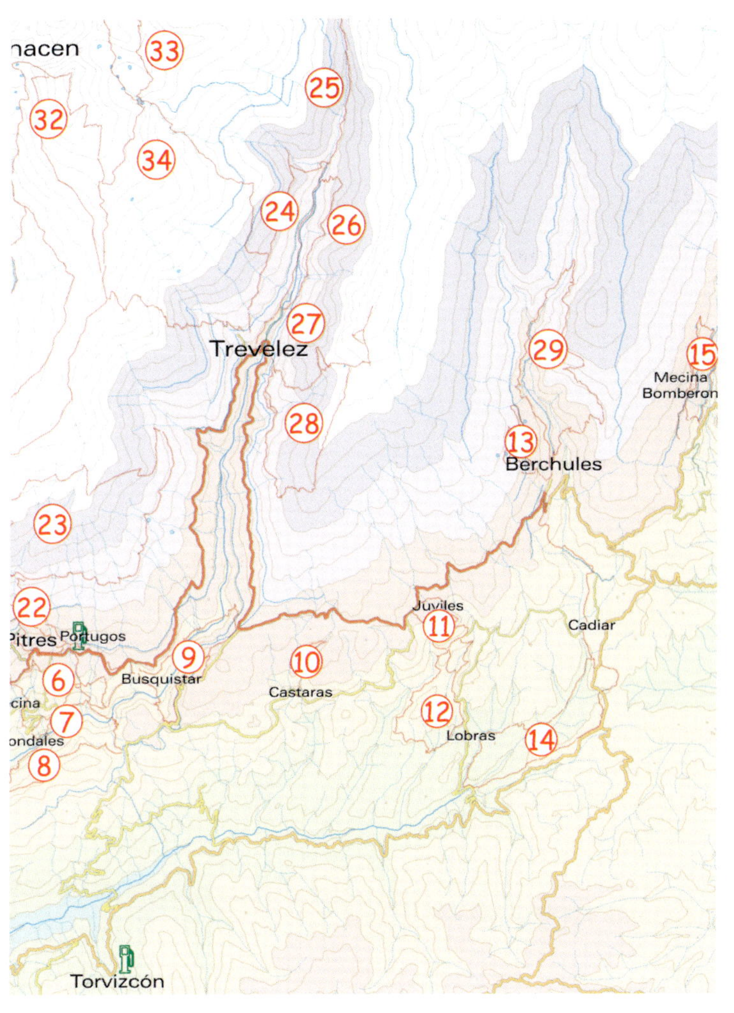

MAP LEGEND

The map sections which accompany the walk descriptions in this book are adapted from:

Alpujarras Tour & Trail Super-Durable Map
(ISBN 9781904946885 published by Discovery Walking Guides Ltd.).

This 1:40,000 scale map is recommended for use alongside this book. It is available from bookshops, from amazon.co.uk and direct from the publishers at:

www.walking.demon.co.uk   www.dwgwalking.co.uk

Altitude

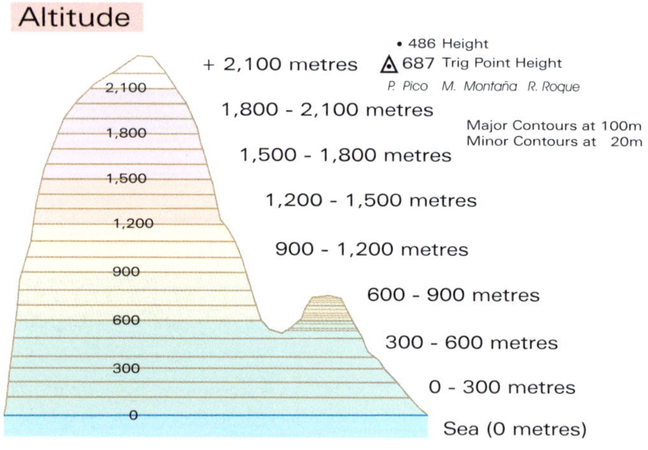

Roads, Tracks & Trails

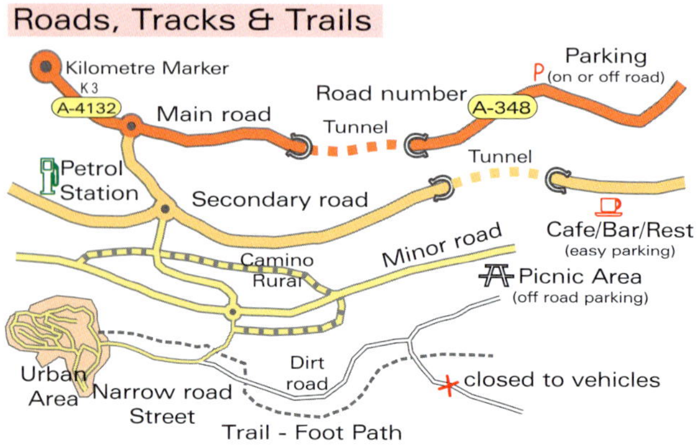

Features

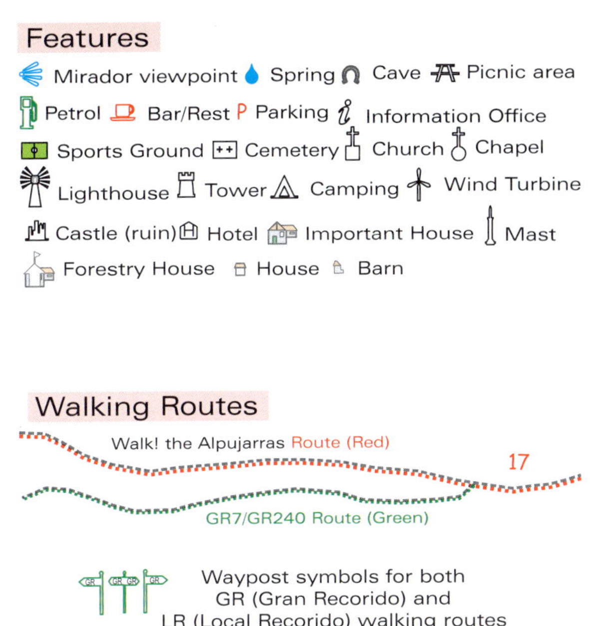

- Mirador viewpoint
- Spring
- Cave
- Picnic area
- Petrol
- Bar/Rest
- P Parking
- Information Office
- Sports Ground
- Cemetery
- Church
- Chapel
- Lighthouse
- Tower
- Camping
- Wind Turbine
- Castle (ruin)
- Hotel
- Important House
- Mast
- Forestry House
- House
- Barn

Walking Routes

Walk! the Alpujarras Route (Red)

17

GR7/GR240 Route (Green)

Waypost symbols for both
GR (Gran Recorido) and
LR (Local Recorido) walking routes

USING GPS IN THE ALPUJARRAS

GPS reception is generally good on all of the walking routes included in our new Walk! the Alpujarras. If it's your first visit to this region then GPS will provide you with the pinpoint navigational accuracy you can rely on while discovering these exciting and adventurous landscapes, plus helping you quickly locate the start of each walking route. The GPS waypoint files for all routes are available as free downloads from our website at:-

www.walking.demon.co.uk/pnfs.htm
www.dwgwalking.co.uk/pnfs.htm

Download the Walk! the Alpujarras zip file, then unzip the file into its individual gpx files, then load the gpx file(s) into your GPS unit.

If you have a modern 'mapping' GPS unit such as an Adventurer or Lowrance Endura then you can use the digital edition of the Alpujarras Tour & Trail Map to give you a real time mapping display showing exactly where you are on the walking route. Our Tour & Trail Maps are also available for use on your 3G phones and tablets using apps from Viewranger, Memory Map and MyTrails.

All of Walk! the Alpujarras' walking routes can be easily navigated without using GPS by following the detailed walk description for each route. However, using GPS gives you the added confidence of knowing exactly where you are on each route, especially if you are using a mapping GPS or phone/tablet equipped with the Alpujarras Tour & Trail Map.

If you want to know about GPS and how it can help your own adventuring, or you are thinking of buying a GPS, then see our 'Choosing and Using GPS' on our website. 'GPS The Easy Way', £4.99 for the book or free as a pdf download on our website, will give you a clear explanation of how these modern navigational aids work and can be used for your benefit:-

'Ask not "What is GPS?"
Ask "What can GPS do for me?"

WALKING EQUIPMENT

Here's a brief summary of the basics we carry during walking research:-
Backpack
A 25-30 litre day pack with plenty of outside pockets with well-padded straps and a waist strap. A ventilated back panel and stand-off frame helps clear sweat on hot days and tough routes.
Footwear
Never compromise on footwear. Choose a thick, hard sole with plenty of grip and a well padded foot-bed. Make sure that you've have covered plenty of kilometres in them before coming to the Alpujarras.
Sun Protection
A comfortable sun hat that stays on in the wind is also useful in rain. Sunglasses and high-factor sun cream are highly recommended.
Water & Food
A couple of ½ litre bottles is the minimum, plus another couple of litres for more demanding routes. Even on shorter routes, carry some survival rations; chocolate bars, dried fruit and the like can provide welcome comfort.
Medical Kit
Antiseptic wipes/cream, plasters, bandage, lip salve, tweezers, pain killers..
Navigation
Buy the best guide book and the best map and carry them with you. A compass is useful but a GPS unit is far more so - see 'Using GPS in the Alpujarras' in this book..
Clothing
Choose loose comfortable clothing and carry a lightweight waterproof jacket and extra warm layers. Be prepared for any conditions (depends when you go)..
Other Equipment
Digital camera, monocular/binoculars, whistle, mobile phone, money inc. coins for machines.

The Editors

Too often, town centred trails are the product of some sedentary functionary despatching a hapless minion with a moped and a pot of paint and a very modest stock of imagination and instructions not to return until he's done a bit of daubing on the crash barriers of the local B-road. The **Sendero Circular de Lanjarón** is something else. Evidently conceived by somebody who knows the landscape intimately and loves it well, the trail is nicely judged to show you the very best of **Lanjarón** (Moorish castle, cobbled mule trails, lovely valley, great views, and corners so recondite that no casual visitor could hope to find them unassisted), taking what appears on paper to be a very domestic walk and lending it a real sense of adventure.

Pathfinding is mildly challenging between Wps.7&11, but I found my way with only a sketchy notion of where we were meant to be going, so the map and description should be sufficient to keep you on trail. The waymarking and wayposting are adequate, but not infallible.

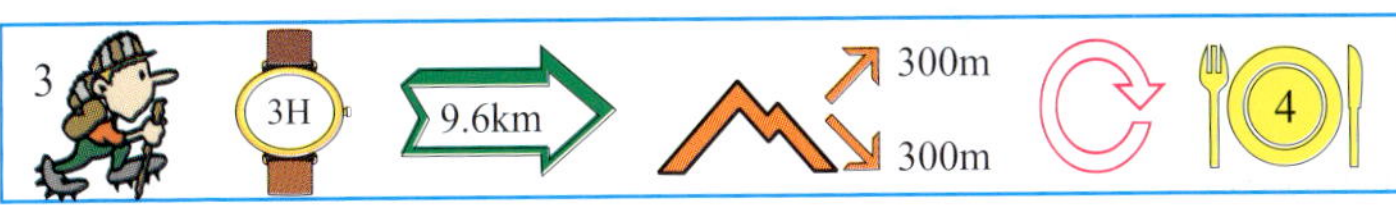

Access: by car/on foot from Lanjarón
The described route is a slight variant on the official version and begins at the entrance to the **Parque del Salado** in front of the **Hotel Balneario** on the A348 at the western end of **Lanjarón**, where there is ample roadside parking. In the unlikely event of all the spaces being taken, additional parking is available 100 metres up the road beside the **Frenazo Restaurant** at the start of **Pista Forestal 1** (see Appendix A).

Directly in front of the hotel entrance (Wp.1 0M), we take the **Paseo al Castillo** through **Parque de Salado**. Descending to the left alongside the watercourse bisecting the park, we reach a waterfall where a broad, stepped trail (4M) descends amid eucalyptus and pine to join the wayposted PR (Wp.2 7M).

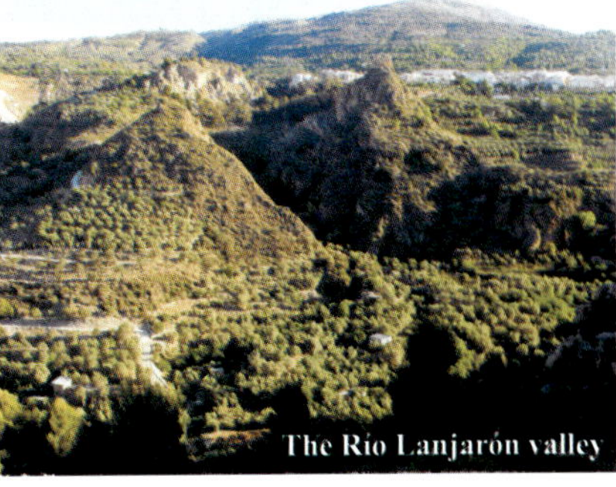

The Río Lanjarón valley

Bearing left, we cross open ground to approach a tall retaining wall, on the right hand side of which our trail continues to descend alongside the watercourse, offering us our first glimpse of the castle. At a junction with a track just short of the castle (Wp.3 13M), we bear left to reach the castle esplanade where we turn left on a concrete track climbing toward the **Lanjarón** bypass. Immediately below the bypass, we fork right (Wp.4 20M) and descend steeply on a surfaced track.

When the track ends at **Cortijo La Mistral** (Wp.5 23M), we continue descending in front of the *cortijo* entrance on a narrow path that soon resolves itself into a cobbled trail, passing a succession of idyllic ruins.

When the trail joins a track (Wp.6 28M), we turn right and follow the track into a terrace path that descends across intermittent cobbling to reach an immaculately tended and heavily gated garden directly below a large date palm (39M).

.. an immaculately tended garden ..

Onward progress appears to be blocked here, but in fact, just to the left of the garden, the PR continues on a narrow overgrown path passing another ruin, where it becomes a clear cobbled trail again.

Zigzagging down toward the **Río Lanjarón**, we pass a derelict cabin with a corrugated roof, in front of which, at an intersection of irrigation channels (Wp.7 44M), we carry straight on. Shadowing the course of the river, we skirt then traverse groves of olive trees and pass in front of a noisy kennel.

Fifty metres after the kennel, just below the end of a dirt track, we bear left, crossing a single log bridge and passing a waypost (52M). After a further fifty metres, waymarks indicate where there used to be a bridge over the river (Wp.8). At the time of writing, the bridge has been washed away, but it's a relatively easy ford and should pose no problems.

The ford at Wp.8

The far bank of the river does pose a problem (albeit a very modest one) of orientation.

Ten metres south of the riverbank, we bear left and climb steeply alongside terraces of olive trees to cross a partially interred *acequia*, above which we climb to the right on a clear path that zigzags up to skirt the western flank of a rocky ridge overlooking the lower reaches of the *río*.

After crossing the back of the ridge and veering left in front of a fence (Wp.9 67M), we pass to the left of a new house. Continuing alongside the fence, initially on a very narrow way then along a broader path crossing a scrub clad slope, we follow the fence until it curls round a reservoir and we maintain an easterly direction parallel to a minor road, which we join 150 metres later

(Wp.10 79M). Turning left, we follow this road for 550 metres until it reaches the A348 (Wp.11 89M).

Fifty metres to the left, just beyond the bend, we cross the A348 (quickly, cars nip round here at a hell of a lick) and continue on a wayposted path climbing towards a canalized torrent. Staying to the left of the torrent, we traverse bare, waymarked rock, heading towards a small antenna, 100 metres short of which, we hop across the canalization to join the end of a concrete track (Wp.12 95M). Turning left, we climb steadily (it's a hard old slog in hot weather) to pass the antenna and reach the charming little **Ermita de Tajo de la Cruz**, which is a good spot for a break early in the morning when the terrace is still shady.

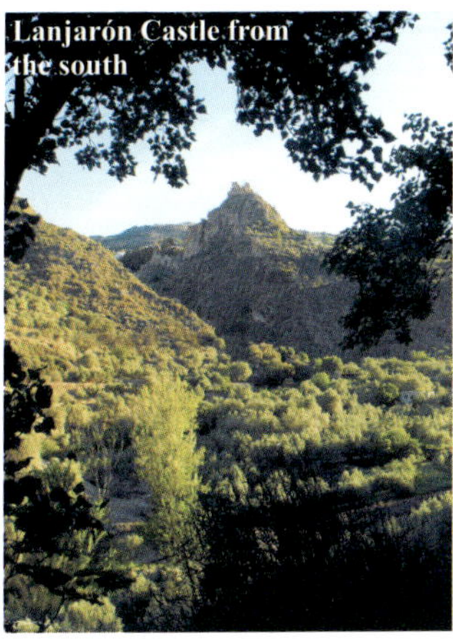

Lanjarón Castle from the south

Directly behind the *ermita*, we intersect with the **GR142** at a crossroads formed by a dirt track off to the right, a rough path climbing directly ahead, and a cobbled mule trail to the left (Wp.13 102M). Turning left on the GR waymarked and PR wayposted trail, we descend to a junction with a concrete lane, at which point the GR and PR diverge (Wp.14 106M). Turning right, we climb gently to the first sharp right hand bend (Wp.15 114M), where we carry straight on along a narrower asphalted branch that winds through a shady dell before crossing the **GR7** (Wp.16 119M).

Thereafter, we ignore all branches and simply stick to the lane as it meanders along the hillside for 800 metres until we come to the signposted intersection with the old **Tello** trail, now designated as the **PR34** (Wp.17 134M).

If the signposts disappear, this junction is just before the asphalted lane dwindles to an even narrower concrete track. Forking left, we descend on a rough, intermittently cobbled path to join a lane behind the road bridge over the **Río Lanjarón** (Wp.18 141M). Turning left, we descend past the **Fuente Hoya del Grillo** and cross the road bridge.

Following the A348 into **Lanjarón**, we pass a petrol station, 300 metres after which we have a choice of routes (Wp.19 151M). If refreshments seem imperative, carry straight on through the centre of town on the road, though bear in mind that, given the variety and quantity of bars en route, there is material here for the mother of all pub crawls. It's also a lot noisier. Alternatively, sticking to PR, immediately before the road sign for 'Granada' and 'Centro Urbano', we turn right, then take the first left into the tranquil back streets of **Lanjarón**. What follows sounds complicated due to all the intersections, but is reasonably easy to follow on the ground.

Adjacent to a baker, we turn right into **Piedra de Castaño** street (Wp.20 155M), at the end of which, we take a narrow, waymarked path to the left (Wp.21 158M) that climbs past a turning on the right to cross a surfaced track (Wp.22) onto another, narrower surfaced track. Climbing amid a scattering of cottages, we fork left at a Y junction (Wp.23 165M) to approach a house called 'El Aguacate'. Officially the PR stays on the surfaced track passing in front of **El Aguacate**, but there is a narrow public path passing behind the house that is more pleasant, rejoining the official route 100 metres later

After another 150 metres, the track reaches a triple junction where we fork left on a narrow path beginning in the crux of the two lefthand forks (Wp.24 171M). The path runs alongside an *acequia* above an embankment, passing behind a ruin before shadowing a retaining wall to reach another track, which is surfaced for its first 50 metres. Ignoring a track on the left with a signpost for 'Lanjarón 15m' (179M), we continue on the main track for another 75 metres to join the broad concreted stretch at the foot of **Pista Forestal 1** (Wp.25 180M), where we turn left to return to our starting point.

A grand walk in every sense, employing the **GR142** (Wps.1 to 10), **GR7** (Wps.10 to 25) and a few bits I made up myself (Wp.26 to the end) to visit two villages, two rivers, and explore the wilder recesses of the western Alpujarras. The highlight is the extraordinary **Dique 24**, a dam built in the 1940s to control flash floods that has engendered an idyllic glade in the bed of the **Río Chico**. It's one of the loveliest hideaways in the area and a perfect spot for a picnic or just lounging about in the shade of the trees.

The lower reaches of the **Río Sucio**, which we skirt in the first part of our itinerary, have long been the demesne of Órgiva's 'alternative'population, and you can expect to see some of their encampments creeping up the sides of the valley. I mention this since unexpectedly coming across a tepee full of hippies might not be to everybody's taste, but experience suggests they are a benign if occasionally noisy bunch, and our walk never approaches the heartland of the community.

The start and end of the itinerary are punishingly hot in the height of summer, so choose your day carefully. Otherwise, in hot weather or if you don't fancy the stiff climb at the start, the linear route between **Cáñar** and **Dique 24** is highly recommended. There is a slight risk of vertigo.

Access by car/on foot:

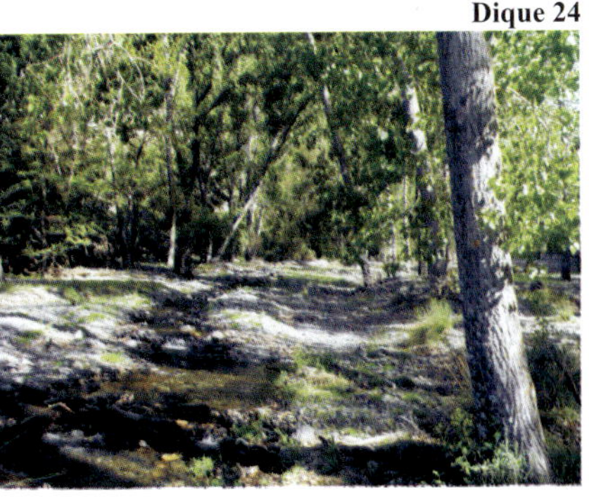
Dique 24

From the BP station at the western edge of **Órgiva** (Wp.1 0M) (where you can usually find parking in the shade), we cross the road bridge over the **Río Chico** and, ignoring a branch to the right, climb to the junction of the A348 and A4132 (Wp.2 4M). 75 metres up the A4132 (Wp.3), we turn left onto a narrow path climbing through a cleft in the rock.

After skirting a fenced property and following a holloway behind a ruin, we traverse terraces of olive and almond trees, beyond which our path becomes a narrow dirt track. When the track rejoins the A348 (Wp.4 11M), we turn right and follow the road for 250 metres until we reach the bridge over the **Río Sucio**, where there is a **GR142** fingerpost and a metal sign for the hamlet of 'Las Barreras' (Wp.5 13M). Sticking with the **GR142**, we turn right on a track along the left bank of the **Río Sucio**, which we follow for a little under 900 metres. Fifty metres after passing a house shrouded in eucalyptus trees, we fork left (Wp.6 27M) on a poorly waymarked track fording the river, immediately after which we fork left again on a path. At a T junction 50 metres above the river (Wp.7 30M), we turn right and promptly start climbing steeply in a westerly direction along a badly eroded path that passes a small reservoir before veering right below a solitary outcrop of rock, the **Rabiete** (Wp.8 47M).

After passing above the dilapidated **Cortijo del Conde** or **de Tejas** (the count in question being the only man wealthy enough to roof his house with tiles), our path runs parallel to a wooded gully, climbing slightly to pass an old reservoir before traversing terraces of almond trees and open scrubland to reach a dirt track 25 metres short of the **GR7** (Wp.9 74M).

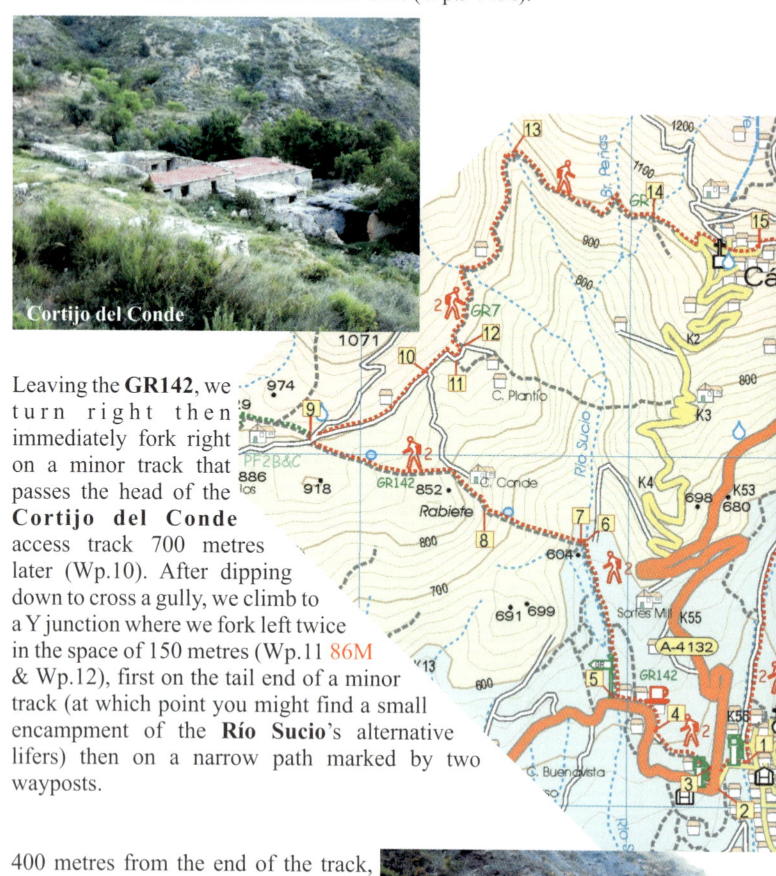

Leaving the **GR142**, we turn right then immediately fork right on a minor track that passes the head of the **Cortijo del Conde** access track 700 metres later (Wp.10). After dipping down to cross a gully, we climb to a Y junction where we fork left twice in the space of 150 metres (Wp.11 86M & Wp.12), first on the tail end of a minor track (at which point you might find a small encampment of the **Río Sucio**'s alternative lifers) then on a narrow path marked by two wayposts.

400 metres from the end of the track, our path traverses a slightly eroded stretch where we have to watch our footing, then dips into a shady affluent of the **Río Sucio**.

We then pass below a ruin and approach the wilder upper reaches of the **Sucio** valley, which is dotted with some fine old holm oak. This is where the rewards of the walk really begin as we descend over an old rockslide to cross the river at

The steep slope after Wp.1

a shady niche (Wp.13 114M).

Five metres up the far bank of the river, a waymarked rock indicates our ongoing path, which climbs steeply away from the river.

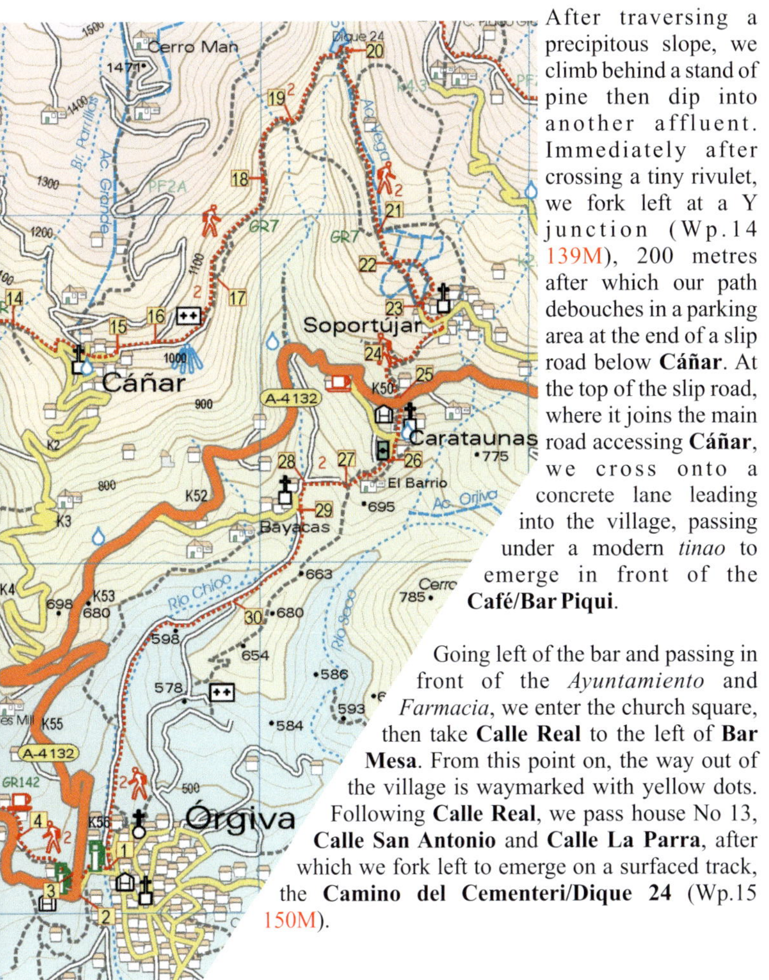

After traversing a precipitous slope, we climb behind a stand of pine then dip into another affluent. Immediately after crossing a tiny rivulet, we fork left at a Y junction (Wp.14 139M), 200 metres after which our path debouches in a parking area at the end of a slip road below **Cáñar**. At the top of the slip road, where it joins the main road accessing **Cáñar**, we cross onto a concrete lane leading into the village, passing under a modern *tinao* to emerge in front of the **Café/Bar Piqui**.

Going left of the bar and passing in front of the *Ayuntamiento* and *Farmacia*, we enter the church square, then take **Calle Real** to the left of **Bar Mesa**. From this point on, the way out of the village is waymarked with yellow dots. Following **Calle Real**, we pass house No 13, **Calle San Antonio** and **Calle La Parra**, after which we fork left to emerge on a surfaced track, the **Camino del Cementeri/Dique 24** (Wp.15 150M).

Climbing along this track, we fork right at a Y junction below the cemetery (Wp.16 155M) and continue on a dirt track leading to a *mirador*, after which the track dwindles to a path curving into the **Río Chico** valley, from where we can see **Soportújar** and **Carataunas** off to our right.

Following a clear path snaking along the hillside, we come to a Y junction a little over 500 metres from the cemetery (Wp.17 164M). The GR forks right on the narrower path, though both routes rejoin 200 metres later and the higher one is slightly easier as a short stretch of the GR descends steeply on unstable ground.

Once the two paths rejoin, a nice balcony path precedes a brief climb to a false Y junction (Wp.18 176M) that's actually just a shortcut across a bend.

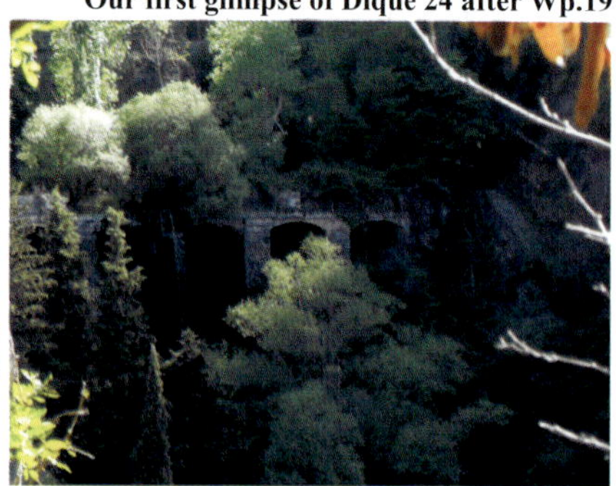
Our first glimpse of Dique 24 after Wp.19

After winding through an ancillary gully defined by a narrow pine-topped spine, we pass a second shortcut Y junction (Wp.19 183M) and the path broadens to a trail from where we get our first glimpse of the arches of **Dique 24**.

We then traverse a fifty metre stretch that has always been prone to landslips (at the time of writing the path is well trodden and easily traversed) and climb briefly twice before reaching the **Dique 24** glade, where there is a log bridge over the **Río Chico** (Wp.20 191M). Take a break. You've earned it!

On the far side of the dam, steps lead down to the continuation of the **GR7**, which soon climbs to cross the **Acequia de la Vega**.

Acequia de la Vega

We recross the *acequia* a couple of minutes later and descend past a new cottage, after which we follow the intermittently interred *acequia* for 500 metres until it swings sharp left at a water inspection hatch above a ruin within sight of a small *cortijo* off to our left (Wp.21 221M).

When we recorded this itinerary, much of the path between here and **Soportújar** had been dug up for the purposes of installing a new pipe. The work should be finished by the time we go to print, but in case not I'll detail two slightly different routes to the village. In both cases, we fork right at the water inspection hatch and descend to the left of the ruin. At an intersection with another *acequia* 175 metres later (Wp.22), the official path carries straight on for 300 metres to reach a junction of concrete tracks directly above the village (Wp.23 230M). Alternatively, if the ongoing path at Wp.24 is still churned up, the junction of concrete tracks can be reached by turning left at the *acequia* then right 150 metres later in front of the black metal gates of an orchard with a white cabin.

Either way, once the two concrete tracks converge, we take the second turning on the left into **Soportújar**, descending along **Calle Real** and passing (possibly not) the **Bar El Correillo**. Thereafter, we keep descending through the village until we see (off to our left) the telephone cabin in the central square, behind which we take **Calle Estacion**. Directly below the intersection with **Calle Xanfilla** and **Calle Moralillo**, we take **Calle Camino Carataunas**, which brings us to a concrete trail (238M).

The trail descends steeply before becoming a narrow terrace path leading to a Y junction 200 metres below the village (Wp.24 241M). Forking left, we keep descending until we pass in front of the gates of a small house called **La Rondilla**, below which the path becomes a concrete driveway leading to the A4132 (Wp.25 245M). Crossing the road, we take a wayposted path twenty five metres to the right and descend into **Carataunas**, where we follow the road down past the church and across **Plaza de Constitución**. We then carry straight on, passing below a block of empty flats to reach a Y junction (Wp.26 252M). Taking the higher of the two forks, we join a surfaced track which we follow down to the left until it ends just short of the largely abandoned hamlet of **El Barrio**. Following a very rough track and then the old path through the centre of **El Barrio**, we join another track below the hamlet (Wp.27 259M) on which we turn right to reach another broader track running along the left bank of the **Río Chico** 200 metres later (Wp.28 263M).

Turning left and staying on the left bank when the main track crosses the river to the hamlet of **Bayacas** (Wp.29 266M), we follow an increasingly rough track past a stand of tall eucalyptus trees. When the rough track ends (270M), we carry straight on along a rough path leading to another better stabilized track. Once again carrying straight on and ignoring a branch climbing to the left three hundred metres later (Wp.30), we simply follow this track and the lane it eventually leads into all the way back to our starting point in **Órgiva**.

I mentioned in the introduction that it's a job to keep up with all the SLs that have been wayposted in the Alpujarras in the past ten years and the **Poqueira Valley** is no exception, although this initiative has not always been a tale of unmitigated success. There is, for instance, a stretch of the **Sendero Local La Atalaya** that has been impassable for at least three years to my knowledge and nobody seems very fussed about it. There are no such problems on the present twin itinerary, though.

Long one of our favourite wild camping spots, the **Barranco de la Sangre** between **Pampaneira** and **Pitres** boasts a less pacific past, being named for a bloody battle between Moors and Christians, after which the Christians claimed their blood flowed uphill to avoid mingling with that of their enemies. There's a good flow of blood and a fair bit of uphill stuff in the first version of the present itinerary, in which we put our cardiovascular systems to the test with a steep climb up the stairs alongside the *tubería* servicing **Pampaneira**'s hydroelectric plant. Thereafter, we visit some of the finest viewing points over the Poqueira valley before taking advantage of the **SL Monte Pecho la Tala** and **GR7** to return to **Pampaneira** via **Bubíon**.

However, not everyone will be enamoured by the prospect of slogging up a steep staircase for forty minutes, so we also feature a second, shorter version of the walk following the official route of the **SL Monte Pampaneira**, a very brief stroll offering effortless views that are almost as good as those enjoyed higher up. We did it as a breakfast picnic walk on our day of departure and were well pleased with ourselves. The early morning light seeping across the **Loma de Mulhacén** is a sight to behold.

Access by car/on foot:
- from **Pampaneira** cemetery which is situated above the village on the A4132. Both walks start from **Pampaneira** cemetery, which can be reached via a surfaced track doubling back to the left 200 metres above the town's limits and marked with a small 'Sendero Monte Pampaneira' fingerpost. There's room to park alongside the track and additional space in front of the diminutive football pitch above the cemetery. The walks can also be reached from the upper car park on the A4132 at the hairpin bend in front of the **Hotel Rural Estrella de las Nieves**. If starting from here, take **Calle La Peseta** below the hotel to pass the **Pizzeria Castañar** then cross the **Calle La Peseta** porch and turn right on **Calle Real** to reach the paved pedestrian way climbing to the cemetery. For the sake of convenience, both itineraries are described from the 'SL Monte Pampaneira' mapboard 50 metres after the cemetery.

a) **Barranco de la Sangre** via the *tubería*

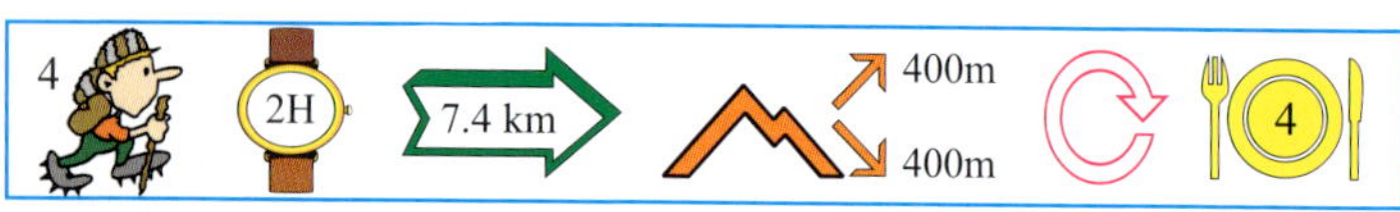

From the SL mapboard (Wp.1 0M), we climb away from the cemetery, carrying straight on along a dirt track when the concrete track doubles back to the right toward the football pitch (Wp.2). Immediately after passing a bright white water hut a little over 100 metres later, we turn right on a path marked

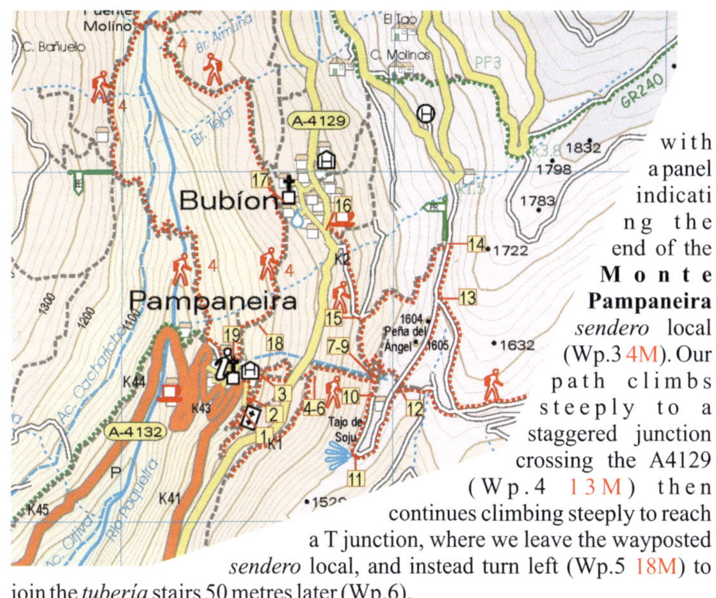

with a panel indicating the end of the **M o n t e Pampaneira** *sendero* local (Wp.3 4M). Our path climbs steeply to a staggered junction crossing the A4129 (Wp.4 13M) then continues climbing steeply to reach a T junction, where we leave the wayposted *sendero* local, and instead turn left (Wp.5 18M) to join the *tubería* stairs 50 metres later (Wp.6).

No doubting what awaits us now as we simply slog up the stairs, very much taking it one step at a time.

The *tubería* and stair

Almost at the top of the *tubería*, at the foot of a massive embankment below the holding dam (Wp.7 38M), we duck under the pipe and follow a clearly trodden path across the scree for 75 metres to reach a bend on a major path where we briefly join the **GR7** (Wp.8). Turning right, we climb along the GR for a further 75 metres to the next left hand bend and a junction marked with SL & GR wayposts (Wp.9 42M). Leaving the wayposted itineraries, we fork right (against the GR 'wrong direction' waypost) to follow a well trodden path traversing the face of the embankment below the dam, beyond

View from above Wp.11 on Walk 3a

which we join the end of a dirt track beside a small house (Wp.10 44M). Following the track, we climb to a left hand bend, on the right of which a succession of small humps furnish some of the finest natural *miradors* overlooking the **Poqueira** valley (Wp.11 47M). How many humps you take in is down to you, but you should probably allow about ten minutes for this diversion (not counted in subsequent timings).

After enjoying the diversion, we return to the main track and follow it to the northeast as it curves along the western edge of the **Barranco de la Sangre**, passing another cottage and the *tubería* reservoir before crossing the **GR7** and rejoining the green and white wayposted **SL Monte Pecho la Tala** (Wp.12 54M). Continuing along the track, we pass below the rocky outcrop of the **Peña del Angel** to reach an inverted Y junction (Wp.13 59M), where we carry straight on along the tail of the Y. We follow the track for another 300 metres until (150 metres after a dentate stone crash barrier in case the wayposts disappear) twin wayposts indicate a path doubling back to the left (Wp.14 63M).

Taking this path, we descend onto a broad trail cutting across holm oak woodland. After a steady occasionally skittery descent, the trail runs into the end of a rough dirt track, which rejoins the **GR7** 100 metres later (Wp.15 76M). Bearing right and staying on the dirt track, we follow the clearly waymarked GR down to **Bubíon**.

After turning right on the A4129 (Wp.16 84M), we fork left on the concrete lane passing below the municipal car park. We then turn left into **Calle Lavadero** following the **Ruta Barrio Bajo** down past House No.2. After turning right in **Calle Parras** and taking the first left past house No.21, we turn right again to reach the church square, on the left of which we find the signposted continuation of the **GR7** (Wp.17 93M). Descending to the southeast, we join the **Camino de Pampaneira**, an intermittently cobbled path. 600 metres later, just below a dog pound 300 metres above **Pampaneira**, we briefly follow a concrete track (Wp.18 102M) before recovering the old trail for the final descent to **Pampaneira**. 30 metres after a mapboard for the 'Poqueira Villages Circuit', we turn left (Wp.19 111M) then descend past **Calle Principe** before turning left again to join the paved way climbing back to the cemetery.

b) SL Monte Pampaneira

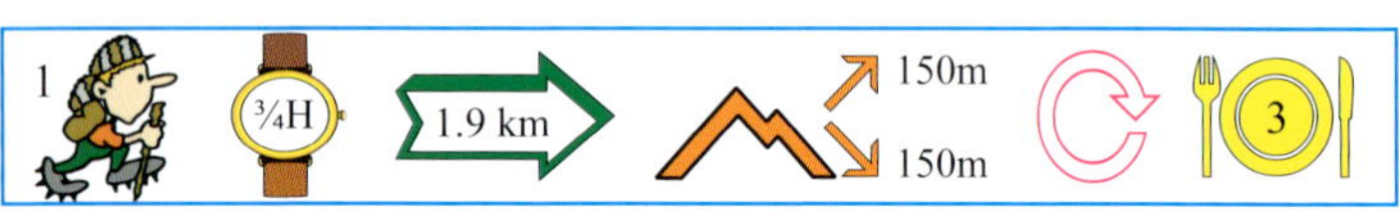

From the SL mapboard (Wp.1 0M), we follow the wayposted trail up to the right, passing below the football pitch. After climbing steadily then gently amid mature holm oak and enjoying fine views to the south over the tail end of the **Sierra Mecina** and, behind us, up the **Poqueira** valley to **Veleta**, we cross the A4129 (Wp.2 10M) and follow a broader trail climbing gently to a junction just short of a large stone bench (Wp.3 13M).

Doubling back to the left, we head toward the *tubería*, enjoying particularly fine views over **Bubíon** and **Capileira**. Fifty metres short of the *tubería*, we fork left on a wayposted path (Wp.4 27M) that descends steeply back to the A4129 (Wp.5 30M).

Bubíon and Capileira

Turning left then almost immediately descending to the right, we follow a nice shady path weaving through the woods down to a 'Fin de Sendero' sign beside a white water hut (Wp.6) where we turn left to return to the start.

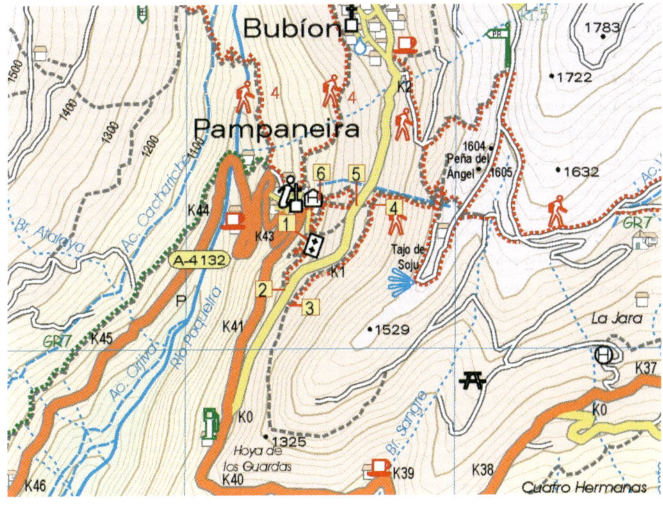

The Poqueira Valley

The catchphrase claims 'the old ones are the best' and, in this classic tour of the **Poqueira** valley, an adage coined for comedy holds true for walking. Our version of the itinerary is a figure of eight that can be done in its entirety or divided into two shorter loops, both of which would make very satisfactory short excursions.

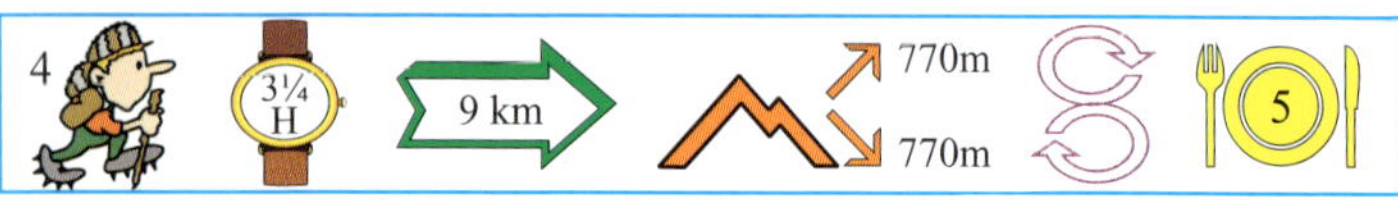

Access: on foot from any of the three villages.

Pampaneira is such a maze, describing the way out of it might constitute a walk description in itself. To simplify matters, from the entrance to the village, take the lane in front of **Hostal Ruta de Mulhacén** and climb at every junction until you pass **Calle Real** and see, off to your left, **Calle Rosario**, at the end of which is a 'Camino de Bubíon' signpost (Wp.1 9M).

Waypoint 1

We follow the paved *camino* as it climbs through **Calle Castillo**, at the top of which we fork left below houses Nºs 1 and 3, as indicated by a waypost. Traversing well-tended terraces, we fork right at the next junction (waymarked and wayposted) (Wp.2 15M) and climb steadily along a cobbled mule trail below a malodorous dog pound.

Just below the pound, we briefly join a track before recovering the old mule trail (Wp.3 19M). Climbing steadily along a chestnut fringed dirt trail, we enter **Bubíon** via the **Fuente Barrio Bajo** (Wp.4 34M).

Climbing past a 'GR7' signpost, we cut across the church square then follow the sign for 'Camino del Río/Los Cortijos/Polideportivo Municipal'. At the northeastern corner of the municipal football field, we take a broad trail marked with a waypost (Wp.5 40M). Ignoring minor branches accessing fields and huts, we descend to cross **Barranco de Tejar**, immediately after which we pass a new trail climbing to the right (Wp.6 47M). Sticking to the old trail as it descends towards the river, we cross **Barranco de Armuña**, 50 metres after which we reach the point where the loops of our figure of eight intersect, a signposted turning on the right for 'Capileira' (Wp.7 58M).

We descend to **Puente Molino**, a great spot for a picnic, beyond which we climb to a T-junction, where the two loops diverge (Wp.8 65M). Turning right, we climb past **Cortijo Enrique** (much barking, mostly benign and, if not benign, timid) and cross an ancient *acequia* layered with black pipes (Wp.9 72M).

After passing an abandoned cabin and a threshing circle, we fork right at the enbrambled carcass of a dead tree (Wp.10 75M), and follow a good level path along a contour into the **Barranco de las Rosas**. After crossing a first watercourse, we bear right at a wayposted junction of paths in a second watercourse (Wp.11 80M), taking either of the forks immediately after the watercourse (they rejoin almost immediately on the bend of a broader trail).

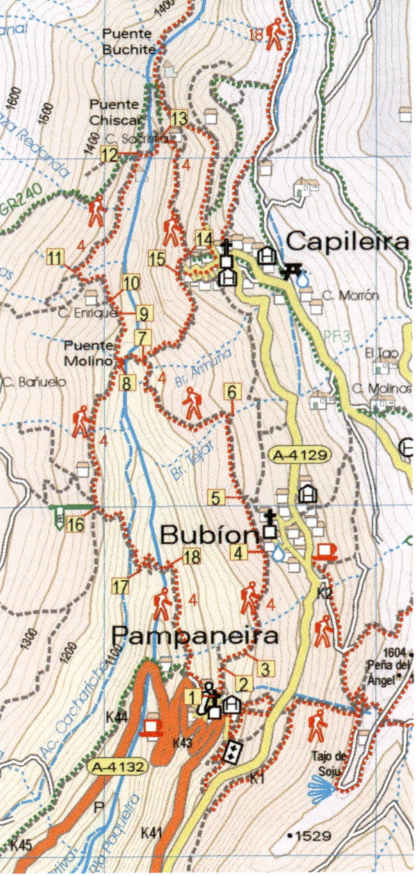

Following a brief climb, the trail levels out, passing below a small cabin and bringing into view on the right bank the yellowish walls of **Cortijo de la Sacristia**, which stands above **Puente Chiscar**. At a wayposted junction below two small *cortijos* (Wp.12 93M), we fork right, descending to the picturesque **Puente Chiscar**.

Back on the left bank of the river, we follow a broad mule trail, climbing steadily to a junction just below **Cortijo de la Sacristia** where we turn right (Wp.13 100M).

The view north after Wp.13

Climbing steadily to steeply, we enter **Capileira** via a concrete track, signposted 'Puente Chistal' and 'Puente Chiscal' (sic) (Wp.14 115M).

We initially follow the concrete track, then carry straight on at the first bend where the main track doubles back into the village.

A corner house in Capileira

When the concrete runs into a cobbled alley, we turn right then bear left in front of **Casa Liliana** and pass under a succession of *tinaos* (the terraces that turn streets into tunnels). At the far end of **Plaza Vieja**, we turn right and descend to the signposted 'Camino de las Higuerillas / Molino de Bubíon' (Wp.15 120M).

After a level stretch, the path descends rapidly, intermittently shadowing a torrent before cutting away toward a two-tiered cabin and descending back to Wp.7 (135M), from where we retrace our steps to Wp.8 (142M). Turning left, we climb steadily to a Y-junction at the stump of a fire-scorched chestnut tree (151M), where we bear left.

After crossing three watercourses, the second two usually dry, we climb through an oak forest to the grassy terraces below a ruin, beyond which a waypost indicates our path down to the **Pozo de Pampaneira** (Wp.16 160M).

The path traverses more woodland then emerges in the open and descends past a fissured pillar of rock. At a wayposted junction immediately after a roofless cabin (Wp.17 174M), we double back to the left and zigzag down to the bridge below the **Pozo de Pampaneira**. On the far side of the bridge, we turn right on a narrow dirt track (Wp.18 180M) which leads to a bend in the main road, where the concrete lane of the **GR7** climbs into **Pampaneira** via **Calle Moraleda** and **Calle Princesa**.

5 PITRES: BALCÓN DE PITRES

A slightly higher balcony than the campsite of the same name, [set] back and with considerably better views, featuring two [...] pleasant stretch of *acequia*, easy walking on dirt tracks, [...] venerable chestnut trees, a lovely hamlet, and a restored cottage with a touch of the Gaudis about its painted window frames.

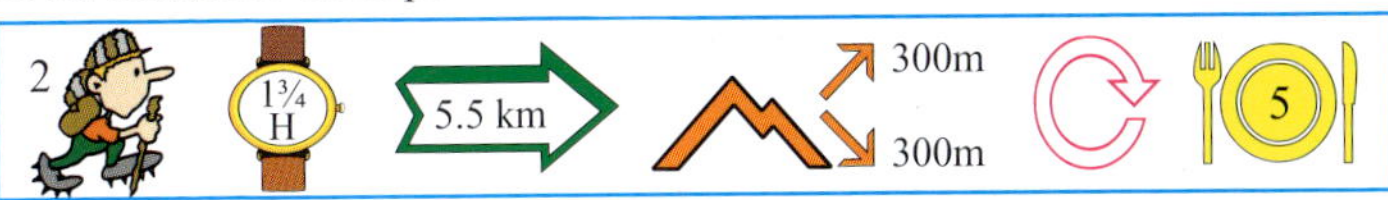

Access:
The A4132 passes through the southern edge of **Pitres**. The walk starts from the town's central plaza, where there is plenty of parking space.

From the northeastern corner of the plaza, we take **Calle San Roque**, the lane climbing in front of the **Bar La Alpujarra** for the 'Lavadero Barrio Alto' (Wp.1 0M). Forking left at the *carniceria* and ignoring all subsequent branches, we follow the narrow paved lane of **Cuesta Molina** up past a fabulous *tinao* to reach the **Barrio Alto Lavadero**, where the lane feeds into **Camino de Capilerilla**, which coincides with the **GR7** (Wp.2 4M).

The *tinao* on Cuesta Molina

Following a broad, shady trail, which is rather touchingly lined with street lamps, we climb steadily alongside a torrent, soon reaching house No.8 at the bottom of the delightful little hamlet of **Capilerilla** (Wp.3 13M). Bearing right, we join the end of the hamlet's access road (Wp.4 16M) at the

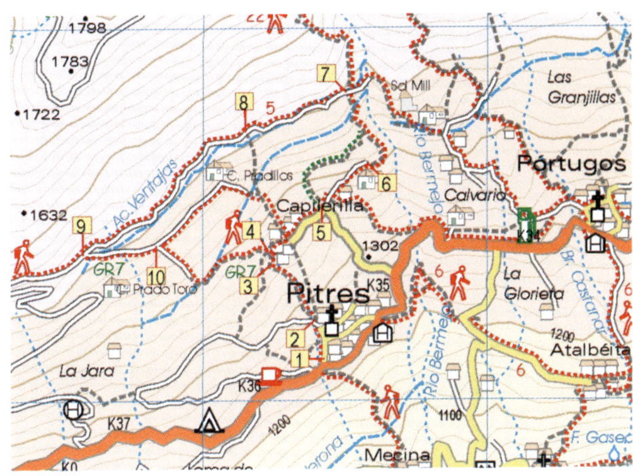

intersection with the **Camino del Monte**.

Turning right, we follow the road for 275 metres until it swings sharp right to descend back toward the A4132 (Wp.5 20M), at which point we fork left then immediately right on a broad dirt track that climbs past some enviably located houses. When the track reaches a water hut and starts to descend, we fork left on a PR wayposted trail (Wp.6 26M).

The path after Wp.6

Climbing steadily along a lovely path shaded by mature chestnut trees and criss-crossing a partially canalized torrent, we pass the Gaudiesque *caseta*, above which the trail broadens to a track shortly before crossing the **Acequia Ventajas** (Wp.7 41M). We leave the wayposted circuit at this point and turn left on a dirt track, signposted 'Bubíon'.

We now simply follow this track until it joins the **GR7** a little under two kilometres later, meandering amid holm oak, and initially shadowing the *acequia*. After ignoring a fork descending past a large reservoir on our left (Wp.8 53M), we enjoy fine views over the **Sierras Mecina** and **Contraviessa**. 500 metres after passing a goat farm, we double back to the left on a broad track used by the clearly wayposted **GR7** (Wp.9 70M), which we follow all the way back to **Capilerilla**, forking right at a wayposted shortcut after 400 metres (Wp.10 76M). After rejoining the track for 100 metres, the GR continues as a path then a broad trail that brings us back to **Capilerilla** and, via a tunnel of three *tinaos*, the Wp.4 junction (89M), from where we follow our outward route back to the start and the perfectly placed **Bar La Alpujarra**.

The **Tahá de Pitres** was the local centre of the medieval silk trade, and still bears the marks in the abundance of mulberry trees off which the silk worms fed, and in the very name **Tahá**, an Arabic administrative district. It's famous for idyllic paths (in a region already famous for idyllic paths), exceptionally pretty villages (ditto), and stunning landscapes (ditto). After the touristy villages of the **Poqueira**, the **Tahá** is a welcome relief. Admittedly, it suffered like everywhere else from the sixties and seventies exodus to the industrial cities of the north and there are plenty of expats buying houses here, but the general atmosphere is still distinctively Alpujarran.

Our route threads its way through the higher villages of the **Tahá**, climaxing with the finest *mirador* in the valley, **La Mezquita**. We follow the **GR7** from **Pitres** to **Busquístar** and the **GR142** from **Busquístar** to below the **Mezquita**, completing the circuit with local trails. Most of it is waymarked and the walking is easy apart from the scramble up to the **Mezquita**.

N.B. Spanish maps identify the highest point of the ridge between Wps.11 & 12 as the **Mezquita**. For the sake of ease and in accordance with local custom, I use 'the **Mezquita**' to refer to the ruins (Wp.11) at the tip of this ridge.

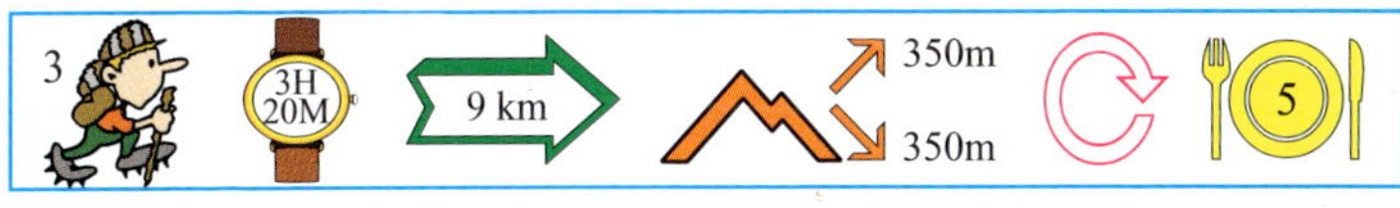

Access by car:
The A4132 passes through the southern edge of **Pitres**. Park along the main road through the lower part of **Pitres**. However, If you want to avoid slogging back up the road from **Atalbéitar** to **Pitres**, start from **Atalbéitar**. You could also easily start from any of the other villages. If you just want to visit the **Mezquita**, start from **Atalbéitar** and turn right at Wp.4.

From the main road through **Pitres**, fifty metres above the **Hotel/Restaurant San Roque** and opposite a sign for 'Youth Hostel', we take the concrete alley descending next to a **GR7** waypost (Wp.1 0M). The concrete alley soon narrows to a dirt path passing under a tiny aqueduct beside the youth hostel/refuge, immediately after which two branches (Wp.2 5M) descend to cross the **Río Bermejo**. The official **GR7** route bears right and descends to a bridge. But for a less steep descent, we bear left, cross the little bridge over the *acequia* and, after a slightly larger bridge over a watercourse, take the path on the right down to the **Fuente Agria de Pitres** (an attractive plunge pool and tiny *fuente*), beyond which a narrow path past a ruined mill rejoins the **GR7**.

The **GR7** then climbs towards electricity pylons where it broadens to a dirt track joining the road to **Atalbéitar** (Wp.3 15M). Ten minutes on the road leads us down to the outskirts of **Atalbéitar**, where we pass the GR7 sign (Pitres 40') and Wp.1 of Walk 7. We cross the village via the **Calle Real**, the **Plaza Candelaria** and the **Calle El Horno** to emerge above the *lavadero* at the end of Walk 7, where we continue on the broad path heading east, signposted 'Pórtugos 30'". After passing two stone huts, we climb to the bridge over the **Barranco del Castañar** and a junction of paths (Wp.4 29M)

where we turn left and continue climbing alongside the *barranco* on an old mule trail until it joins a dirt track (Wp.5 35M).

We bear left here, then right fifty metres later, where a junction dips into the *barranco*. From here you can see the large white block of the **Hotel Nuevo Malagueño** in **Pórtugos**. When the track swings right, we continue past a large chestnut tree to pick up the old mule trail again. After a steepish climb along the mule trail, ignoring all the branches into fields, we bear left just below the road. The path crosses an evil looking effluent pipe, passes below the hotel garden and, judging by the bottle caps cobbling the path, the bar, too, before bearing right to join the main road (Wp.6 48M) at a **GR7** signpost ('Atalbéitar 30").

We then cross the road and follow the concrete alley climbing into **Pórtugos**, taking the third turning on the right (at house Nº 9) into the **Plaza de la Iglesia**. We continue on the main street through the **Plaza Nueva**, passing the **Hostal/Bar Mirador**. After bearing right out of the **Plaza Nueva**, we leave the main street, turning left in front of the Telefonica installations onto the concrete track signposted 'Busquístar 15'. The track soon turns to dirt before descending to the road, which we'll follow for the next 500 metres. If you haven't yet tasted the ferruginous waters of the **Tahá**, it's worth pausing at the **Fuente Agria** next to the *ermita*, just after we join the road.

After the *fuente*, the road goes through a long bend to the right before joining a straight avenue of plane trees, at the end of which (Wp.7 68M), we take the broad path climbing to the left just before the road itself bends sharp left.

After fifty metres the path bears right across an *acequia*. It then passes above fields of raspberries and cultivated blackberries, and goes through an overgrown section, before joining a dirt track behind a breeze-block byre, from where we can see **Busquístar**.

The track descends alongside the road, crosses a stand of poplars, then joins the road which the **GR7** follows all the way into **Busquístar**.

We also follow the road, but ten metres before the village limits sign and (on our left) a *no potable fuente*, we leave the GR and turn right onto a dirt path descending steeply behind a black lamppost (Wp.8 89M).

The path descends into the lower part of **Busquístar** between another *no potable fuente* and a couple of concrete benches below shady plane trees. Beyond the *fuente*, we continue in the same direction down a concrete lane passing a sign for the 'Camino al Río & Ferreirola'. Descending at each junction, we pass **Las Lillas Bar**, after which a final steep descent emerges between a PR waypost and (hidden round the corner) a sign for the 'Camino a Ferreirola' (Wp.9 101M). We take the dirt path on the right towards **Ferreirola**. The path descends past a goat farm (your nose will tell you!) then climbs to briefly follow an *acequia*. Just after it crosses the *acequia*, peer through the trees ahead and you should be able to pick out some stone walls nestling in a rocky outcrop: this is the **Mezquita**.

After a level section alongside another *acequia*, the path joins a new dirt track down from the road. We climb the dirt track for fifty metres then, when it bears sharp right, take the old mule trail on the left, from where we can see the path beyond the *río* climbing the **Pechos de Carriguelas** (see Walk 8). Five minutes later, the path passes an overhanging rock and a concrete triangulation post, thirty metres after which there's a junction. Ignore the path descending on the left and take the path on the right towards **Ferreirola**.

If you don't want to climb the Mezquita
Follow this path to **Cortijo de la Guarda** and return to **Atalbéitar** via Walk 7.

To climb the Mezquita
Take the Ferreirola path and, ten paces after the junction, next to an old red arrow on a rock, turn right to follow a very faint path climbing between two small holm oaks (Wp.10 115M).

The path, marked by occasional red dots, is reasonably clear at first as it winds up past mini-terraces, but higher up it tends to get lost in brambles. After 4-5 minutes, about halfway up, you should find yourself faced with a red cross telling you not to climb straight ahead. In fact, though the path does bear right, it's so embrambled that you're better off ignoring the cross and going straight up to the right of the rocks for an easy scramble onto a clearer stretch of the path. Behind the cross, we bear left to traverse a slab of rock with a red line in the middle, and head towards a half-dead olive tree, shortly after which we reach the **Mezquita** (Wp.11 126M).

This is an exceptional site, well worth the climb, with the best views to be found anywhere in the valley. More recently, it's been used as a byre, but in Moorish times (possibly as far back as the eighth century) it was a stronghold controlling the passes over the **Sierra Mecina** that were vital to the silk trade: to the south is the **Carriguelas** pass (Walk 8), to the west the path snakes up from **Fondales** bridge (Walk 8), and to the east the **Busquístar** 'Camino al Río' (Walk 9). There's also a remarkable threshing circle built into a huge slab of rock.

To return to **Atalbéitar**, we will circle the valley dividing it from the **Mezquita**, passing the ruined mill perched on a promontory midway between the two. To start, we take the path between the buildings and the threshing circle, then cross the rock immediately below the **Mezquita** (N).

La Mezquita

Ducking under the skeleton of the chestnut tree directly behind the **Mezquita**, we then follow the waymarks along the ridge, climbing onto the rocks just to the left of another concrete triangulation post, and squeezing between the boulders at the highest point of the ridge (the cartographic **Mezquita**).

After the 'peak', litter and beer cans mark the favoured picnic spot of the agricultural labourers who work the nearby fields. The path crosses the fields within sight of the road and the avenue of trees (Wp.7) to join a dirt track (Wp.12 141M) where we turn left and, when the track bears left some fifty metres later, continue straight ahead onto a path between the fields. Two fields later, the path dips to the left of a small house with a pretty garden. We bear right below the garden onto a narrower, shadier stretch.

After descending past another little house, we bear right again at a junction beside a waypost (Wp.13 150M) shortly before the mill. Five minutes after winding round the mill promontory, we come to the junction with the **GR7** (Wp.4). We return to **Atalbéitar** and/or **Pitres** on the **GR7**.

A ferruginous spring

Four linked strolls between the lower villages of the **Tahá** along pleasant, peaceful, easy paths and mule trails with one slightly rougher section between **Fondales** and **Ferreirola**. **Ferreirola** is the last toponymal link with another phenomenon for which **La Tahá** is famed, the extraordinarily high iron content of its springs, which give the water such a distinctive taste (hence the **Fuentes Agrias** at **Pitres** and **Portúgos**; *agrio* meaning sour) and lends the riverbeds their startling ochre tint - some rocks literally seem to be bleeding rust. The **Tahá**'s original name was *Ferreira*.

This route is ideal for a relaxing day after some of the more strenuous mountain walks. In summer, keep an eye open for the pungent white-flowered oregano. All these traditional routes between villages are peppered with slip paths into the fields. Unless otherwise stated, always stick to the main path. For simplicity's sake, I use 'path' to describe all the routes taken, though several would qualify as mule trails. Park along the road leading into **Atalbéitar**.

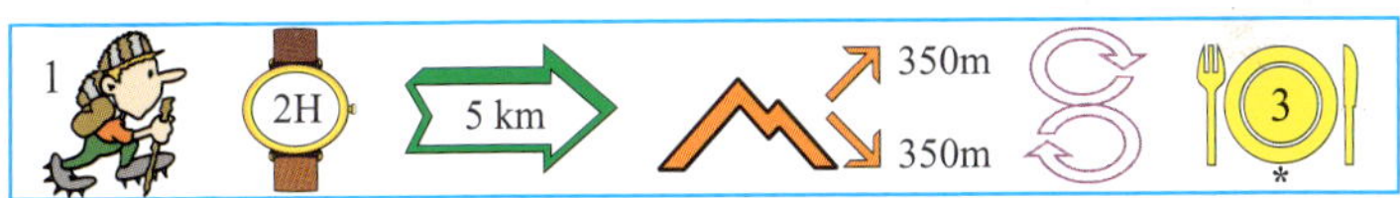

* if anything's open, which it probably won't be, in which case 0. The **Al Jipe** bar in **Mecinilla** and the hotel in **Mecina** are more reliable and are only about 10 minutes away from **Fondales**.

Access:
Drive to **Atalbéitar** which lies at the end of a minor road branching off the A4132 between **Pitres** and **Pórtugos**. The walk starts from the first house on the western edge of the settlement.

N.B. Since many people will probably want to break this up into shorter strolls, waypoint timings are given between villages, not on the basis of the entire walk. You'll probably take longer than the stated time, not because you have to stop to catch your breath or because we went belting round like maniacs, but because you'll want to savour the tranquillity of the place.

Atalbéitar - Ferreirola 15 minutes
Ferreirola - Fondales 20 - 25 minutes
Fondales - Ferreirola 30 - 40 minutes
Ferreirola - Atalbéitar 35 minutes

ATALBÉITAR - FERREIROLA

From the first house on the western edge of **Atalbéitar** (Wp.1 0M), we take the short concrete drive down towards the dark red doors and immediately bear right onto a dirt path winding down past almond groves, agave, blackberry and mulberry.

After crossing an *acequia* (Wp.2 7M), we bear left below a peach and plum orchard within sight of **Ferreirola** church. We then pass a long, narrow water hut and the path broadens, bringing us into **Ferreirola** a little over ten minutes from **Atalbéitar**.

Maintaining direction into **Ferreirola**, we pass between a *lavadero* and the **Villa Kiko**, then follow the alley descending below the church square, passing on our left the **Calle El Cerezo**, the **Villa Paquita** and **Los Monteros** before climbing slightly to reach a tiny stone cabin beside a signpost, 'GR142 Mecina-Fondales 30 mins' (Wp.3 21M).

The sign at Wp.3

FERREIROLA - FONDALES

Fifteen metres after the GR sign, the path bears left at a waypost, and winds down above an olive grove. At a Y-junction halfway along the olive grove, we take the upper path climbing past a fig tree, shortly after which we see **Fondales** ahead.

After descending over a rocky section, the path winds along the slopes through tangled blackberry bushes and dense *retama* dotted with occasional acacia, olive, chestnut and fig trees. Climbing slightly between huge rocks it crosses a concrete bridge (Wp.4 9M) over the **Río Bermejo**. A brief climb past some poplars precedes a section between an *acequia* and another olive grove before we cross the *acequia* and continue past an immense chestnut tree and a water reservoir. The path follows another *acequia* till, about fifty metres after the chestnut tree, we dip down below the *acequia* (Wp.5 15M) and descend to a stream and a tiny *fuente* with benches, a few minutes from **Fondales**.

In **Fondales**, we bear left after the **GR142** waypost ('Ferreirola 30 mins') to descend along the outskirts of the village. We keep bearing left till we pass underneath a broad *tinao* with brown garage doors on the left, immediately after which we see a GR142 sign 'Órgiva 5h30 mins'.

FONDALES - FERREIROLA

We follow the **GR142** concreted lane down past a *fuente/lavadero* where it turns into a dirt path. The subsequent descent is clear except for one slightly ambiguous moment where the path divides next to a pomegranate tree with a prickly pear bush behind it.

We take the narrower, rougher path to the left, descending through a small poplar wood to an idyllic spot beside a Roman bridge (Wp.6 10M) over the **Río Trevélez**.

Bearing left at the bridge, we leave the **GR142** and follow the right bank of the **Río Trevélez**, almost immediately crossing a stream over large slabs of smooth stone.

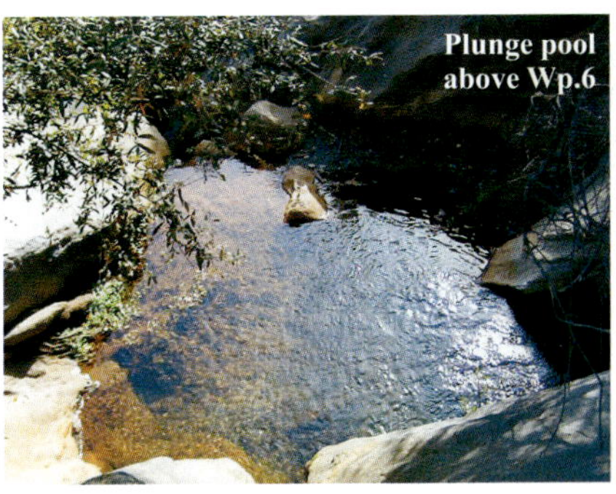

Beyond the stream, a yellow waymark indicates a rough path that zigzags up through big bushes of *retama*.

We follow this path, crossing an eroded, rocky section and climbing towards a small chestnut tree where there's a very old, very faint yellow dot on a rock, and the path becomes clearer. After winding through a small stand of chestnut, the path climbs steeply then bears right on a gentler slope below a long rocky outcrop topped with a couple of dead chestnuts.

The rocks give way to stone retaining walls until the path bears left then right to pass a partially dead chestnut, after which it winds up below an acacia to rejoin the outward route (Wp.7 24M). Turning right here, we reach **Ferreirola** five minutes later, where we retrace our steps to the church square. (If you started this route from **Fondales** or the Roman bridge, you'll find the church by continuing straight on past the GR sign and bearing left after the **Villa Paquita** to climb to the *fuente/lavadero* next to the church square.)

From the *fuente/lavadero*, we follow the GR waymarks in the lane below the
Villa Kiko (Calle Rosario) across **Ferreirola** until **Calle Rosario** bears right
and then left to join the path marked 'Busquístar 50 mins'.

FERREIROLA - ATALBÉITAR

A few minutes from **Ferreirola**, we come
to the celebrated **Fuente La Gaseosa**
(Wp.8 3M), decorated with ceramics
depicting the seasons. At least a sip of its
extraordinary tasting waters is obligatory.

After the *fuente*, we cross the bridge over
the **Barranco del Castañar** and follow a
broad path above a large threshing circle
before climbing to cross another bridge
over the watercourse from **Pórtugos'**
Fuente Agria.

Fuente La Gaseosa

Fifty metres later, a third bridge leads onto an open sheet of rock, **Cortijo de
la Guarda** (Wp.9 15M), with fine views down the **Río Trevélez**. The **GR142**
continues east, linking up with Walk 6.

Immediately after **Cortijo La Guarda**, we leave the GR and take the clear
path on the left (NE) up to another junction, where we bear left again.
Climbing steeply, we cross the **Fuente Agria** watercourse again, after which
the gradient moderates and we come into a shady area.

After crossing an *acequia*, we follow the main path up past various branches
until it emerges from the tree cover, where it swings left and climbs alongside
a terracing wall to another bridge over the **Barranco del Castañar** (Wp.10
30M).

We cross the *barranco* and an *acequia* to climb a narrow, possibly water-
logged path densely lined with brambles. Just after a sign on the left saying
'Propiedad Particular - Ganado', we bear right, away from a terrace (Wp.11
32M) and climb to **Atalbéitar** fifty metres later. Turn left to cross the village
and return to Wp.1 (35M).

An easy walk (despite the extraordinary descent after Wp.5) using the GR142, dirt tracks and PRs, and taking in two of the Moorish silk-route passes. The views are spectacular. *Cabra montés* can occasionally be seen near **La Corona** (see map). And it's worth pausing at Wp.6; the bridge appears to be man-made, but in fact is built on a natural arc of rock spanning the spectacular gorge.

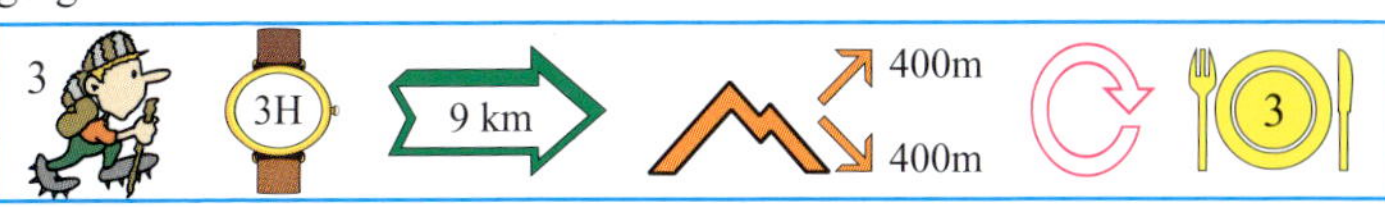

Access by car:
Park in the tiny car-park at the entrance to **Fondales** or if full, a little way up the road.

Access by bus:
If arriving by bus, the track from **Pitres** to **Fondales** starts on the main road opposite the **Paseo Maritimo**. Take the concrete lane to the right of **La Meta** restaurant and follow the mule trail down to **Mecina** (15M). Bear left on the concrete lane into **Mecina**, then take either the second or third turning on the right down to the *Ayuntamiento de la Tahá* noticeboard. Bear right, and follow the road round the hotel and church down to **Mecinilla** (20M). Enter **Mecinilla** to the right of **Al Jipe** bar and follow the main alley to a *fuente* dated '1964'.

Bear left, then right, then left again to join the path to **Fondales**. At the road take the path on the right of the garage with red and white doors down to **Fondales** car-park (Wp.1 30M; subsequent times from 0M).

Fondales Bridge

Start from Fondales car park

From **Fondales** car-park (Wp.1 0M), we follow the lane into the village and take the first right next to house Nº3. We then continue descending till a lane on the left passes under a *tinao* and joins the **GR142** down to **Fondales** bridge (see Walk 7).
Crossing the bridge, we follow the **GR142** (SW) as it climbs above the river on a broad, easy path. Twenty minutes from the bridge, the path crosses a rockslide then zigzags up **El Aguadero** to join the end of a rough dirt track (Wp.2 45M).

We follow the dirt track up behind a newly built house to join the main **Sierra Mecina** dirt track (Wp.3 55M). Leaving the **GR142**, which bears right for a long, dry, dreary drag down to **Órgiva** (it's all tarmac and *retama* - if you want to go to **Órgiva**, get a bus), we turn left to follow the track along the **Sierra Mecina**.

The track climbs gently with fine views of the **Tahá**, the cliffs of **Carriguelas** and **Helechones**, and the old iron mines at **Cerro Conjuro**, before descending toward a group of houses just above the **Torviscón** road.

At the houses, just before Number 4, we take the wayposted track on the left (Wp.4 95M) to descend past the ruins of the *Baños de Panjuila* (on our right and virtually imperceptible) to the cliffs of the **Pecho de las Carriguelas** or **Carihuelas** (Wp.5 105M) where the track turns into a path.

The houses before waypoint 4

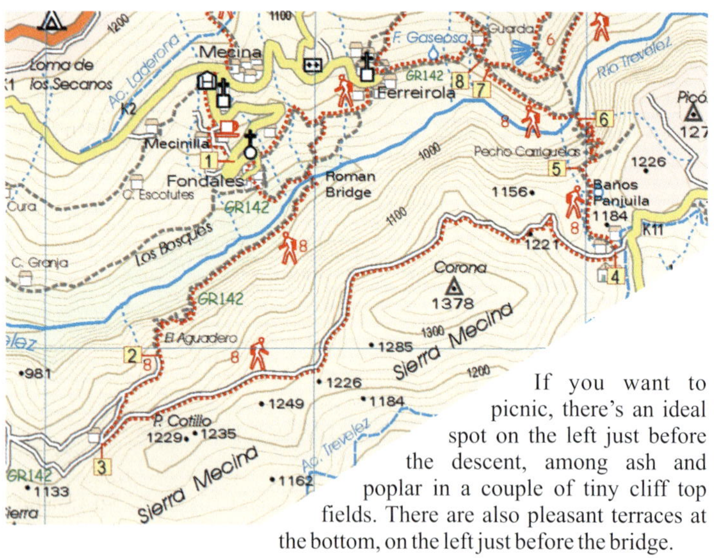

If you want to picnic, there's an ideal spot on the left just before the descent, among ash and poplar in a couple of tiny cliff top fields. There are also pleasant terraces at the bottom, on the left just before the bridge.

From the top, it's hard to believe there's a way down to the river, but in fact an easy path zigzags down causing no difficulty, even for those who suffer acute vertigo. We cross the bridge (Wp.6 125M) and take the path climbing past the ruined mill. Ignoring a branch on the right ten metres later (climbing to **La Mezquita** and **Busquístar** - see Walk 6), we stay on the main path to pass another waypost and a ruined cabin before rejoining the **GR142** (Wp.7 135M).

Bearing left here, we cross the rock shelf at the **Cortijo de la Guarda** (Wp.8 136M) and follow the **GR142** (Walk 7 in the opposite sense) across a series of watercourses to the **Fuente Agria** and **Ferreirola**. After the first *tinao*, turn right up an alley that immediately bears left and crosses **Ferreirola** to the *fuente/lavadero* in front of the church. To return to **Fondales**, follow Walk 7 back.

A glorious, wild walk exploring a little-known, scarcely visited end of the **Tahá**, climbing to the **Cerillos Negros** firewatch hut to take in stunning views of the **Trevélez Gorge**, then descending by the easternmost 'silk-route' pass over the **Sierra Mecina**. The only drawback is that it also involves a couple of kilometres on the road. There's very little traffic though, the views from the road are excellent, and the ascent and descent out of and into the **Tahá** are so exceptional, I suspect most walkers would happily do double the distance on the road. *Helecho* translates as bracken or fern, not that it's much in evidence nowadays.

N.B. Since we 'discovered' this walk, the stretch between **Busquístar** and **El Portichuelo** (Wps. 1 to 7) has been incorporated into the **PR299 Ruta Medieval** between **Pórtugos** and **Juviles**.

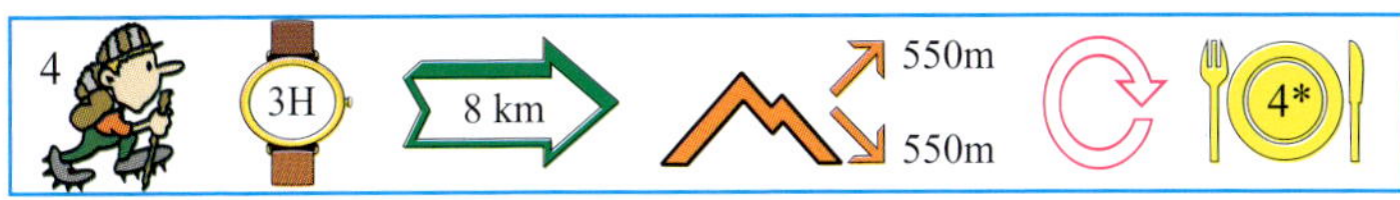

* in **Busquístar**

Access by car:
Park on or near the main square in **Busquístar**.

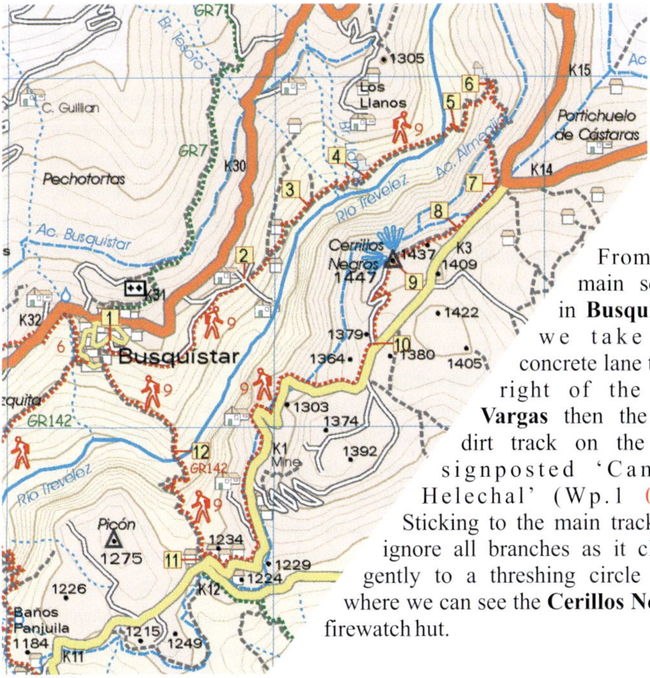

From the main square in **Busquístar**, we take the concrete lane to the right of the **Bar Vargas** then the first dirt track on the left, signposted 'Camino Helechal' (Wp.1 0M). Sticking to the main track, we ignore all branches as it climbs gently to a threshing circle from where we can see the **Cerillos Negros** firewatch hut.

We then follow the increasingly narrow dirt track as it passes behind a two-storey concrete house and ignore all branches until we come to a cross-roads (Wp.2 13M) with a new dirt track. The track we've been following continues on the far side as a narrow path that eventually leads to **Los Llanos**.

We, however, bear right on the new dirt track to pass behind a white-painted *cortijo*, beyond which a narrow path descends to a second, gated *cortijo*. Immediately after the gate, there are two paths on the right. We take the second path to pass below the pasture in front of the *cortijo* and descend (NE) towards the river.

Fifty metres above the river, we bear right at a Y-junction (Wp.3 31M) and descend to another gate, after which the path dips and rises across the watercourses of the **Barrancos del Tesoro** and **de los Llanos** before climbing steeply to a third gate. We continue climbing to a small chestnut tree then bear right, heading upriver to pass in front of a ruin (Wp.4 40M).

From the ruin, we descend to a small wood where the path is eroded by a couple of torrents. Beyond the wood, there's yet another gate, after which a gentle climb and brief descent lead to the bridge (Wp.5 49M), which looks terrifying as you approach but seems solid enough once you're on it. Beyond the bridge, a clear path climbs below the cliffs to cross a meagre watercourse next to a ruin (Wp.6 61M) (visible from before the bridge) where the way up to **Portichuelo** begins.

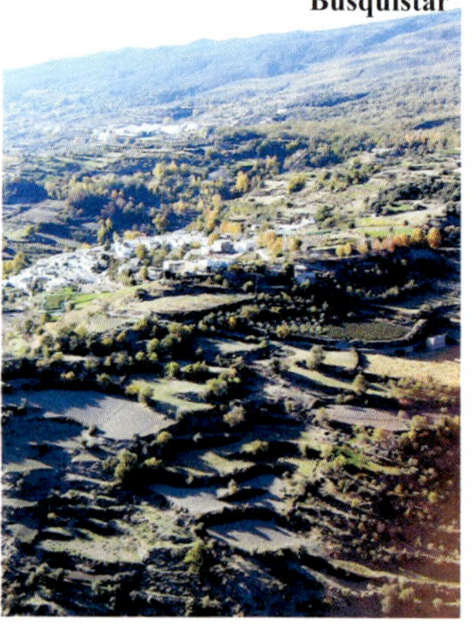

Busquístar

It's worth pausing here, partly for a breather beneath the ruin's shady walnut tree, partly to enjoy the fine views back towards **Busquístar**, but also to orient yourself.

If you look up from directly behind the ruin, you can see some of the concrete crash barrier along the **Trevélez** road and, to the south, the firewatch hut. Like most climbs, this one's a lot easier than it looks.

We take the path that bears right behind the ruin to re-cross the watercourse a little higher up, after which it climbs steeply, hopefully passing occasional cairns. If the cairns have been knocked down, stick to the clearer traces (most of the others are shortcuts) as they wind up to cross the broad **Acequia de Almegíjar** in a little under fifteen minutes.

Beyond the *acequia*, the increasingly broad and clear path continues climbing, meandering through some massive rocks before emerging at the junction of the **Trevélez-Juviles & Torviscón** roads (Wp.7 85M). Turning right, we follow the **Torviscón** road for just under 300 metres. As it comes into a slight rise, we leave the road to take a faint path on the right (Wp.8 91M) climbing through the pine trees.

The path soon loses definition, but if you stick to the right of the pine wood, a series of goat tracks along the ridge lead up to a little pass between two rocky outcrops where the path becomes clearer, winding along the cliff tops (near enough for gawping, far enough for comfort) before climbing gently to the firewatch tower (Wp.9 102M) for exceptional views of the **Trevélez Gorge** from its headwaters all the way down to the western end of the **Tahá de Pitres**.

To descend from the firewatch hut, we take the dirt track down to the road (Wp.10 110M). Bearing right, we follow the road for 2.3kms until it reaches the junction of roads to **Cástaras** and **Almegíjar/Torviscón** where we join the **GR142** (Wp.11 135M). As indicated by the GR fingerpost, we turn right on the higher of two paths.

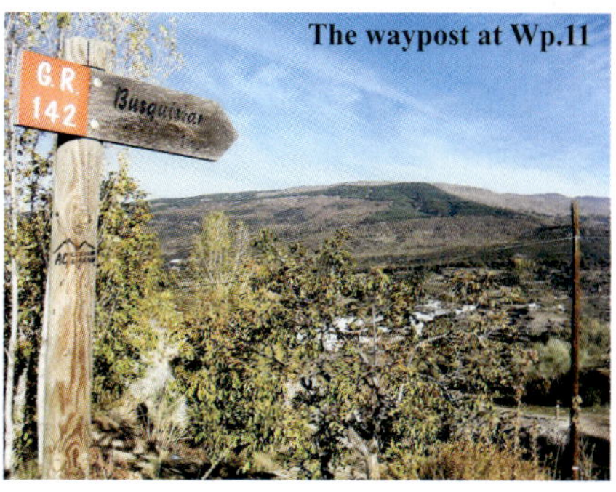

The waypost at Wp.11

After swinging left, the GR crosses a shelf of rock and descends toward the **Río Trevélez** on a broad, rocky and very dramatic trail. We then cross a bridge over the river (Wp.12 156M) and climb back to **Busquístar** along a clear path known as the 'Camino al Río'.

Stranded between the verdant valleys of the high Alpujarras and the desiccated hills of the **Contraviessa**, the delightful sleepy little villages and hamlets strung along what has become the **PR299 Ruta Medieval** are virtually devoid of the scars of tourism, and are blessed with a profusion of lovely short walks, each seemingly more exquisite than the last. Most, it must be said, are best avoided in hot weather, but this is an exception, almost exclusively following shady paths alongside abundant watercourses, where the untenanted land has become the demesne of so much wildlife that the spoors near drove our dogs to distraction.

Don't be deceived by the brevity of this itinerary, nor of Walks 11 & 12. They are complete unto themselves and amply repay the effort of getting off the beaten track.

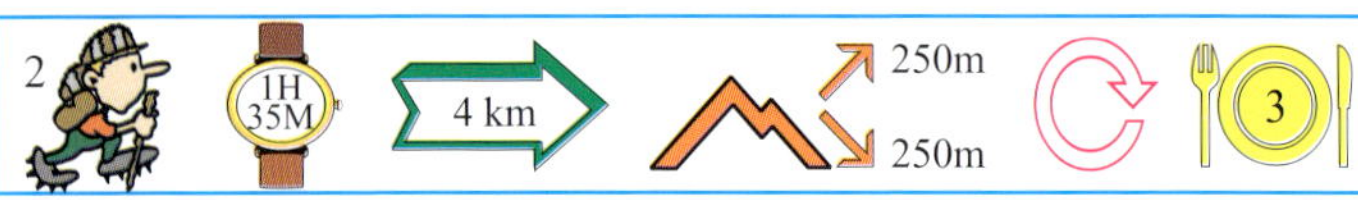

Access by car:
The walk starts from the circular *plaza* in front of **Cástaras** town hall (the be-flagged building with a clock face) where there's plenty of parking.

Cástaras *plaza*

From the *plaza* (Wp.1 0M), we follow the **Trevélez / Torviscón** road for 250 metres up to the **Barrio Medio**, where we turn right, just before the 40km speed limit sign, on a concrete surfaced track (Wp.2).

Above the houses of the

Barrio Medio, we ignore a concrete trail climbing to the right (Wp.3 7M) and fork right ten metres later at the junction with the wayposted **Ruta Medieval**, then left 25 metres after that on a roughly cobbled trail climbing behind a partially derelict house.

A steady climb takes us into the **Barranco de Fuente Medina**, where the trail levels out briefly, passing a path off to the right and an orange waymarked route to the left (Wp.4 13M). Carrying straight on and climbing steadily again, we pass a second path on the right 50 metres later (Wp.5),

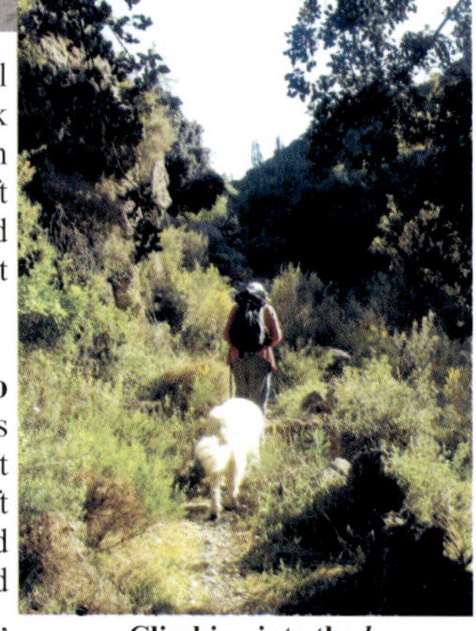
Climbing into the *barranco*

the **Caminillo Vieja** which the **Ruta Medieval** follows to **Nieles**. For our part, we carry straight on, climbing through lovely woodland along the right bank of the **Fuente Medina** stream, following an intermittently cobbled trail bejewelled with cistus and broom.

After fording the stream below a small waterfall, we continue climbing along the left bank. Following a narrower but always clear path, we re-cross the stream, after which path and watercourse diverge as we climb across abandoned terraces (NE) to join a dirt track (Wp.6 43M).

Turning left, we follow this track for a little over 500 metres to a Y junction with a minor track where we fork left on the minor track (Wp.7 50M).

When the track bottoms out in front of a smallholding, we turn left (Wp.8) on a narrow, occasionally muddy path, running alongside the

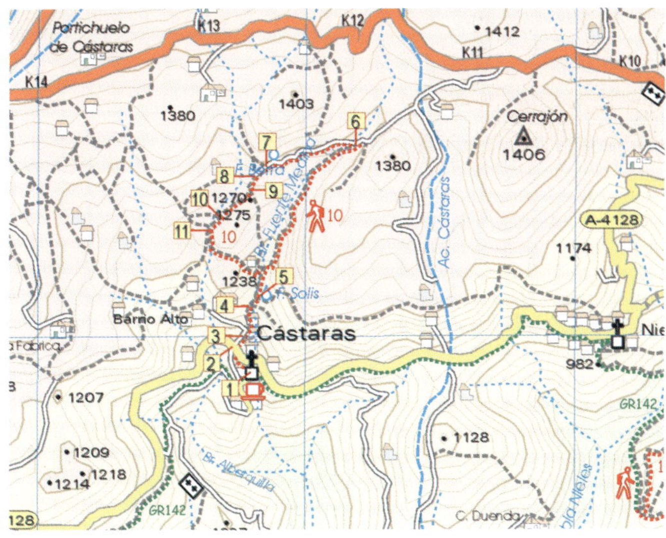

remains of an overgrown *acequia*. At a Y junction just below the summit of **Cerro de las Catifas** (Wp.9 54M) we fork right, contouring round the northern flank of the *cerro* amid shady holm oaks high above the **Barranco de Alberquillas** watercourse.

After ignoring a waymarked turning down to our right (Wp.10 59M), we zigzag down to a T junction beside a stand of poplar (Wp.11 63M). Turning left and staying on the left bank of the **Alberquillas** stream, we contour round the southern side of **Cerro de las Catifas** and follow a narrow path to the right of an almond grove before descending gently behind terraces of olive trees, again on an intermittently cobbled trail that rejoins our outward route a little way above Wp.5, some 700 metres from the start.

A fabulous little walk packing more wildness into its brief span than most itineraries achieve in triple the length as it traces a loop between **Juviles** and **Tímar** via **El Fuerte**, formerly the site of a Moorish fortification, before returning through the extraordinary upper reaches of the **Rambla de Nieles**. If the fortifications were 'fuerte', so are the emotions as we piece together exiguous paths in spectacular terrain with magnificent views. Not for the faint of heart, nor, I would hazard, anyone in hot weather, but definitely a case of less is more - short but very intense. If you don't fancy picking out the barely existent path below **El Fuerte**, this stretch can be avoided by the simple expedient of following the **GR7**. See Wp.4 for details. For a full day's outing, this itinerary could be combined with Walk 12 to make a figure of 8 circuit.

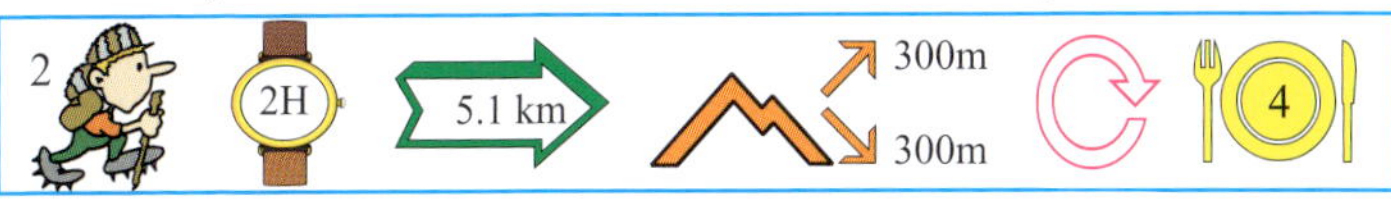

Access by car:
There's plenty of roadside parking on the A4130 through **Juviles**. If you don't find room here, there are more spaces to the right of the **Trastienda de Juviles** grocers (see text) on the road leading to the *mirador*.

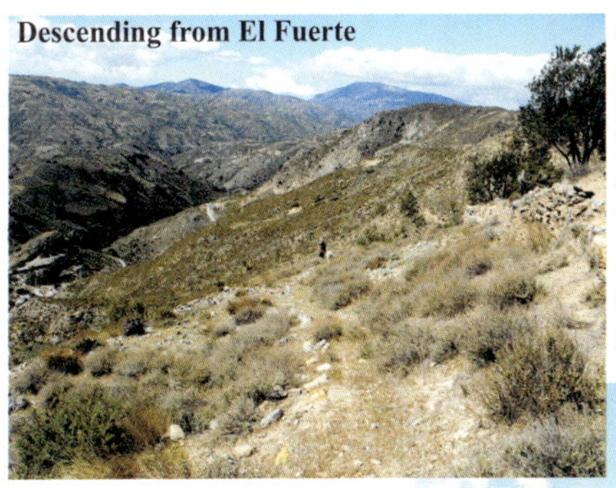

Descending from El Fuerte

Our itinerary starts at the eastern end of **Juviles** next to the large **Jamones de Juviles** building on **Calle Escuela**, where there's a signpost for 'Fuerte de Juviles / Fuente Agria / Cueva de la Umbria' (Wp.1 0M). We descend along **Calle Escuela** toward the

Wp.1

Trastienda de Juviles grocers. 75 metres from the main road, just in front of the grocers, we bear left for 'Fuerte de Juviles' and follow the **GR7** as it descends on a dirt track into one of the valleys that subsequently form the **Rambla de Nieles**.

On the nearside of the stream, a stone *acequia* wall (Wp.2 8M) leads into the shady crevices of the **Fuente Agria**, a ferruginous spring that makes for a pleasant diversion, but beware, the rocks can be extremely slippery. Returning to the main track, we cross the stream and climb above a cabin, passing a fork off to the left (Wp.3 20M), after which the track dwindles to a trail that follows a contour line before climbing onto the narrow spine behind **El Fuerte**, where we come to a signposted Y junction (Wp.4 25M). To avoid

The Y junction at Wp.4

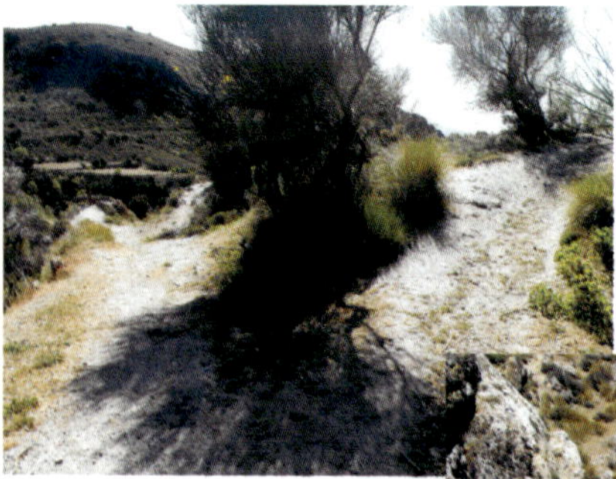

any pathfinding problems, fork left here and follow the **GR7**, which crosses a dramatic pass ten minutes later before descending to rejoin the main walk in **Tímar**. For views and more challenging terrain, we fork right.

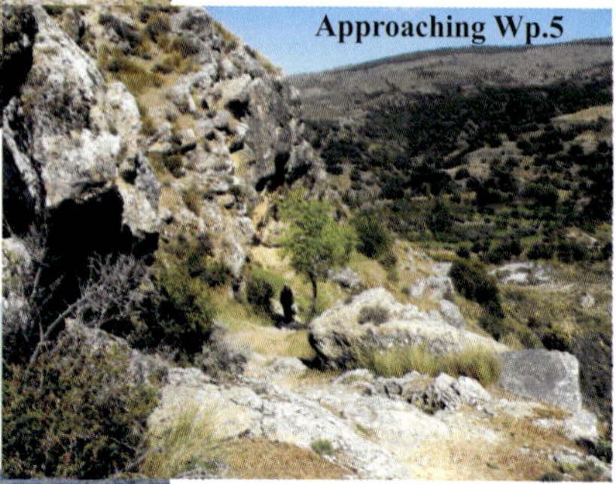

Approaching Wp.5

Following a clear path, we climb past a reservoir and pass to the left of the **El Fuerte** crags, where we reach a second Y junction, this one unmarked (Wp.5 33M). Forking left and skirting the summit, we maintain a south-easterly direction to pass the remains of an *aljub* (a Moorish cistern).

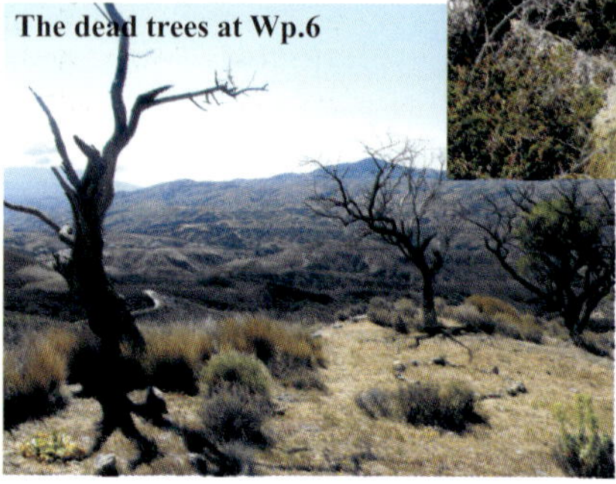

The dead trees at Wp.6

Following a faint path along the ridge to the south of **El Fuerte**, we soon see **Lobras** then (off to our left once we reach the tip of the ridge, where there are two dead trees on a tiny terrace) **Cádiar** (Wp.6 38M). Five metres to the left of this point, a line of stones define the very faint continuation of our path.

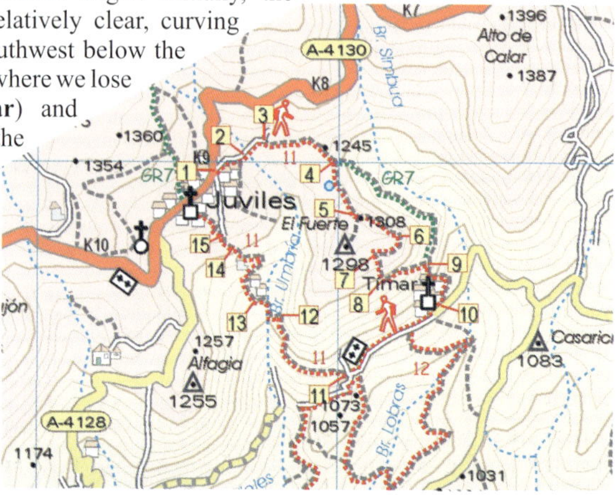

Descending below a retaining wall, we see **Tímar** for the first time, and can pick out a couple of stone lined zigzags in our ongoing path. This is where the pathfinding problems begin. Initially, the path remains relatively clear, curving round to the southwest below the retaining wall (where we lose sight of **Tímar**) and descending to the

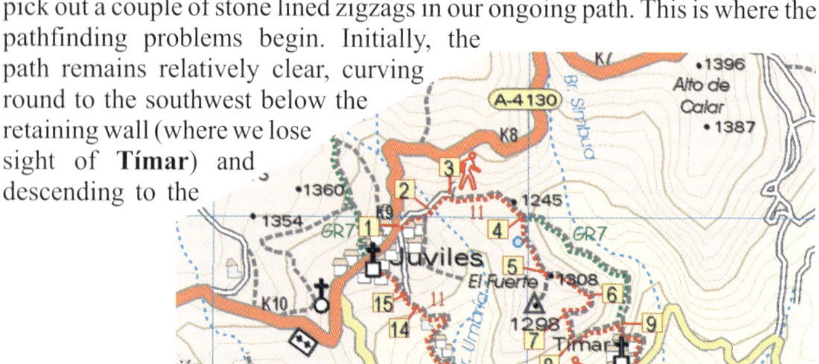

stump of a dead tree daubed with large green waymarks. At the waymarked tree (Wp.7 44M), we descend to the left, apparently off path, but passing regular green waymarks that confirm the very faint remains of an infinitesimally narrow path, soon bringing **Tímar** back into view (Wp.8 47M). Following the green waymarks (which appear every 25 metres), we head east (basically aiming for the road climbing away from **Tímar** toward **Cádiar**), cutting across the untenanted terrain below the southern bluffs of **El Fuerte**, gradually descending until we join the broad, but at this stage unwaymarked, path followed by the **GR7** (Wp.9 53M).

Turning right, we follow the GR down to the exquisite little hamlet of **Tímar**, which from above, barring the odd TV antenna, looks much as it must have done half a millennium ago. Entering **Tímar** (Wp.10 60M), we bear right and descend to the left of house No.15, after which we keep descending until we reach the lane in front of **Tímar** church, where we again bear right. We follow the lane for 600 metres until the cemetery, where we join the wayposted **Ruta Medieval** (Wp.11 71M). Directly below the cemetery, we fork right, climbing to an information panel about the old mercury works of the **Minas de la Retama**. Immediately behind the information panel we fork left on a narrow path passing below a chimney stack.

Following a rough, but distinct path picked out with orange waymarks, we curve round into the spectacular **Rambla de Nieles** gully, bringing **Juviles** church into view. Crossing occasional cobbled stretches, we descend briefly before climbing past the remains of an *acequia* to the densely wooded confluence of the two streams that form the **Río Nieles** (Wp.12 89M).

Crossing the meagre course of the more easterly affluent, we shadow the more westerly, climbing steeply then steadily to the end of a narrow track below an abandoned cabin (Wp.13 96M). Staying on the nearside of the stream, we climb behind a second, better maintained cabin that has the remains of a bread oven in its exterior wall.

We then walk along a terrace wall before zigzagging up across patchy cobbling to reach a junction directly below a massive holm oak sprouting from a fissured rock, to the right of which there is a large outcrop of reddish rock (Wp.14 106M). The reddish rock is the **Pisada del Gigante** or **Giant's Footstep**, allegedly named after an imprint on the face of the rock, one that I signally failed to decrypt, contriving only to fall over and dislocate my forefinger (these sort of things never happened to Harrison Ford). 150 metres later, the trail broadens to a track (Wp.15 108M), at which point we can either carry straight on to return to our starting point or, for refreshments, turn left on the **Ruta Medieval** wayposted path that climbs into the centre of **Juviles** village. Bearing left to pass in front of the church, we emerge on the A4130 just east of **Bar Fernandez**, then follow the road to the right past the **Bar Alonzo** to return to the start.

This is one that most emphatically does what it says on the tin, cobbling together two sublime and hitherto unpublished balcony paths between **Lobras** and **Tímar**, the one following the excellent **Acequia de los Castaños** *sendero local*, the other a stretch of the **PR299 Ruta Medieval** above the **Rambla de Nieles** as it cuts a swathe through banks of cistus, poppy, broom, and wild oats in an atmosphere pungent with the perfume of rose hip. Utterly lovely, utterly tranquil, utterly lost - in the figurative sense: we know where we are throughout; it's the cares of the world that slip away into oblivion.

Frankly, the idea that such a pure and simple pleasure should be marred by consulting a book en route is almost offensive. Happily, apart from one short stretch climbing from the *acequia* into **Tímar**, you should be able to stash the book and just enjoy the walking. For a full day's outing, this itinerary could be combined with Walk 11 to make a figure of 8 circuit.

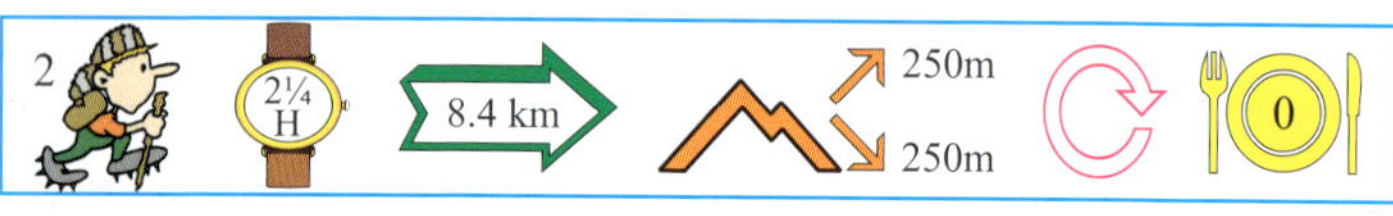

Access by car:

We start at the northern end of **Lobras** beside a white water hut, where there's a fingerpost for the 'GR7' to 'Timar', an information panel for the **Acequia de los Castaños** *sendero local*, and a concrete lay by with room for four or five cars.

From the top of the lay by

(Wp.1 0M), we follow the signs for the 'GR7/SL' and 'Timar', taking a broad track to the north. When the track doubles back to the left 25 metres from the road, we carry straight on, already following the **Acequia de los Castaños**, though the actual irrigation channel is interred for the first hundred metres or so.

When the **GR7** forks left 250 metres later to descend into the **Barranco de Lobras** (Wp.2 3M), we simply carry on along the *acequia*, which curls around the hillside bringing **Tímar** into view.

After 1200 metres strolling in the intermittent shade of mature oak, we cross a dirt track (Wp.3 18M) and, 400 metres later, a footbridge over the **Barranco**

The footbridge at Wp.4

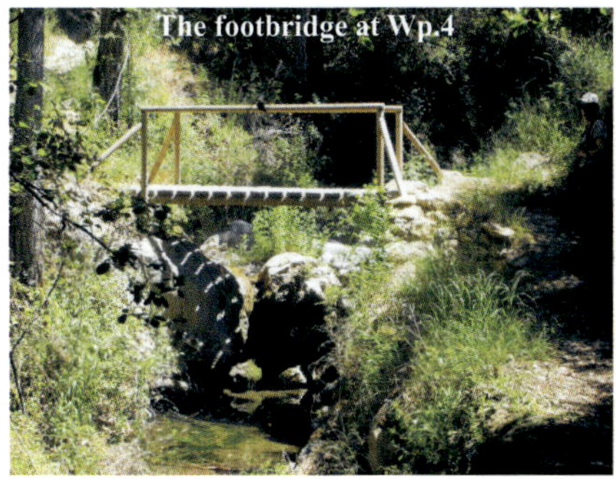

de Lobras stream. 50 metres after the footbridge (Wp.4 26M), we double back to the left on a dirt track.

At successive triple forks, we carry straight on along the central tine, the first time (50 metres from Wp.4) on dirt track, the second time on a narrow path (Wp.5 29M).

The road down from Nieles into the Rambla

Climbing amid terraces of olive and almond trees, we come to a lane below **Tímar**, where we turn left on the **GR7** (Wp.6 36M). We follow this lane into the **Rambla de Nieles** passing in quick succession the cemetery, where we join the **Ruta Medieval**, an old mercury mine works, and the point (not signposted) at which the **GR7** descends to the left past a pebble-dashed threshing circle (Wp.7 44M).

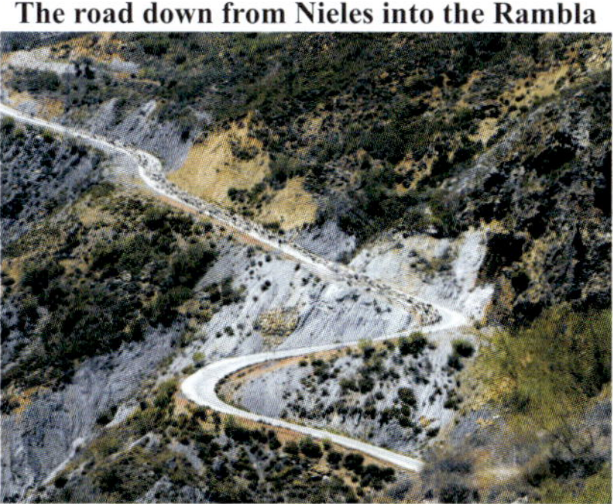

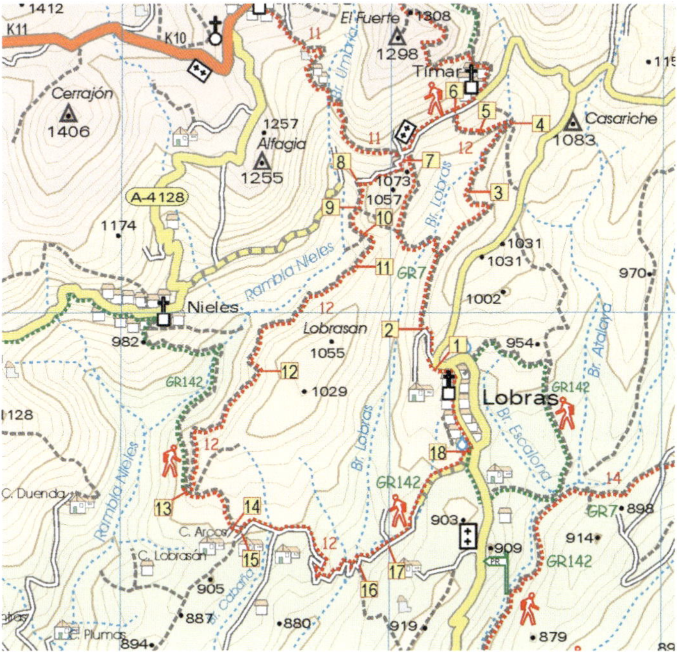

Just before the lane bottoms out in the **Rambla de Nieles** (Wp.8 48M), we turn left on a signposted track, still following the **Ruta Medieval**, then fork right 125 metres later (Wp.9).

After passing a branch descending to the right a little under 450 metres from the lane (Wp.10), the track dwindles to an overgrown path running along an interred pipe, which we follow for almost two kilometres, passing en route two minor obstacles. The first and superficially more significant is an erosion hole bridged by the exposed canalization pipe (Wp.11 57M).

This is a 'hands and bottoms' job, but scrambling into and out of the hole poses no significant problems. The second, 500 metres later, is a very modest slew of rubble (Wp.12 71M). Otherwise, there's no going wrong here as we simply follow the interred pipe along a contour line between the tree-lined *rambla* on our right and the humped rise of **Cerro Lobrasan** on our left.

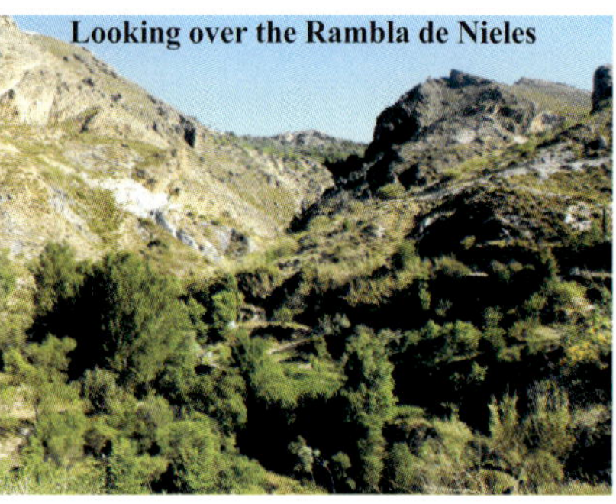

Looking over the Rambla de Nieles

At the tapering southern tip of **Cerro Lobrasan**, the path broadens then joins the GR142 (Wp.13 85M).

Still following the interred pipe, our path swings round to the east to reach a rough dirt track behind the semi-derelict **Cortijo de los Arcos** (Wp.14 91M). Bearing left, we cross an almond grove to join the *cortijo* access track (Wp.15 94M), where we again turn left. We now follow this track all the way back to **Lobras**, coiling into the **Barranco de Lobras** where we pass a signposted turning on the right for the 'Sendero Ventilla PR292' (Wp.16 110M). Climbing out of the *barranco*, we pass a track on the left (Wp.17 115M) and continue on the main track until it joins the road at the southern limit of **Lobras** (Wp.18 125M). Turning left, then forking left into **Calle Real**, we cross **Lobras** via the church square, then follow the main road back up to our starting point.

A most bucolic walk climbing amidst the immaculately tended market gardens and pastoral highlands on the western flank of the **Bérchules** valley, following two very pretty *acequias* with excellent mountain views. The way out of the village is steep, but thereafter, the walking is on the level, except for a brief, optional climb extending the *sendero local* via the **PR Sendero Vereica**. Note, if you're walking with dogs or are particularly timid around dogs, the extension is not recommended as it passes a sheepfold protected by a pack of mastiffs who weren't hugely pleased to see our two mutts. They didn't attack, but it wasn't exactly 'hale fellow, well met'.

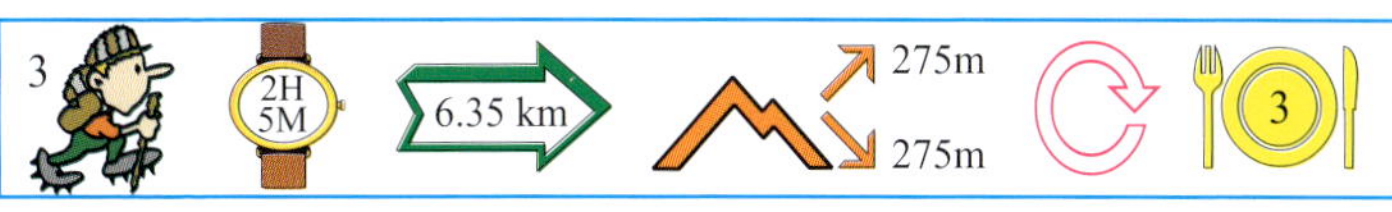

Access by car:

We start from the parking area on the right beside the **Bar Duende** at the entrance to **Bérchules** village, where there is generally plenty of room, the space reserved for the bus stop notwithstanding.

Opposite the entrance to the car park (Wp.1 0M), we take the road climbing away from the centre of the village signed toward the 'Mirador Era de la Platera' and the 'Mirador Apartamentos'. 200 metres later, we turn right at the **Fuente Platera** into **Calle Fuente Platera**, and climb along the pitted pedestrian alley of **Calle Platera**

At the junction with **Calle Nueva** and **Plaza Zapata**, we continue climbing into **Calle Fuentecilla**, passing a mapboard for the *sendero local*. At the top of **Calle Fuentecilla**, just over 400 metres from the start, we continue climbing steadily to steeply on a broad path (Wp.2 9M).

After crossing a lane above the village (Wp.3 14M), we follow a wayposted track, which is surfaced for the first 150 metres, still climbing steadily.

At the end of the concrete, we ignore two paths doubling back to the left (Wp.4 18M & Wp.5) then fork left at a PR and SL wayposted Y junction (Wp.6 22M) for the last stretch of unavoidable climbing to a small white house where we join the **Acequia Real** (Wp.7 27M). And that, unless you opt for the detour along the PR at the end, is pretty much it as far as exertion goes. Following an unusually broad path along a lovely, deep *acequia*, we enjoy fine views over the highlands and the rugged land round the **Junta de los Ríos Chico** and **Grande**, which we explore in Walk 29.

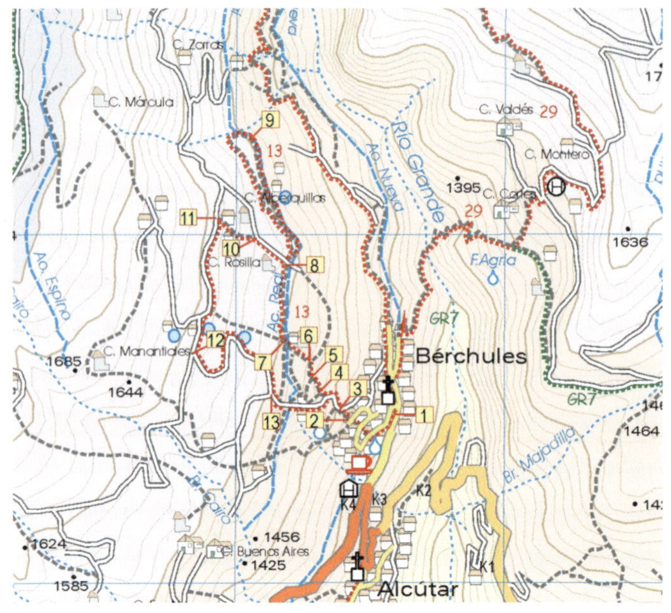

When the *acequia* crosses a dirt track (Wp.8 36M), we ignore the PR waypost on the left and carry straight on, passing between two large reservoirs, to continue along the **Acequia Real**, now following a much narrower path.

After traversing patchy woodland of chestnut, birch, eucalyptus, and poplar, we

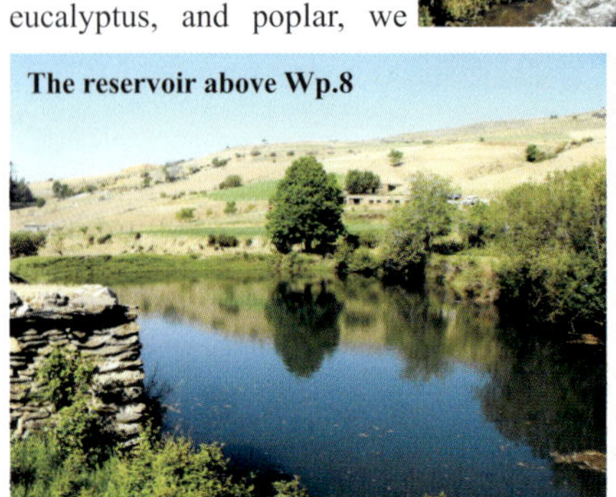
The reservoir above Wp.8

Acequia Real

pass above three large reservoirs, where the **Acequia Real** crosses a rough dirt track (Wp.9 51M).

There are no wayposts here, but the *acequia* path becomes much narrower and overgrown, indicating that this is the turning point for the *sendero local*.

Fifty metres up to the left, we head back
the way we came alongside another,
narrower *acequia* that brings us back to
Wp.8 (63M). From here, we can either
return to **Bérchules** by our outward route
or, to extend the walk and expand the
views, climb to the right on the dirt track
marked with a PR waypost, which soon
passes, on our left, **Cortijo de la Rosilla**.

When the main track bears right behind a
cabin, we fork left on a minor PR
wayposted branch (Wp.10 70M) and
climb steadily to join the main track
circling the uplands of the **Bérchules**
valley (Wp.11 76M).

The return *acequia*

Turning left, we stroll along this track, enjoying grand views to the southeast
until we come to a major junction with a track descending to the left (Wp.12
88M).

Turning left, we simply follow this track all the way back to Wp.3, passing en
route the sheep-shielding mastiffs, and bearing left when our track runs into
concrete at a junction with another track (Wp.13 103M).

Cádiar is not the best walking country in the Alpujarras, but there's a decent bit of Winter walking in the vicinity, and since the town is home to what appears to be the largest British expat community in the region apart from **Órgiva**, it seemed reasonable that a guide book directed at English speakers should show something of what's on offer in the area. The present itinerary is not recommended in hot weather, but on a blustery day it offers fine views of the high mountains, and one short stretch of wild walking that lends an agreeable air of adventure to what is otherwise a very domestic outing exploring the agricultural landscape around the town.

The route follows the **GR7** and **GR142** which are adequately waymarked and wayposted though some titivation is required.

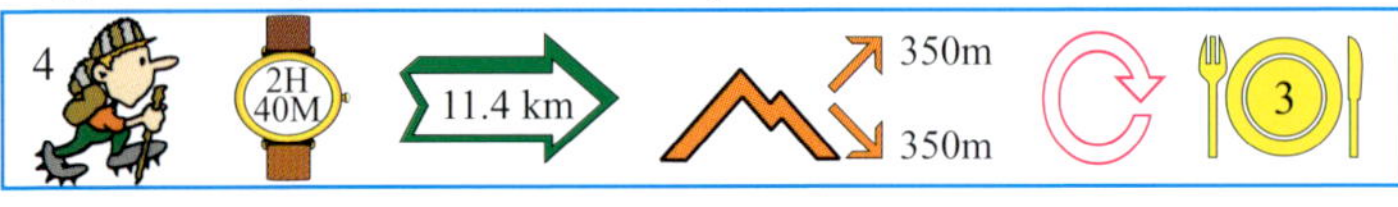

Access by car:

Our itinerary starts from the A348 directly to the south of **Cádiar**, a little way short of the fire station and immediately before the **British Café** and the signposted turning for the cemetery. We park on the western side of the road in the long lay by beside the large mosaic identifying **Cádiar**, a little optimistically, as being the heart of the Alpujarras.

From the lay by (Wp.1 0M), we take the lane into **Cádiar**'s **Barrio Bajo** and immediately turn left, zigzagging down through the unnamed, largely pedestrian alleyways of the *barrio*. At the left hand end of the black railed lane at the bottom of the *barrio*, a pedestrian ramp accesses a road between the bridge over the **Río Cádiar** and the fire station (Wp.2 3M).

Turning right, we cross the bridge then bear left on a dirt track, joining the **GR7**.

After traversing allotments and orchards, we ignore a fork on the right (Wp.3 13M), and stick with the main track as it crosses an almond grove, forking right at a Y junction 700 metres later (Wp.4 20M) to shadow a narrow *acequia*.

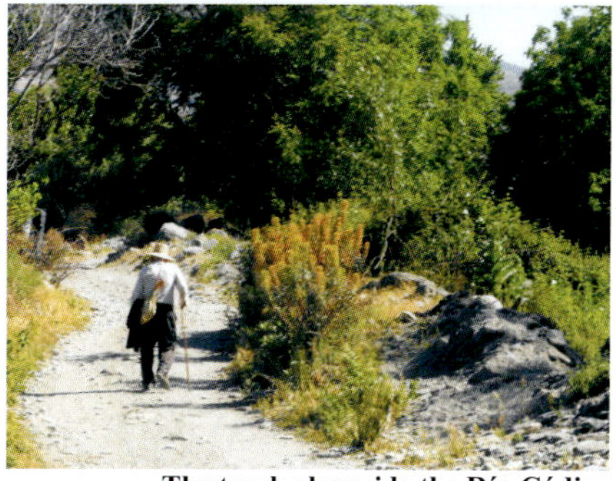

The track alongside the Río Cádiar

At the next two junctions, the first a crossroads where the trail on the left leads to the **Alqueria de Morayma** tourism complex (Wp.5 28M), the second when the track doubles back to the left and the **GR7** becomes a path (Wp.6 30M), we carry straight on. Crossing the *acequia* behind a small reservoir, we follow its narrow interred course to a Y junction (Wp.7 34M).

Forking right then left thirty metres later, we leave the course of the *acequia* and climb across dessicated hillside to a crossroads with a rough firebreak and a path (Wp.8 39M). Carrying straight on along the main path, we climb more gently to cross a dirt track in the middle of a field of fig trees (Wp.9 44M), from where we can see **Lobras** directly ahead of us and fine views open out over the highlands behind **Bérchules**.

A long, gentle descent traversing the flank of the hill behind the fig field brings us down to the rough **Rambla de Albayar**, where we bear left to reach the signposted intersection of the **GRs7** and **142** at the confluence of the **Barrancos de Escalona** and **Atalaya** (Wp.10 54M). This is where the adventurous stretch begins.

Turning left for **Cádiar**, we follow a faint trail across a field of olive trees beside the riverbed of the **Rambla Vereda**, on the far side of which, all traces of a path disappear and we take to the riverbed itself, splashing in and out of a shallow stream. When the riverbed widens, we pass a GR signpost, 100 metres after which, directly in front of a breeze block byre on the right bank of the stream (Wp.11 64M), a faint path runs along the edge of an olive grove. After 100 metres, the path crosses back onto the left bank, where it resolves itself into a rough track crisscrossing the watercourse before emerging on the **Lobras** road (Wp.12 69M).

Turning left, we follow the road over the first of two bridges crossing the **Río Guadalfeo** and **Barranco Lagarto**. At the ruined mill between the two bridges (Wp.13 73M), we descend to the right of the mill then scramble up the embankment behind it to pick up a faint firebreak track. The firebreak climbs directly behind the mill, gently for the first 50 metres, then steeply, then very steeply. Fifteen metres up the very steep stretch, we fork left on a GR wayposted path (Wp.14 81M) that joins a dirt track 125 metres later (Wp.15).

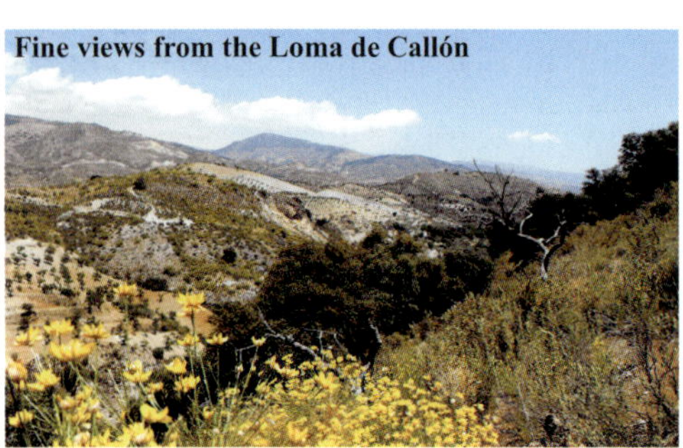
Fine views from the Loma de Callón

Bearing left, we follow this track along the spine of the **Loma de Callón**, crossing the top of a steep field (where the trail is usually ploughed up) of almond and fig trees, beyond which we come to a junction of tracks beside a white hut (Wp.16 93M).

Taking the narrower track which continues climbing (NE) along the ridge beside a field of vines, we pass in front of a new, two-tiered *caseta*, 100 metres after which, the track tapers to a path, which soon disappears in ploughed land. Slightly to the left of the point where the path disappears, there's a small col (Wp.17 100M), from where a faint trail climbs steadily (NE) toward the summit of the *loma*, where we join a broad dirt track (Wp.18 106M). Bearing right, we follow this track round the southern flank of the *loma*, which is crowned with a large holm oak, bringing **Cádiar** back into view. After the strenuous climb from the **Guadalfeo**, easy walking resumes as we stride along the ridge, enjoying excellent views toward the high mountains.

When the track descends to the A348 at the entrance to the **Alqueria de Morayma** tourist complex (Wp.19 117M), we continue on the road, which we follow for 600 metres until the junction with the A345 (Wp.20 123M), where we turn left. The GR stays on the road here, but it's more agreeable to scramble onto the terraces alongside it, joining a track branching off the road 200 metres later (Wp.21 127M). At an unmarked Y junction of tracks 100 metres later (Wp.22 128M), we fork right. After running parallel to the A348, the track bears round to the left, bringing into view a cluster of *casetas*, at which point we double back to the right on a wayposted path (Wp.23 132M). The path continues to shadow the road before descending (very steeply and dustily towards the end) to rejoin the track.

30 metres to the right is a signposted junction indicating **Cádiar** is on the left (Wp.24 138M). However, to avoid additional road walking, we turn right, signed for **Jorairatar**, passing under the A348 to join a waymarked track, which we follow to the east for 300 metres. Immediately after passing a rough branch track and a ruin on the left, we turn left on a dusty track marked with a **PR25** signpost (Wp.25 143M). The track climbs steadily before joining a concrete lane in front of the cemetery (Wp.26 147M), where we turn left to return to our starting point.

Mecina-Bombarón has long been a 'must visit' for lovers of acequias and chestnut forests, offering ramblers some of the finest woodland walking in the Alpujarras along one of the region's loveliest man made aquifers. The present 'two for the price of one' itinerary is the result of a clever idea that not everyone will find quite so clever in practice. I had intended replacing the **PR111** (15a) with a new route (15b) trailblazing a cunning link between the village's two *acequias*, which have both been designated *senderos locales* since the publication of the previous edition of this book. Unfortunately, the cunning off path bit I'd devised in the middle proved a tad more cunning and a tad more off path than I had anticipated. For those of us who love tramping through pathless woodland, it's the most tremendous fun. For those who don't, it's not. Hence the two in one.

As it happens, the two itineraries are complimentary and I recommend doing both if you can. That said, if you don't want to walk with your head buried in a book (unavoidable on the **PR111**, since the waymarking is very wayward) or don't positively relish paths that appear to be made up literally on the hoof (as in the link between the *senderos locales*) treat each itinerary as a linear stroll, continuing along the **Acequia de los Castaños** at Wps.4&9 of the **PR111** to reach its source in the **Río Mecina** 900 metres later, and simply following the **SL Acequia Baja** to Wp.4 and back again.

(a) PR111 Acequia de los Castaños

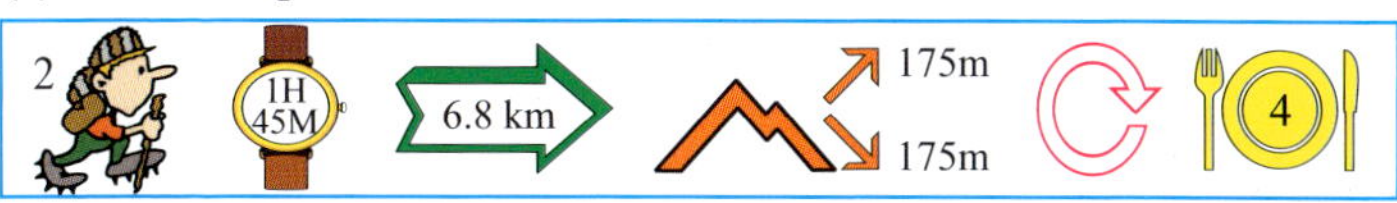

Access by car: take the concrete track from the western limit of **Mecina-Bombarón** up to **Calle Plaza Vieja** and park in the **Plaza Vieja** itself. From the *plaza*, take the narrow street climbing beside the *fuente* (signposted 'Bérchules 2h') and bear right onto **Calle Castillo** (signposted 'Sendero de las Acequias 4h') (Wp.1 0M).

From the top of **Calle Castillo**, we continue on a mule trail till it crosses the **Acequia de los Castaños** (Wp.2 3M), where we bear right on a minor path passing a large reservoir. Beyond the reservoir, we follow a narrow path bearing away from the main *acequia* feeding the reservoir. We then climb slightly alongside a minor, dry *acequia*, passing above a small house, behind which we rejoin the **Acequia de los Castaños**.

The *acequia* path soon runs into a broad trail (an alternative, waymarked access from the village) (Wp.3 13M), which shadows the channel for 125-metres then forks left (Wp.4), rapidly becoming a partially cobbled trail climbing to join a dirt track (Wp.5 18M). We now simply follow this track to the north through a delightfully bucolic landscape peppered with well-maintained *cortijos* and enticing country cabins enjoying great views up toward the head of the **Río Mecina**.

After a gentle climb we reach a major, waymarked Y-junction, where we fork right, away from the 'Propiedad Privada' track (Wp.6 28M), and dip down briefly.

We stick with the main track until oak begin to mingle among the chestnut and poplar, and we come to another major waymarked junction, where we again fork right (Wp.7 46M).

Our branch track descends past twin threshing circles, a small cabin and ancient threshing machine, after which we leave the track, forking right on a broad trail descending to a crumbling *cortijo* with large waymarks on the corner of the main building (Wp.8 50M).

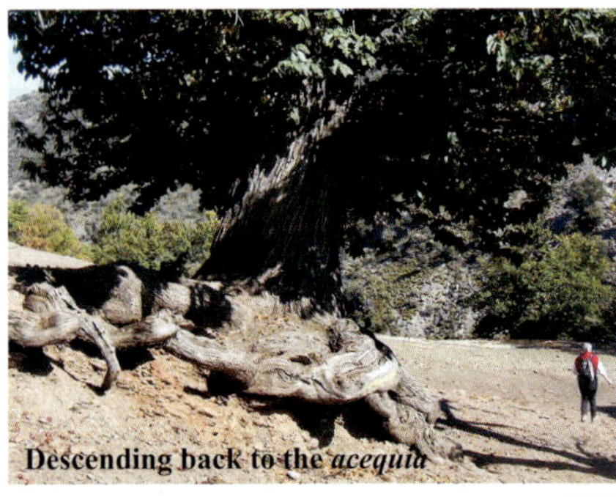

Descending back to the *acequia*

The onward route is not immediately obvious, but descending to the right of the *cortijo* then immediately bearing left along its lower edge (WITHOUT descending into the gully below it), we recover a minor track at the eastern end of the *cortijo*, which descends past a PVC-lined reservoir and a small cabin to rejoin the **Acequia de los Castaños** (Wp.9 56M).

Having negotiated the *cortijo* descent, pathfinding problems disappear, as we now simply turn right and follow the *acequia*, crossing a dirt track leading to a *cortijo* that lies below the *acequia* (Wp.10 75M) before rejoining our outward route at Wp.4 (87M).

We can either bear left at Wp.3 and follow the broad trail back to the village then bear right and keep bearing right round the outskirts of the village to return to the **Plaza Vieja** or (more direct and more attractive) follow the outward leg along the *acequia* back to the start.

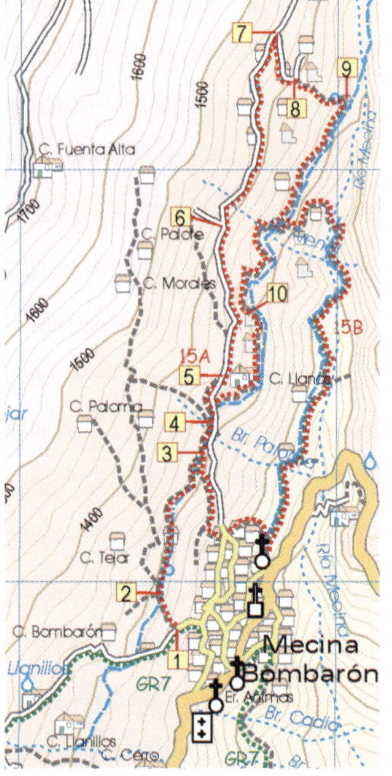

(b) SLs Acequia Baja & Acequia Alta

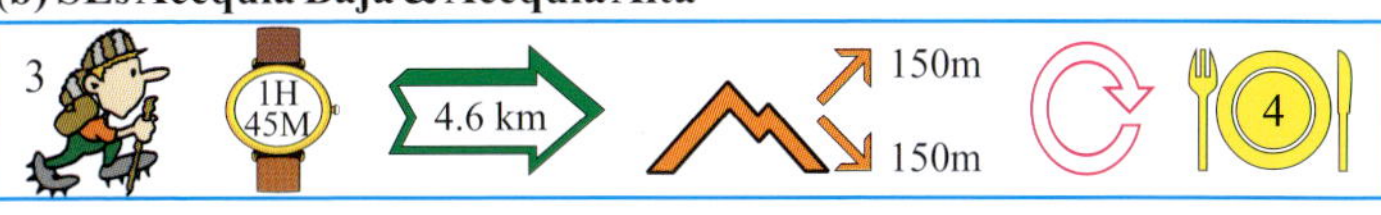

Access by car:
The walk starts from the A4130, just past the **Ermita de los Remedios** at the eastern limits of **Mecina-Bombarón**, where there is an information panel for the **Sendero Local Acequia Baja** and ample parking in the lay bys on either side of the road.

The start couldn't be more straightforward as we simply set off along the *acequia* path beside the information panel (Wp.1 0M) and follow the *acequia* until its terminus at source in the **Río de Mecina**, tunnelling through chestnut woods nearly all the way.

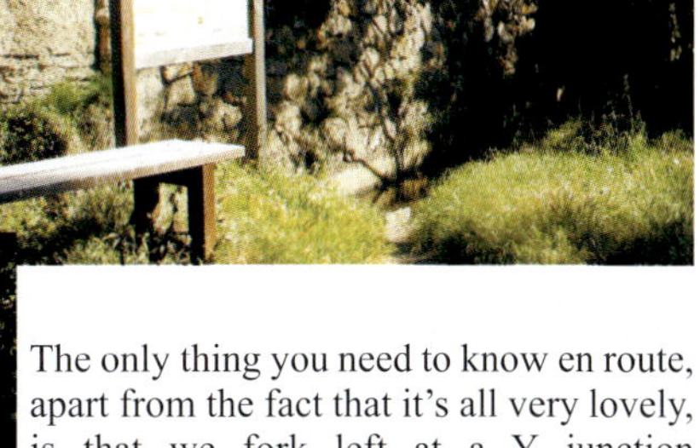

The only thing you need to know en route, apart from the fact that it's all very lovely, is that we fork left at a Y junction immediately after crossing a small stream (Wp.2 10M) and climb behind a house to avoid going through the garden, which the waypost suggests we do.

Acequia Baja

After passing in front of another gorgeously located house, we briefly diverge from the *acequia*, crossing a small rise where we ignore a faint fork down to the right (Wp.3 17M) seventy five metres before rejoining the *acequia*, which ends at source in the river 750 metres later (Wp.4 35M).

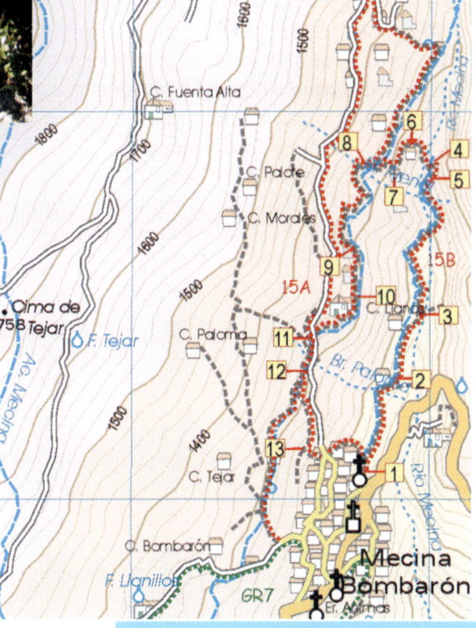

To do the full loop, we retrace our steps fifty metres to a point just short of the mesh fence that has run alongside the *acequia* for the last few hundred metres, where there is a rough fork descending to the left (Wp.5) and, on the right, a white waymark on a rock. Hopping across the *acequia*, we climb steeply between the fence and a large chestnut tree, bearing right behind the tree on a faint way confirmed by another white waymark. Climbing steeply amid magnificent chestnut trees, we continue trending to the right (NNW) on the clearest traces.

Passing to the right of a small stone cabin built into the hillside (Wp.6 47M) (above which another white waymark confirms that we're on path, not that there are any paths to speak of), we bear left (S) and continue climbing, soon recovering clearer traces of a trodden way passing between a waymarked tree and a second cabin (Wp.7 57M).

Still climbing, though now in a more westerly direction, we see off to our left the breeze block and stone walls of the *cortijo* at the head of the fenced area, from which point another fifty metres climbing brings us onto the **Acequia Alta** (Wp.8 64M).

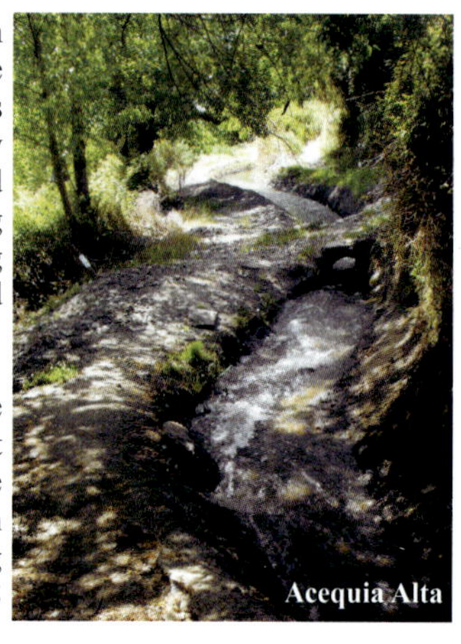

The tricky bit is over. From here, we simply turn left and follow the *acequia* back towards **Mecina**, crossing the track accessing the *cortijo* (Wp.9 74M). When the path broadens to a track (Wp.10 78M), we bear left, recovering the *acequia* path fifty metres later, after which the village comes into view.

After a further 400 metres, a footbridge takes us onto a broader path on the right hand side of the *acequia*, though it is possible to continue on the lower path (Wp.11 85M). Either way, the two paths rejoin 100 metres later, at which point we follow the broad trail forking down to the left (Wp.12) and descend to join a concrete track that takes us into **Mecina**. At the *lavadero/fuente* on the edge of the village (Wp.13), we turn left and keep descending to the left into **Calle Fuente Romera**, from the end of which an intermittently surfaced track takes us back to our starting point.

The three thousand metre **El Caballo** (see Walk 30) is the undisputed star of the western Alpujarras and rightly so, but there's much to recommend its sister summit of **Peña Caballera**. There's no punishing climb for one thing, the views of the **Contravessia**, **Almijara**, and **Tejeda** *sierras* are quite splendid, and there's a gloriously airy feel to this comparatively easy high mountain walk, which almost exclusively follows dirt tracks. The summit itself is undistinguished and its western flank is littered with the debris of the 2006 forest fire, the damage of which, experts say, will take fifty years to repair.

Nonetheless, this little visited summit is not to be dismissed and, for those of you who can't quite face the full on slog up **Caballo**, but want to do the extraordinary drive up **Pista Forestal 1** (see Appendix A) and wander about a bit when you get to the end, this is the ideal itinerary. There's a steep firebreak descent, but otherwise there is little to take a toll on lungs, knees or any of the other vulnerable bits walkers tend to abuse.

Access by car:
There is ample trackside parking in the shade of the oaks on the hairpin bend at km 16.1 of **Pista Forestal 1** (see Appendix A).

The Rules reservoir

From the hairpin bend (Wp.1 0M), we simply continue along the main track, climbing to pass between two metal posts beside a solitary pine (the starting point for Walk 30) (Wp.2 10M), where the track narrows dramatically as it embarks on a long, gentle descent with nothing to distract us but the views - prepare to be thoroughly distracted!

A grand panorama gradually opens out, first over the **Río Lanjarón** valley, then up toward **El Caballo**, as we pass a path climbing from the **Tello** helipad, which is visible down below us (Wp.3 22M). The track then zigzags up to pass behind a white roofed weather station, the zigs breached by a succession of

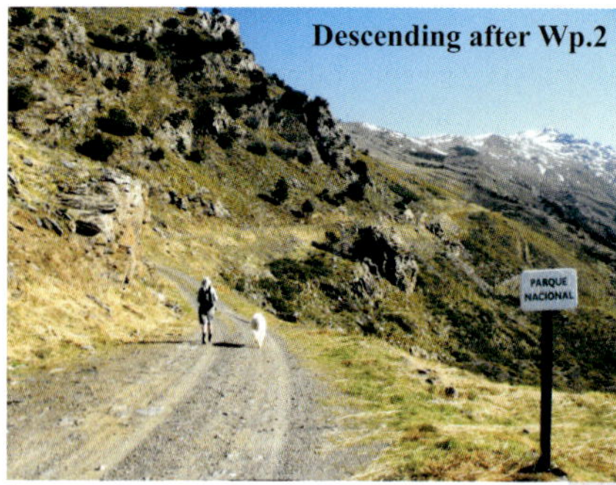

shortcuts, each framed by sentinel standing stones, the last of which brings us to the end of the track, where there is a sign for 'Cerro del Caballo / Ventura' (Wp.4 55M).

Following a clear path picked out with standing stones, we cross a gully and a small rise then zigzag up towards the **Ventura** refuge, a simple stone cabin, directly above which we can see the horizontal scar of an *acequia* running along the hillside.

At **Ventura** (Wp.5 72M) (which is semi-derelict, but provides adequate shelter if required from excessive heat, rain or cold - though ideally you wouldn't be up here if any of the above pertain), we stick to the main path climbing (NE) behind the refuge, approaching a dense hanger of pine.

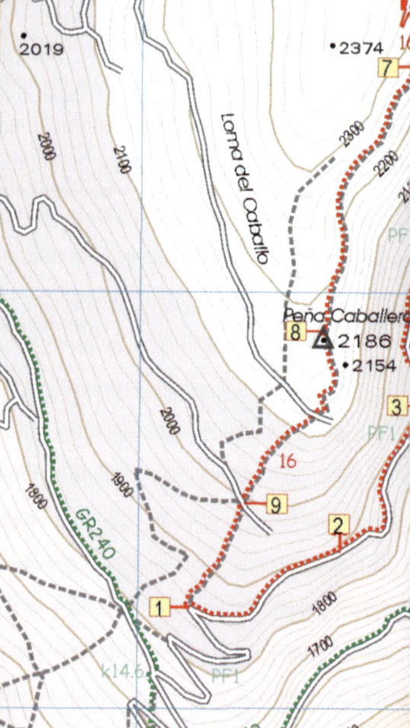

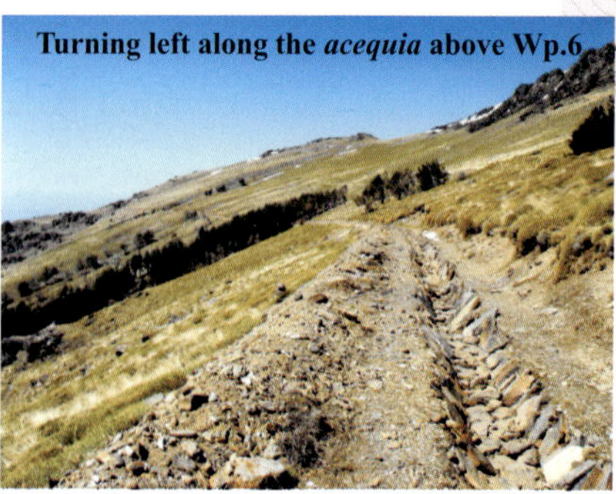

Immediately before the pine, we leave the main path and fork left on a less well defined path (Wp.6 77M) climbing to join the *acequia* twenty metres further up the slope. At this point, the present itinerary and Walk 30 diverge as we turn left along the *acequia*.

After almost a kilometre of easy strolling, the *acequia* path feeds into a track (Wp.7 102M) that climbs above the contour followed by the *acequia* for 200 metres then snakes along the hillside to **Peña Caballera**, a knobby rock topped with a cylindrical trig point, directly below which (Wp.8 122M) we pass two very faint branches doubling back to the right onto the **Loma del Caballo**.

Carrying straight on for another 500 metres, we join a firebreak where we come to a Y junction overlooking the **Rules** and **Beznar** reservoirs (Wp.9

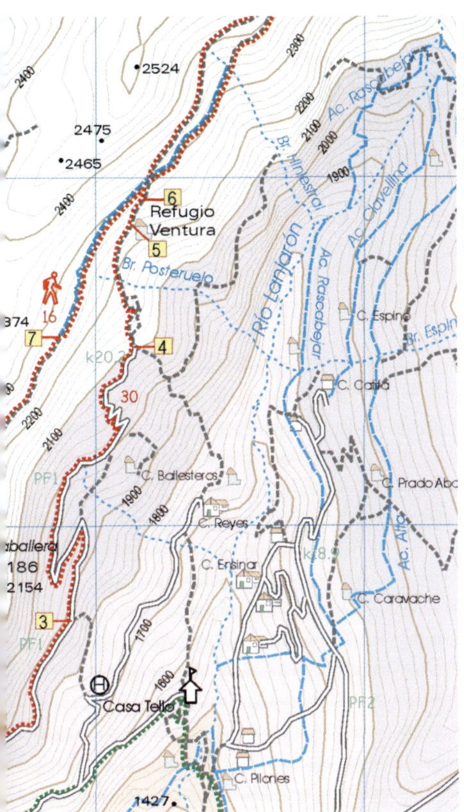

127M). Forking left, we descend steeply then steadily toward the more northerly of the two reservoirs, then steeply again to a second major Y junction (Wp.10 137M), where we carry straight on along the left fork for a final steady descent back to our starting point.

Despite my strictures in the introduction concerning the track-hugging **Sendero Sulayr**, at its best the **GR240** is quite sublime, in this instance incorporating a path of which I was wholly ignorant, but which I reckon may well be the most beautiful in the entire Alpujarras. Beginning with an easy climb on dirt tracks traversing some really beautiful woods, we join the GR above the Buddhist retreat of **O.Sel.Ling** and follow it along the **Acequia Almiar** to the *área recreativa* at **Puente Palo**.

Frankly, words fail me when it comes to describing just how delightful this path is. It's so lovely it's sinful. Well, you know what it's like with sin. Once you get a taste for it, you can't leave it alone. In this instance, when the official route diverges from the *acequia* we just thought, "We can't be having that", so we continued along the *acequia* to see what happened. What usually happens in these cases is a combination of terror and entanglement followed by a humiliating retreat, but for once the gamble paid off and took us to extraordinary places.

If you prefer to avoid the slightly rougher walking and just want to keep things gentle, fork left at Wp.7 to descend to Wp.13. Thereafter, the descent on the **PR22** follows another lovely path about which I would be going into raptures if it featured in any other walk, but which pales a little in comparison to the **Acequia Almiar**. AN ABSOLUTE MUST DO.

Part of the climb crosses private property and involves passing a 'Prohibido el Paso'sign, but the sign is intended to deter motorized traffic and the English owner is relaxed about responsible walkers. So long as nobody does anything silly and dogs are kept on a lead, there is no reason to suppose this track will be closed.

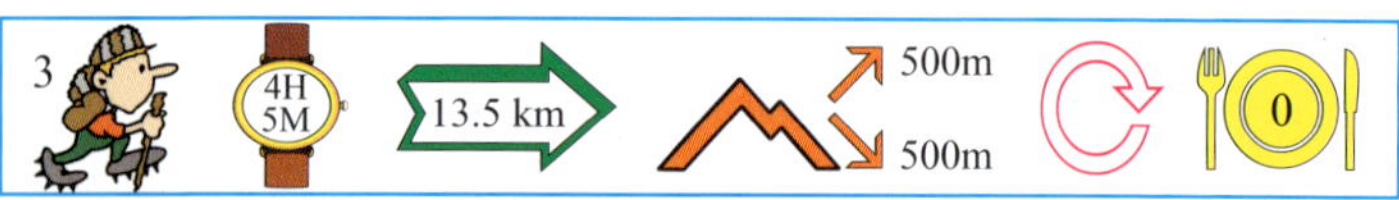

Access by car:
The walk starts from km4.7 of **Pista Forestal 2** (see Appendix A) where there's a mapboard for the **PR22**, a sign indicating that the **Puente Palo Área Recreativa** is 6km away, and ample trackside parking.

From the **PR22** mapboard (Wp.1 0M), we simply continue along the main **Puente Palo** track for two and a quarter kilometres, ignoring all branch tracks and enjoying fine views to the southwest toward the **Rules** dam.

Views from the main track near the start

After a long easterly trend, the track doubles back to the northwest and, 750 metres later, we turn right to go through large black gates on a minor track marked with a 'Prohibido el Paso' sign (Wp.2 33M), taking all necessary precautions to avoid any disturbance that might jeopardize this exquisite itinerary for future walkers.

This is where the real pleasure begins as we climb into shady oak woods, passing a cluster of *casetas*, and carrying straight on at a junction with a major branch off to the right (Wp.3 44M).

After climbing above the houses and crossing a couple of partially canalized watercourses, the track levels out in a lovely, bucolic landscape tessellated with coppicing and patches of denser woodland.

The track above Wp.4

Forking left at a Y junction (Wp.4 58M), we resume our gentle ascent, intermittently converging with the upper watercourse, which is now a consistently canalized *acequia*. Passing a small pond, we fork right (Wp.5 79M), a few minutes after which, the track fades, the tree cover thins, and we cross the **Acequia Almiar** to join the GR wayposted **Sendero Sulayr** (Wp.6 84M).

Acequia Almiar

Turning left and immediately returning to shady woodland, we follow a lovely sun dappled path weaving through the woods above the *acequia*. 800 metres later, we cross a firebreak and the path cleaves more closely to the *acequia*, pine gradually supplanting the oak as grand views open up towards the **Loma de Cáñar** (see Walk 31).

After a little over 600 metres walking along the wall on the southern side of the *acequia*, we cross back onto the northern side via a footbridge and pass above a large pasture, skirting a second, larger pond. A little less than a kilometre after this second pond, we come to a crossroads with a major signed and wayposted track '1.4km' from the *área recreativa* (Wp.7 132M).

At this point, the **GR240** descends to the left to join **Pista Forestal 2** at the intersection with the top of the **PR22**. Chances are that you will find this as regrettable as we did. If so and if you don't mind a little rough walking, stick with the *acequia* path, which continues to the north, passing a fallen tree that we have to duck under before reaching a small waterfall (Wp.8 152M).

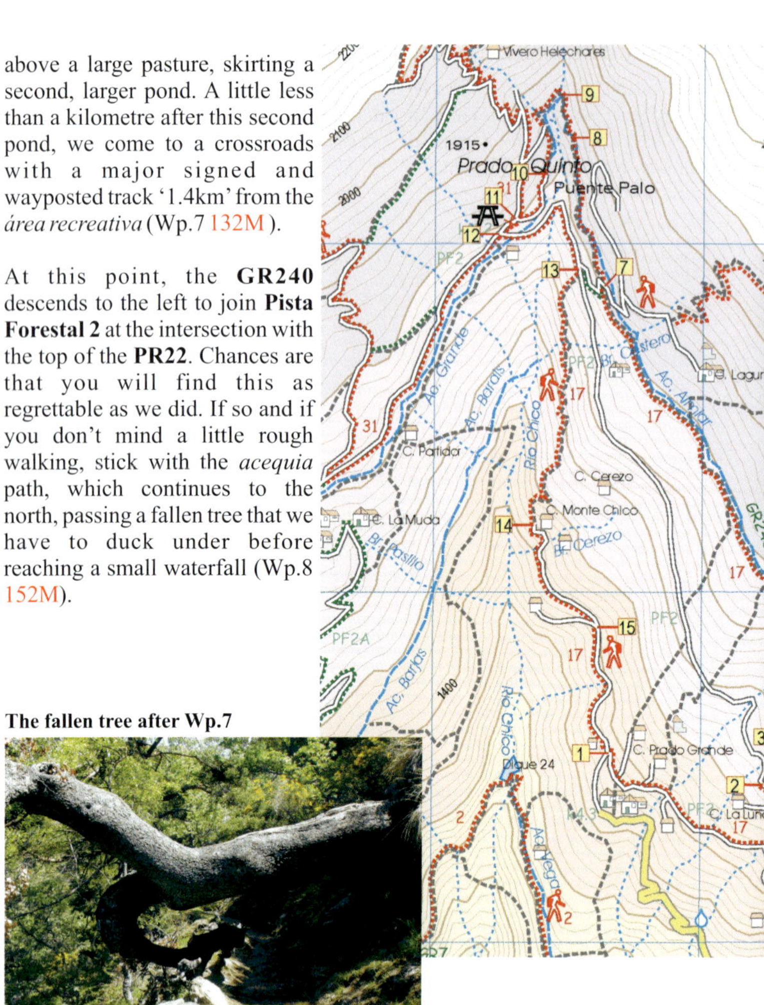

The fallen tree after Wp.7

Scrambling up to the left of the falls, we recover a good path that brings us to the *acequia*'s source in the **Río Chico** (Wp.9 159M). Five metres above the right bank of the river, there is another *acequia*, on which we bear left.

After descending alongside two brief but swift races, we come to a clearing used for stockpiling logs. On the far side of this clearing and 25 metres to the left of the *acequia*, there is the end of a logging track (Wp.10 172M) which promptly crosses the course of the *acequia*.

When the logging track joins another, broader track (Wp.11 178M), we turn left to descend to **Pista Forestal 2** at the **Puente Palo Área Recreativa**, where we again turn left (Wp.12 181M), once more on the **GR240** and joining the tail end of the yellow and white wayposted **PR22**, which we now follow for the rest of the walk.

A little under 600 metres after the *área recreativa,* at a sign and wayposted intersection when the GR forks left on the track climbing to Wp.7, we descend to the right (Wp.13 190M) on a broad trail signposted for the 'Casa Forestal'. The trail dwindles to a path descending through mixed woodland that includes a scattering of centenarian oaks, between which we enjoy great views over the **Río Chico** valley.

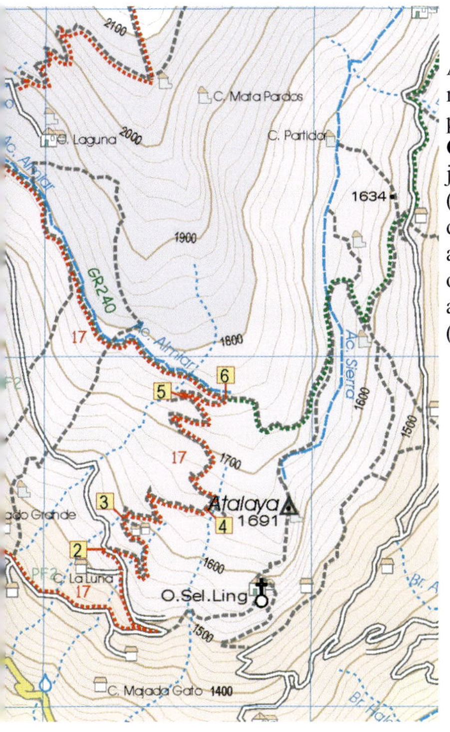

After a kilometre, the path veers round to the right to skirt the green perimeter fence of the **Monte Chico** arboretum, below which we join the arboretum access track (Wp.14 226M). The track descends steeply, then levels out and follows a contour line back to our starting point, passing en route a branch doubling back to the right (Wp.15 236M).

This is the well-known **Red Route** from **Capileira** to **La Cebadilla**, the abandoned hamlet built to service the **Central Poqueira** power-station at the junction of the **Ríos Toril** & **Naute**. On the way back, we pass **Puente Buchite**, one of the loveliest picnic spots in the gorge, but get there early if you're visiting in the summer, as it's popular with local expats and guided parties. If it's not your habit already, take a towel.

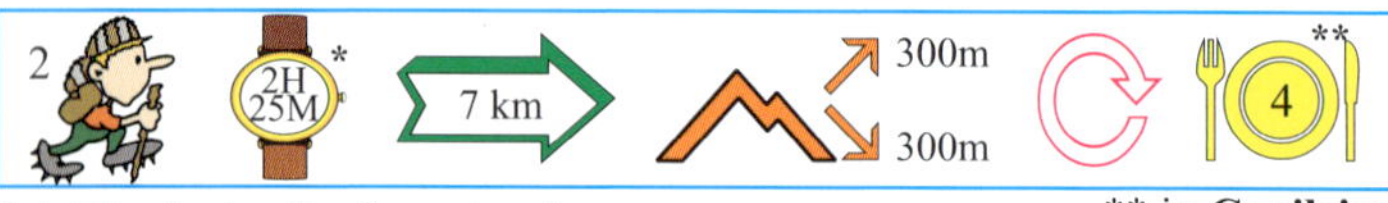

* + 20 minutes for the extension   ** in **Capileira**

Access by car:
You can park in the municipal car-park or, if you don't fancy negotiating the narrow alley down to the car-park, on the main road one hundred metres above the **Café-Bar Rosendo**.

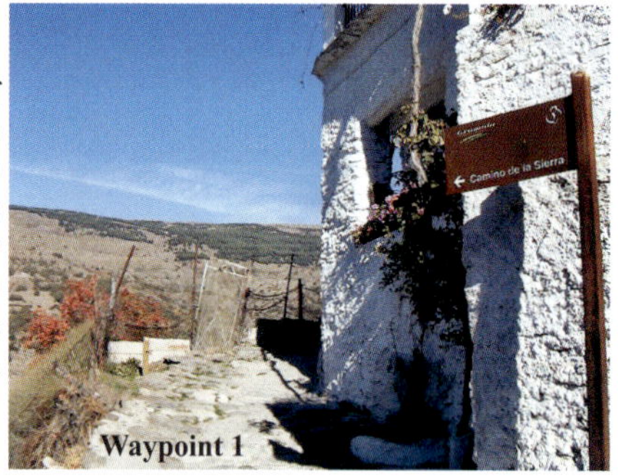
Waypoint 1

Starting at the northern end of **Capileira**, we take the slip road next to the *Aparcamiento Municipal* sign just past the **Café-Bar Rosendo**, then bear left on the **Caidero de las Ramones** and turn right opposite the *fuente* on a cobbled path (Wp.1 0M).

Climbing past the mapboards, we cross a dirt track at the edge of the village and take the broad path past a Blue Route mapboard. This path passes two water huts (Wps. 2&3, 10M & 15M): after the first hut, we continue up the main path towards the electricity pylons; after the second, we turn left on a narrow dirt track leading to the **Acequia de Lugares** at a waypost and new stone building.

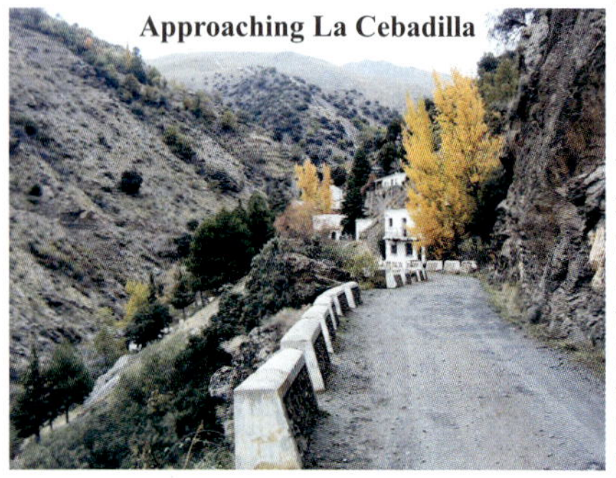
Approaching La Cebadilla

We then follow the *acequia* (which occasionally disappears underground, notably where the track widens near a recently restored *cortijo* ([Wp.4 40M]) till a gentle five minute climb leads to **La Cebadilla** forestry track (Wp.5 50M). We turn left here and follow the track through **La Cebadilla** to the **Puente Hondero** (Wp.6 70M).

Extension

From **Puente Hondero**, take the concrete track behind the red and white barrier, cross a second bridge at the junction of the **Ríos Toril** and **Naute**, and a third, **Puente Naute**, to a *Parque Natural* mapboard. When the path upriver bears left and starts climbing, carry straight on to descend to the river and a pleasant bathing spot, ten minutes from **Puente Hondero**.

To return to Capileira

To return to **Capileira**, we take the track climbing south from **Puente Hondero** along the right bank of the **Río Poqueira**.

Puente Hondero

After ten minutes of steady climbing, the track bears sharp right below a *cortijo* (Wp.7 80M). Immediately after the bend, a waypost indicates a narrow path climbing between the main farm buildings and a tall pylon with a small aerial on top. We follow this path between the fields beyond the *cortijo* until it goes to the left of a ruin and joins the **Blue Route**.

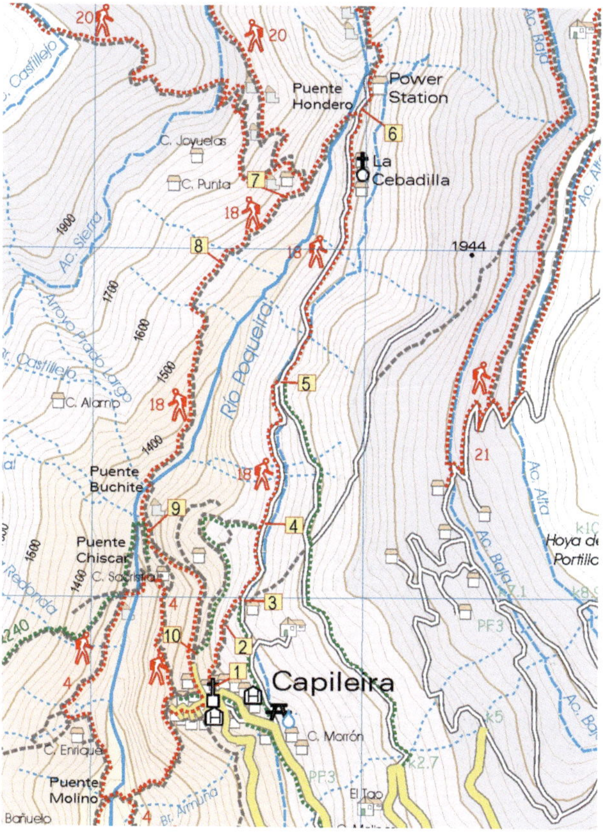

Continuing on the lower **Red Route**, we eventually cross a small torrent among poplar trees, where the path divides. The branches soon merge again, but in dry weather it's probably nicer to take the lower path along the stream. Once the paths rejoin, we climb beside a narrow, cement-lined *acequia* to a small bridge over another torrent, after which a muddy stretch and a brief climb lead to another *acequia* and waypost (Wp.8 95M).

After another *cortijo*, the path bears round to cross two gates and a *barranco*. We ignore the tracks climbing beyond the *barranco* into a field and continue on the lower path to pass below a small stone cabin/corral and above a ruin.

The path then starts winding down towards the river. You'll soon see a stand of poplars downriver and beyond them the path climbing to **Capileira** from **Puente Buchite**, which we reach in thirty minutes from Wp.8. Once over the bridge, a scramble across rocks on the left leads into a lovely picnic spot on the riverbank underneath the poplars.

Mirador de Aldeire

The final climb to **Capileira** follows the stony path up from the bridge, soon passing a waypost (Wp.9) marking a branch down to **Puente Chiscar**. We continue on the main path to join the dirt track into **Capileira**, arriving at the **Mirador de Aldeire** threshing circles (Wp.10 145M) after a twenty-five minute climb from the river.

We then follow the paved track, the **Paseo de Aldeire**, into **Capileira**. The alley on the left just before the **Apartamentos Vista Veleta** leads back to the start of the walk, while **Calle del Cubo** in front of the *apartamentos* brings us up to **Plaza Calvario** and the **Bar El Tilo**.

An exceptional itinerary combining beauty and grandeur in equal measure, climbing from **La Cebadilla** into increasingly wild terrain with fabulous views evoking an altitude considerably more elevated than it actually is. After passing the water captation installations at **Fuente La Raja** in the **Río Veleta** (lots of concrete yet possessed of a curiously untrammeled and untamed atmosphere), we descend from the **Cámara de Carga** charging chamber along the *tubería* supplying the turbines in the **Central Poqueira** power station. Never did electricity generation look so good!

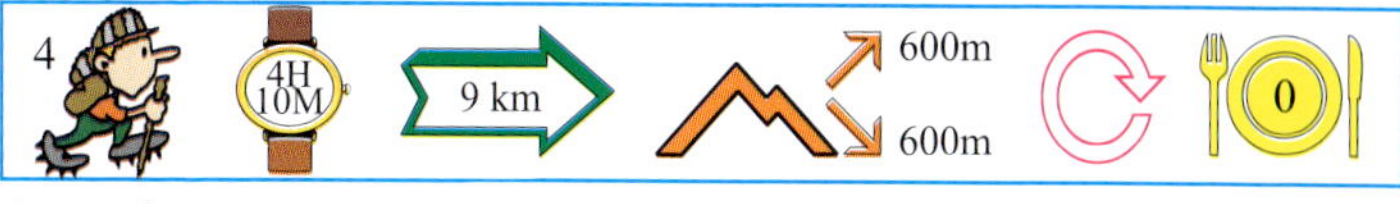

Access by car:

To reach **La Cebadilla** by car, follow **Pista Forestal 3** (see Appendix A) to km2.7 then turn left and take the branch track down to **Puente Hondera**. Park in the shade of the cliffs just west of the bridge.

From **Puente Hondera** (Wp.1 0M), we take the concrete track up to the power station and cross bridges over the **Ríos Toril** and **Naute** to a mapboard outlining a version of this walk. We then cross the concrete ledge after the mapboard and take a mule trail climbing away from the **Río Naute**.

The power station at Puente Hondera

Ignoring a minor branch on the right five minutes later, we continue climbing using the shortcuts according to taste, haste and lung capacity. One shortcut (emerging at a trig point) (Wp.2 20M) has virtually replaced the original route. After a series of zigzags and a long steady climb, the trail levels out just before a branch to the left (Wp.3 25M), which climbs to **Puente Toril**.

This is our return route, but for the present, we continue on the main, level trail (NE), as it dwindles to a dirt path passing a *cortijo*/byre before climbing gently to a wayposted junction at the ruins of **Cortijo Masagrande** (Wp.4 35M). Again, we ignore the **Puente Toril** branch and stay on the main path, descending very slightly to pass immediately behind a white painted *cortijo*. Thereafter, another gentle climb takes us past two large walnut trees to reach a wayposted path descending towards the river and **Cortijo de la Isla**.

Following a clear but eroded path down to the banks of the **Río Naute**, we cross three bridges to reach **Cortijo de la Isla** (Wp.5 55M), beyond which the landscape becomes much wilder and greener. Following the path behind the *cortijo* (NE), we cross a knoll and pass a waypost (Wp.6 60M), after which two more bridges bring us to a marshy green meadow on the right bank of the main river. After climbing past another ruin, the path diverges from the river and steepens as we zigzag up a paved stretch, ignoring a branch on the right.

Río Naute valley

The gradient then eases and a gentler climb brings us to a Y junction (80M). Taking the wayposted path on the right, we descend back towards the river, where the path disappears in a water-logged meadow before reappearing on the far side, after which it follows the **Río Naute**, passing through successive dry and waterlogged sections to reach a bridge over the **Río Veleta** (Wp.7 90M).

Beyond the bridge, a very narrow path climbs through dense vegetation, briefly following the left bank of the **Río Veleta** before veering back towards the **Naute**.

The landscape becomes wilder and drier as the path climbs past occasional cairns before circling a large rocky outcrop to another junction (Wp.8 105M) marked by two wayposts. The main path on the right leads up to **Cortijo Las Tomas** and the **Poqueira Refuge** (see Walk 21), both of which have been clearly visible for much of the preceding hour. We, however, turn left onto a rough narrow path climbing the rise between the **Ríos Veleta** and **Naute**.

The path climbs steeply, occasionally losing definition, but the route is clearly marked by cairns and concrete posts. To the left, we soon see the installations at **Fuente La Raja**, our next objective.

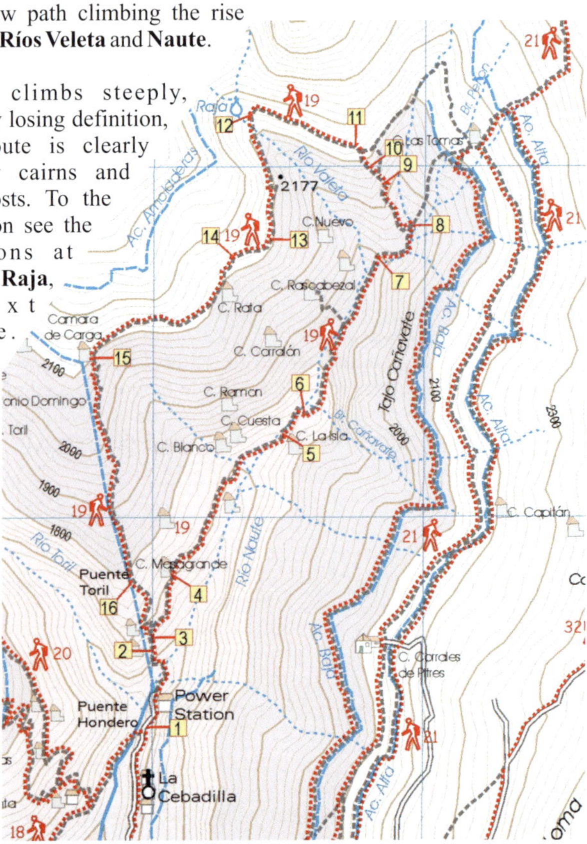

Bearing left at the remains of a threshing circle (Wp.9 125M), we follow the cairn marked path till it bears right at a waypost (Wp.10 127M) where we take a shortcut. Fifty metres to the left of the waypost, we climb (NW) a shaley slope, heading for a sharp rock tipped with a trig point. Bearing left ten metres below the trig point, we continue climbing towards a large cairn on a rock below the cliffs (Wp.11 140M).

At this point, we rejoin the main, waymarked route as it follows a rough path along the interred pipe taking water from the **Río Naute** to **Fuente La Raja**, **La Cámara de Carga** and, eventually, the **Central de Poqueira**. On the far bank of the **Río Veleta**, a little way above the clear green line of an open acequia, we can see the **Ramal del Naute**, the continuation of the pipe linking **Fuente La Raja** with the **Cámara de Carga**.

Ramal del Naute (as seen from the south-east)

Despite the daunting looking pinnacle of rock rising above it (the 2177 metre point on our map), this marks our route. The faint path climbing behind the pinnacle is where we're heading and it's nothing like as horrifying as it looks from a distance. Promise!

Just after the installations at **Fuente La Raja**, the path divides in front of a tiny hut with a faded green door (Wp.12 155M). Ignoring the branch descending on the left to the *acequia*, we follow the interred pipe for 100 metres to an inspection hatch (a stone tower with a concrete lid), ten metres after which, we bear right onto a very rough path marked with cairns that climbs to a pass behind the pinnacles. At first, the path beyond the pass is indistinct, but picking our way down the slope for ten metres, we recover a clear if rough path that passes above a stone waterhut. After climbing briefly, the path becomes smoother and another gentle climb leads to a waypost (Wp.13 180M). We then contour round the hillside before descending back to the **Ramal del Naute** waterpipe at an inspection hatch five minutes from Wp.13 (Wp.14), from where it's easy, level walking all the way to the **Cámara de Carga** and its *tubería*, the unmistakable silver pipe descending to **La Cebadilla**.

As we approach the **Cámara de Carga**, the trail splinters. We can either take a shortcut (the first branch on the left) or continue toward the captation chamber until, fifty metres from the **Cámara** fence, two cairns (Wp.15 200M) indicate the main path down the eastern side of the *tubería*. The path descends parallel to the *tubería*, gradually broadening and tracing long loops to break the descent, before coming directly alongside it and steepening for the last stretch down to the wooden **Puente Toril** bridge (Wp.16 225M). Bearing left, we zigzag down to a small outcrop of rock tipped with stubby holm oak. Bearing right at a large cairn, we take a rough but clear path to the right of the outcrop to rejoin our outward route at Wp.3.

Along with the **Naute**, the **Río Toril** is one of the principal streams that feed the **Río Poqueira**, and as such is one of the Alpujarras' most important water sources. It's a wonderful wild little valley with few trees and a wide open high mountain feel to it, and its *acequias* (the **Amoladeras, Sevillana, Nueva**, and **Castillejos**) are a delight.

The classic tour is a loop via Puente **Toril** and the **Acequia Nueva**, but a landslip above the *cortijos* on the river's northern bank makes that outing a little heavy going. The present itinerary is, in its way, no less arduous, since it involves a long central climb off path on rough ground, but walking two *acequias* in one itinerary (the **Nueva** and the **Castillejos**) is such a glorious indulgence the exertion and pathfinding challenges are amply recompensed.

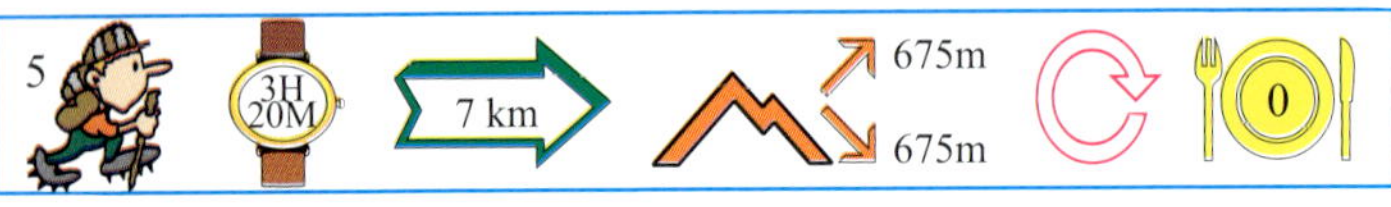

Access by car:
To reach **La Cebadilla** by car, follow **Pista Forestal 3** (see Appendix A) to km2.7 then turn left and take the branch track down to **Puente Hondera. Park** in the shade of the cliffs just west of the bridge.

Starting from **Puente Hondero** (Wp.1 0M), we take the dirt track for 'Puente Abuchite'. After a steady climb, the wayposted path to **Capileira** forks left (Wp.2 9M), but we stay on the track, climbing steadily to steeply to a second wayposted path, this time doubling back to the right, at which point we leave the dirt track (Wp.3 23M). Our stony path zigzags up between stumpy oaks, passing a succession of crumbling ruins and a faint branch path doubling back to the left (Wp.4 35M).

Eventually, we climb above the main growth of wood, fine views of **Mulhacén** and the **Cebadilla** *tubería* opening out on our right. The gradient gradually eases as we approach then join the **Acequia Nueva** (Wp.5 45M), where we bear right and begin a delightful stroll along the level *acequia* path into the **Río Toril** valley.

The Río Toril Valley

There's no call for talk here, just walk and enjoy, however if you intend doing the full walk, it's worth noting that the patch of pine that soon comes into view up to our left defines our return route along the **Acequia Castillejos**. After passing a branch trail doubling back to the right (Wp.6 71M), we see ahead of us, toward the head of the valley, **Cortijo de las Mergas**. Our off path ascent begins on the narrow nose-like ridge defined by two torrents immediately south of the *cortijo*.

Fifty metres after crossing the first of these torrents, **Barranco de las Carreras**, which feeds directly into the

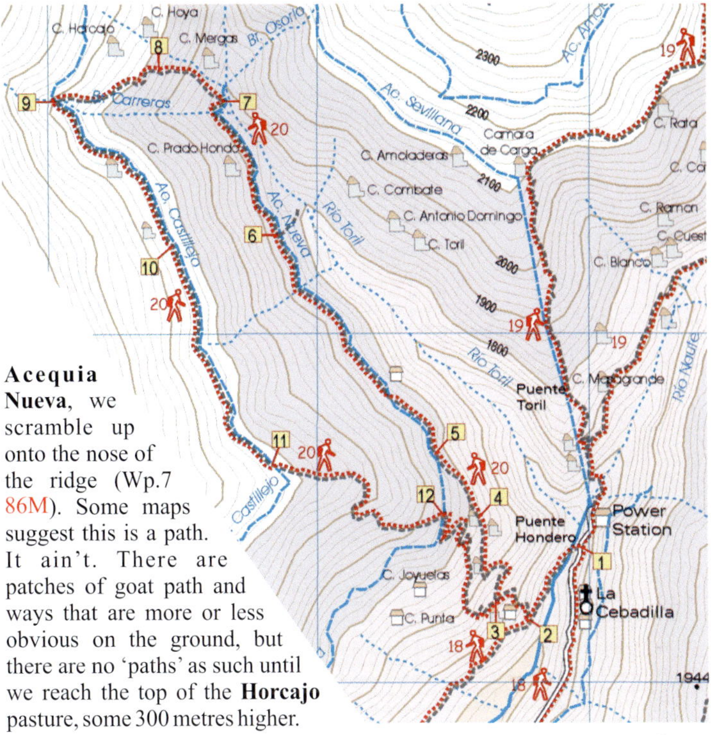

Acequia Nueva, we scramble up onto the nose of the ridge (Wp.7 86M). Some maps suggest this is a path. It ain't. There are patches of goat path and ways that are more or less obvious on the ground, but there are no 'paths' as such until we reach the top of the **Horcajo** pasture, some 300 metres higher.

Acequia Castillejos

So it's best to approach this as an off path climb. Staying as near to the centre of the ridge as the rough ground permits, we climb steeply until we come to a tiny, grassy *acequia*, from where the line of the **Acequia Castillejos** is already visible as it cuts away from the top of the **Barranco de las Carreras** toward a small *cortijo* off to our left (Wp.8 107M).

Following the mini-*acequia* round to the west, we cross its feed spring then scramble (still very much off path) onto the foot of the **Horcajo** grazing ground, a high, ragged pasture splashed with patches of bracken. Maintaining a westerly direction, taking advantage of the occasional tiny patches of cow path, and climbing whenever compelled by one of the swales feeding the **Carreras** torrent, we contour round the **Horcajo** pasture.

There's no one way here, but as a rough guide we stay between the 2140-2175 metre mark, until we reach the canalization point at the intersection of **Barranco de las Carreras** and **Acequia Castillejos**, the line of which is visible throughout our traverse of the pasture (Wp.9 122M). Relax, the rough bit's done and we're back to pure pleasure again!

After that stiff little scramble across the pasture, the way south along the *acequia* and past the *cortijo* seen from below is a blast and the only advice I can give is not to stride out too fast and miss the magnificent views. We draw abreast of the pine wood more or less at the halfway mark of our stroll along the *acequia* (Wp.10 137M). Shortly after crossing a gully of grey shale and just before the *acequia* swings southwest, we fork left on a clear but <u>unmarked</u> path (Wp.11 152M).

The path descends to the southeast, gently at first then more steeply as the **Poqueira** villages come into view off to our right.

Acequia Nueva

After passing a solitary boulder, our way veers south toward the top of the oak wood, then resumes an easterly direction, rejoining the **Acequia Nueva** just south of Wp.5 (Wp.12 170M). Crossing the *acequia*, we join the end of the track climbing from **La Cebadilla**, which we follow down to rejoin our outward route at Wp.3 (185M).

A glorious, easily accessible high-mountain walk taking one of the traditional routes to visit the impressive **Poqueira Refuge** and returning by one of two lovely *acequia* paths. If you want to have lunch at the refuge, make sure you arrive before 3 p.m. as the kitchen is closed between 3 and 5.30 p.m.

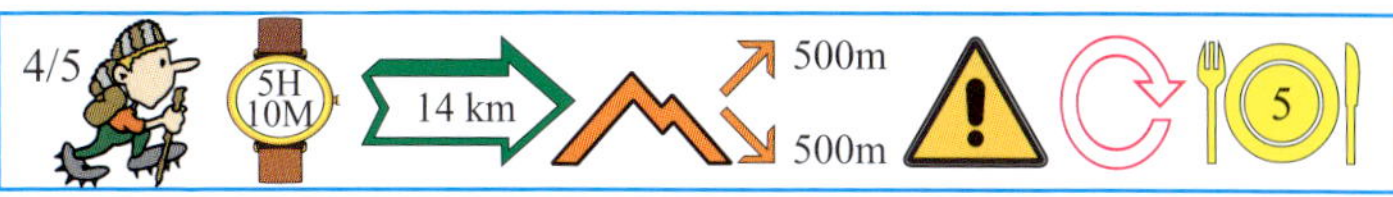

Access by car: To reach the start of the walk, take the **Hoya del Portillo** road from **Capileira (Pista Forestal 3)**, setting your odometer at zero when you leave the tarmac. At km2 the road bears sharp right and we turn left onto a dirt track just after a nicely restored *cortijo*. Eight hundred metres along the track, park at the triangular chimney wall of an unfinished house just before the **Acequia Baja** (Wp.1 0M). If you don't have a car, you can ask the Parque Natural bus from **Capileira** to drop you off at the 2km turning. If you're walking in winter and there's a risk of snow, park at the end of the tarmac.

One hundred metres after crossing the **Acequia Baja** we turn left on another dirt track (usually chained off) which soon brings us in sight of the **Poqueira Refuge** below the **Mulhacén**. A little under one kilometre from the chimney, the track goes through a sharp right-hand bend then swings back north.

Acequia Baja

Just before it bears right again, we take the faint path (Wp.2 15M) on the left below some rocks. The path soon becomes clear, winding along the contour lines and crossing a series of watercourses until it joins a broader, waymarked path (Wp.3 40M) climbing from **Capileira** (an alternative return route if you came by bus, though bear in mind it's a 600 metre descent from here to **Capileira**). After crossing a torrent a few minutes later, we continue along the waymarked path to the goat pens at the **Corrales de Pitres** (Wp.4 55M) where the dirt track we left at Wp.2 ends and a lot of barking begins. Passing below the stone cabins and ignoring the track climbing to the right, we follow the waymarked path to the left, after which you can see in a direct line below the refuge, the **Cortijo de Las Tomas**, our next objective.

The path joins the **Acequia Alta** (Wp.5 65M) beside two wayposts, but bears away from it one hundred metres later for a descent that gives fine views of the **Picos de Pulpito** and **Sabinar**, which when seen from further away tend to be swallowed up by the higher peaks behind them. After passing a ruined stone corral with two wayposts in front of it, we follow the main path and descend to cross a meagre torrent.

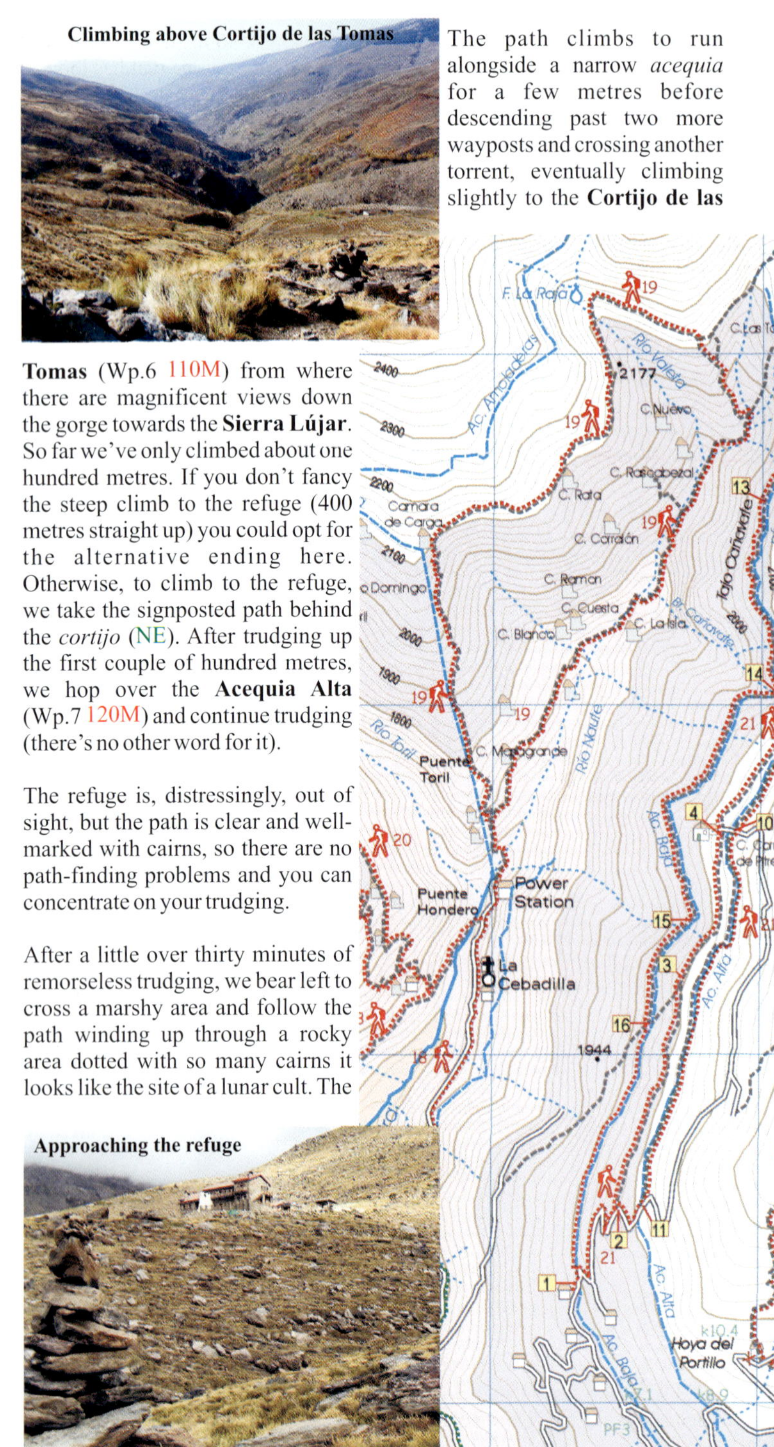

Climbing above Cortijo de las Tomas

The path climbs to run alongside a narrow *acequia* for a few metres before descending past two more wayposts and crossing another torrent, eventually climbing slightly to the **Cortijo de las Tomas** (Wp.6 110M) from where there are magnificent views down the gorge towards the **Sierra Lújar**. So far we've only climbed about one hundred metres. If you don't fancy the steep climb to the refuge (400 metres straight up) you could opt for the alternative ending here. Otherwise, to climb to the refuge, we take the signposted path behind the *cortijo* (NE). After trudging up the first couple of hundred metres, we hop over the **Acequia Alta** (Wp.7 120M) and continue trudging (there's no other word for it).

The refuge is, distressingly, out of sight, but the path is clear and well-marked with cairns, so there are no path-finding problems and you can concentrate on your trudging.

After a little over thirty minutes of remorseless trudging, we bear left to cross a marshy area and follow the path winding up through a rocky area dotted with so many cairns it looks like the site of a lunar cult. The

Approaching the refuge

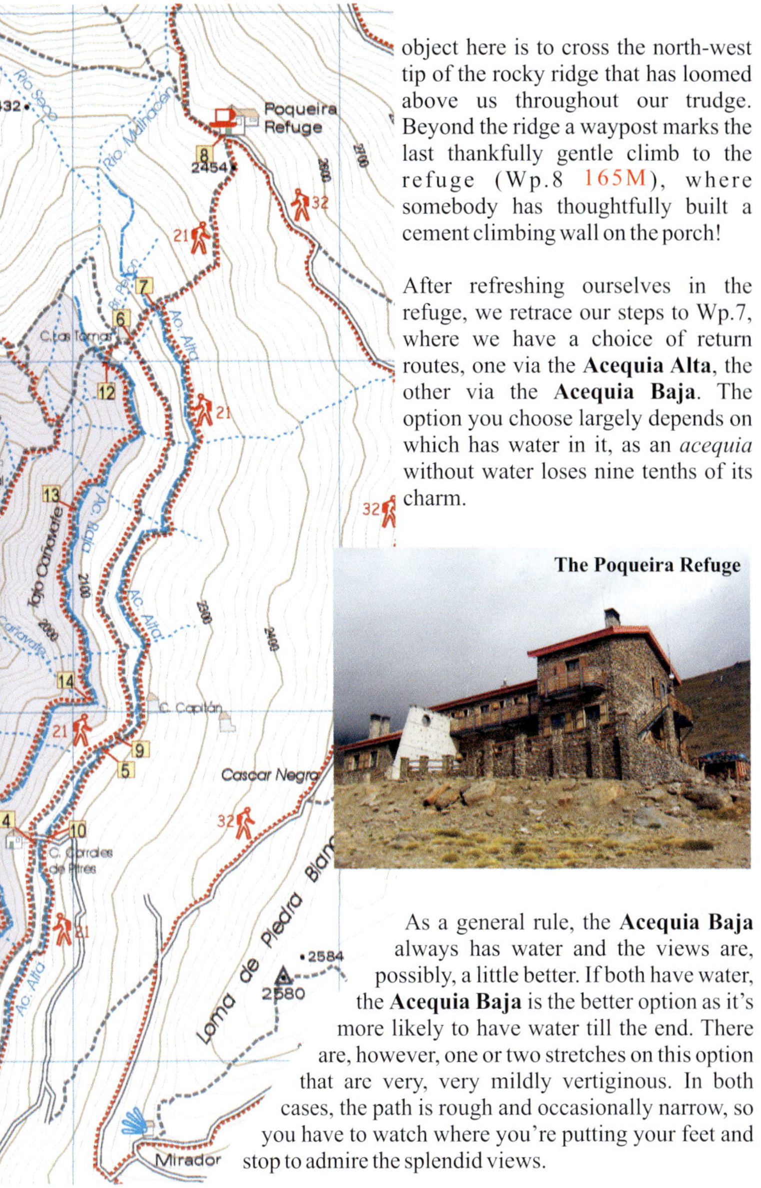

object here is to cross the north-west tip of the rocky ridge that has loomed above us throughout our trudge. Beyond the ridge a waypost marks the last thankfully gentle climb to the refuge (Wp.8 165M), where somebody has thoughtfully built a cement climbing wall on the porch!

After refreshing ourselves in the refuge, we retrace our steps to Wp.7, where we have a choice of return routes, one via the **Acequia Alta**, the other via the **Acequia Baja**. The option you choose largely depends on which has water in it, as an *acequia* without water loses nine tenths of its charm.

The Poqueira Refuge

As a general rule, the **Acequia Baja** always has water and the views are, possibly, a little better. If both have water, the **Acequia Baja** is the better option as it's more likely to have water till the end. There are, however, one or two stretches on this option that arc very, very mildly vertiginous. In both cases, the path is rough and occasionally narrow, so you have to watch where you're putting your feet and stop to admire the splendid views.

Option A Acequia Alta

It's hard to get lost following an *acequia*, but note the following Waypoints:

(Wp.9 240M) we briefly rejoin the outward path (see Wp.5).

(Wp.10 250M) we cross the dirt track above the **Corrales de Pitres**, after which an overgrowth of eglantine obliges us to drop down occasionally on goat tracks. Beware of irrigation gates concealed by marsh grass.

(Wp.11 290M) we rejoin the **Corrales de Pitres** dirt track two minutes above Wp.2, 20 minutes from Wp.1.

Option B Acequia Baja

Descend to Wp.6 and continue descending past **Cortijo de las Tomas**, off path for 100 metres, down to the **Acequia Baja** (Wp.12 202M). We hop over the watercourse onto the *acequero*'s path, turn left and off we go. Once again, there's no call for description, but for the purposes of pacing progress:

(Wp.13 221M) the *acequia* passes between a fissured rock obliging us to drop down below it very briefly;

(Wp.14 237M) we cross **Barranco Cañavate**

(Wp.15 266M) after traversing a gaping scar of shale, two makeshift bridges take us onto the left bank of the *acequia* to avoid damaging the narrow outer wall;

(Wp.16 276M) we cross the wayposted path descending on the right to **Capileira**, after which we simply continue along the *acequia*, traversing the band of pine visible ahead to return to Wp.1.

The classic walk to the **Junta de los Rios** above **Pórtugos**, now designated as a PR and clearly wayposted throughout, is marred by a brief but dodgy bit of road walking including a dangerous bend, but by cutting across the fabulous *acequias* behind the ruined **Molino del Sol**, our new version of the itinerary takes a classic and upgrades it to vintage status. The *acequia* path is very mildly vertiginous and there's a short stretch on a narrow and very steep path that would be virtually impossible to find from the other way round if you didn't know it already, but otherwise this is an easy walk blessed with superb views, a fine oak forest, and the spectacular waterfalls at the **Junta de los Rios** itself, where the **Barrancos de Jabali** and **Chorreras** converge to form the **Río Bermejo**.

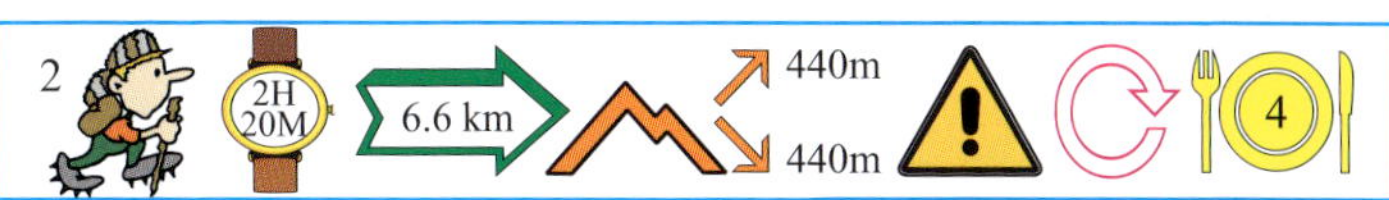

Access by car:
We park in the **Plaza Nueva** at the end of the main road into **Pórtugos**, next to the church and the **Mirador de Pórtugos** hotel.

From the **Plaza Nueva** (Wp.1 0M), we cross the church square and, ignoring the 'PRA70 Sendero Río Bermejo' fingerpost indicating the way up to the right along 'Calle Las Cuatros Esquinas' (this is our return route), carry straight on along **Calle Abaulagillas**, which swings round to the

right to reach the **Plaza de Churriana**, where we bear left and follow **Calle Rosario** until it ends at a concrete track (Wp.2 7M).

Turning right on the concrete track, we pass a large white cross, 50 metres after which we leave the wayposted route of the PR, and instead fork right on a surfaced track signposted **Molino del Sol Área Recreativa Junta de los Rios** (Wp.3 9M). We follow this track for 750 metres through one steady climb and into the chicane of another where it crosses an *acequia* (Wp.4 22M). At this point, we leave the track and turn left along the *acequia*, which passes under a goat farm.

150 metres later, at a Y junction directly below the ruined **Molino del Sol** (Wp.5), we fork right, leaving the *acequia* path and climbing behind the ruin to join another *acequia*.

Fifty metres along this second *acequia*, we hop over a small mill race, and continue along the *acequia*, occasionally on quite a narrow wall, to a waterfall, where we cross the **Río Bermejo** via a concrete footbridge (Wp.6 36M)

The mill race after Wp.5

On the far bank of the river, a very narrow path climbs steeply through dense woodland to join a dirt track that crosses the **Acequia Ventajas** (see Walk 5) a few metres up to our right (Wp.7 43M). At this point we rejoin the clearly wayposted route of the PR.

Crossing the *acequia*, we follow the wayposted route climbing to the right on a rough track that gradually dwindles to a trail as the gradient steepens alongside a dry affluent of the **Bermejo**.

After a good old slog up through the woods, throughout much of which the cleft of the **Junta de los Ríos** is clearly visible off to our right, our trail joins the broad dirt track between the **Poqueira** valley and **Trevélez** (Wp.8 75M). Bearing right and enjoying superb views across the interfolding sierras to the south, we follow the track across the bridge over the river until we come to another track doubling back to the right (Wp.9 90M), which we follow down to the *área recreativa*.

At the end of the *área recreativa* track (Wp.10 94M), the PR descends to the left on a broad trail, but first it's worth descending to the right on the narrow path leading to the waterfall. Once we've spent a few moments snapping photos and splashing about, we retrace our steps to Wp.10 and descend below the **área recreativa** installations for 175 metres to reach a narrow wayposted path descending to the right (Wp.11). After a steady descent on an unmistakable trail amid the lovely woodland that is such a feature of the slopes above **Pórtugos**, we come to an intersection of dirt tracks (Wp.12 120M). Ignoring the branches to left and right, we carry straight on for 75 metres to recover the old path descending to the right (Wp.13).

When the path joins another track beside a sign for the 'Mirador Camino Jabali' (Wp.14 124M), we bear right, descending to cross an *acequia* and another track (Wp.15) below which we follow another *acequia* path.

When the *acequia* divides, one branch turning right alongside a track (Wp.16 128M), we carry straight on, going behind a flat roofed cabin with a tall chimney, where the path starts descending again, passing some remarkably venerable chestnut trees.

.. passing venerable chestnut trees ..

We then pass a path doubling back to the left for 'Piedra Ventana' and 'La Loma' (Wp.17 134M) shortly before arriving back in the village via the fingerposted route we passed at the start.

The balcony walk to beat all balcony walks as nearly seven kilometres of it is on a level and very drivable dirt track, made bearable by brilliant views over the **Contraviessa** and the **Trevélez** valley, and the fact that the very drivable dirt track is evidently very little driven. The rest of the itinerary is something else, a superb alpine promenade taking in high pastures and pine woods. It's another of the highlights of the **GR240 Sendero Sulayr**, not quite as enrapturing as the **Acequia Almiar** (Walk 17), nothing is, but very fine nonetheless, a lovely bit of easy high mountain walking. Except for one brief stretch 200 metres short of **Hoya del Portillo**, the GR is clearly wayposted throughout.

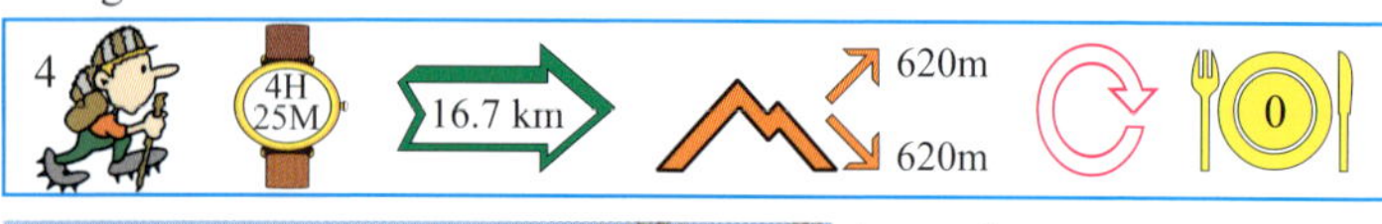

Our start and parking place at Wp.1

Access by car:
From **Pórtugos** *ayuntamientio* (on the road climbing from the A4132 into the central **Plaza Nueva**) we turn right for the 'Área Recreativa Junta de los Ríos',

immediately turning right in front of the *farmacia*, then follow the paved lane behind a small block of flats 50 metres later to join a concrete track. When the concreted section doubles back to the left 800 metres from the *ayuntamiento*, we carry straight on along a good dirt track for roughly five kilometres (apologies, a problem with the odometer on our vehicle here) until it joins the main track between **Capileira** and **Trevélez** at a major junction where a sign indicates that the *área recreativa* is 2.6km away, at which point there's ample track side parking. NB If you're staying in **Capileira**, the *área recreativa* can be reached from km3.8 of **Pista Forestal 3** (see Appendix A).

From the intersection of tracks (Wp.1 0M), we

simply continue along the main track to the west, which we follow all the way to the *área recreativa*. After two and a quarter kilometres, we pass the signposted track descending on the left into the *área recreativa* itself and, 100 metres after that, a minor track doubling back to the right (Wp.2 30M). 250 metres later, immediately after the bridge over the **Junta de los Rios** waterfall, we leave the dirt track, turning right then immediately forking left, first on a broad trail signposted 'Área Recreativa Hoya del Portillo 2.8km', then on a narrow stony path picked out with cairns (Wp.3 37M).

The path, which is very faint in places, climbs parallel to the **Capileira** track for 200 metres before veering north across bare rock to pass a waypost, where we resume a more westerly course, zigzagging up to join a minor dirt track (Wp.4 45M). Turning right and ignoring a branch doubling back on the left to a *cortijo* fifty metres later, we climb past a large reservoir to join the **GR240** at a sharp bend (Wp.5 54M). Bearing right, we climb steadily along an alleyway of pine, going through a hairpin bend, to reach a wayposted junction with a path on the right, at the foot of which there are three stone steps (Wp.6 59M). Turning right, we climb to the northeast, traversing a strip of open scrub before crossing a footbridge into pine woods. We now embark on a long, steady slog up through the woods, which are usually agreeably fresh, the gradient gradually easing as we converge with the flank of

View south after Wp.7

Barranco de las Chorreras, alongside which we cross a second footbridge over a dry affluent (Wp.7 74M). We subsequently cross the *barranco* itself and climb gently to join a rough logging track (Wp.8 84M). Turning left, we follow this track for 250 metres then, just before it re-crosses the **Chorreras** watercourse, fork right on a wayposted path (Wp.9 91M), crossing a third footbridge 100 metres upstream. Our path climbs briefly before traversing a level stretch of forest where it effectively disappears under a carpet of twigs, but maintaining a northwesterly direction, we pass to the right of a tiny patch of scrub and rock, from where you should be able to glimpse through the trees, 200 metres to the northwest, the retaining wall of the **Hoya del Portillo** car park, which we reach at the vehicle barrier on the **Carretera de Veleta** (Wp.10 102M).

Turning right, we follow the *carretera* for 1.3 kilometres to the foot of the first long hairpin bend (Wp.11 122M), where we fork right on a sign and wayposted path that contours across the hillside before traversing another pine forest. After crossing a ferruginous torrent, our path becomes more rugged, dipping up and down amid less densely planted woodland.

The second ferruginous spring

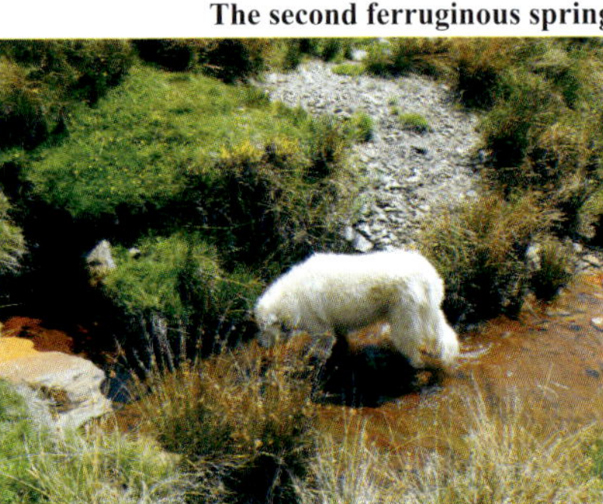

We then cross a second ferruginous spring and bear south above the **Barranco del Jabali** to join the end of a firebreak (Wp.12 154M), which we follow to the south along the back of the **Loma del Jabali**. When the firebreak runs into woodland (Wp.13 162M), we fork left then double back to the northeast on a clear path that descends gently across an immense, sparse pasture. Down to the right, we can see the **Balsa de los Lotes** helipad and reservoir, which are two kilometres from our starting point.

Descending after Wp.13

After crossing a footbridge over an erosion scar (Wp.14 174M), we continue to the northeast for nearly a kilometre before doubling back to the right toward a small reservoir, 50 metres short of which (Wp.15 187M), we veer left and descend across rocky scrubland patched with holm oak to reach a second small reservoir shaded by a large walnut tree (Wp.16 198M). We then wind down through an attractive oak wood to rejoin the **Capileira - Trevélez** track at a junction with the **GR7**, (signed as 11.1km from Pórtugos and 4.8km from Trevélez) (Wp.17 210M). From here, we simply turn right and follow the main track back to the start, ignoring all junctions, including the point at which the **GR7** forks down to the left 300 metres later.

Yes, if you know any Spanish, it does mean what you think it means. If you don't, *culo perro* is an indelicate way of describing a dog's bottom. I don't care to delve into the toponymy of this, but despite the name it's a fine walk made exceptional if you have the pathfinding skills to link it with the lower half of Walk 25. It's especially worthwhile finding the way down in summer as returning via the shady river path is cooler than staying on the exposed path above the **Crestones de los Posteros**. If you do take the 'link' please add to the cairns. Apart from the walk through the village, the way up is nearly all gentle climbing.

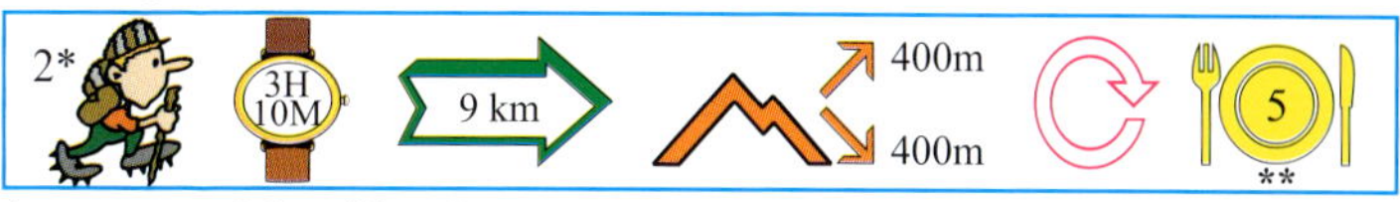

* once out of the village!   ** in **Trevélez**

Access by car:

If you intend doing the loop, park in the **Plaza de la Iglesia**. If not, park in the **Plaza Barrío Medio** and follow Walk 34 through the village.

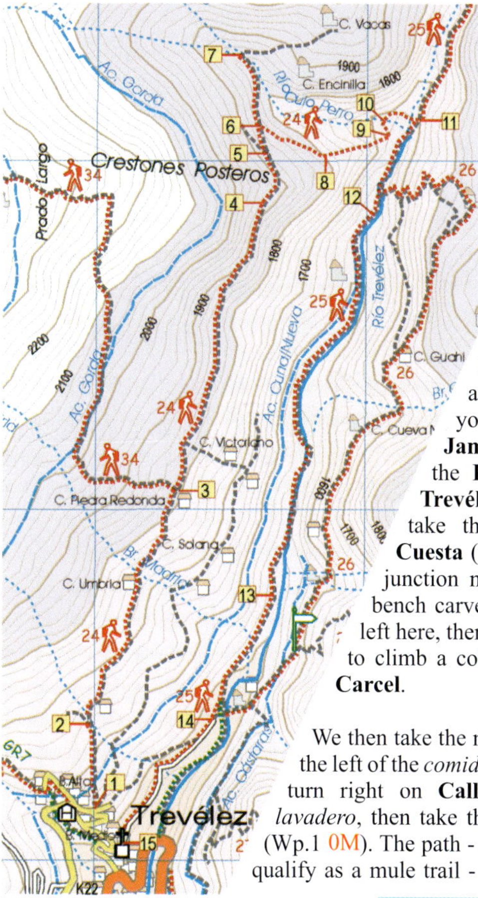

To reach the parking spots from the main square/tourist strip, take the road signposted for the *ayuntamiento* up past the Spar supermarket, until it bears round towards **Restaurante Casa Julio**. Carry straight on for the **Plaza de la Iglesia**. For the **Barrio Medio**, turn left after the restaurant and then sharp right when you come to the hostal and **Jamones Fernando**. From the **Plaza de la Iglesia** in Trevélez' **Barrío Bajo**, we take the aptly named **Calle Cuesta** ('Hill Street') up to a T-junction next to a *fuente* with a bench carved in the rock. We turn left here, then right fifty metres later, to climb a cobbled lane up to **Calle Carcel**.

We then take the narrow concrete alley to the left of the *comidas/camas/jamones* sign, turn right on **Calle Horno**, left at the *lavadero*, then take the first path on the left (Wp.1 0M). The path - in fact broad enough to qualify as a mule trail - climbs steadily to a Y-junction (Wp.2 10M) beside a stand of poplars, where we bear right to continue on the main trail, climbing past two *cortijos* and ignoring occasional branches into fields. Fifty metres after the mule trail passes between a large stone *cortijo* (on the left) and a byre (on the right), we

The path at Wp.1

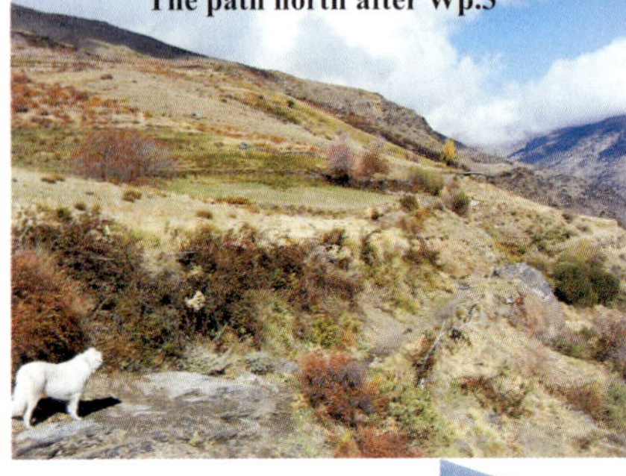
The path north after Wp.3

ignore the waymarked route on the left up to **Siete Lagunas** (Wp.3 42M) and continue along the mule trail (N), which soon dwindles to a dirt path. The path becomes stonier and drier, gradually climbing to pass a plaque (Wp.4 74M)

Fine views south en route

commemorating two *Guardia Civiles* ostensibly killed in a gun battle with Republican guerillas, actually (according to locals) ambushed by the people of **Trevélez** who were fed up being exploited by a couple of rapacious fascists operating a winner takes all policy!

It then winds up to cross the **Crestones de los Posteros** into the **Río Culo Perro** valley, where it gradually descends (NW) to a Y-junction (Wp.5 85M). We take the right-hand branch descending into the valley to a faint cow path branching off to the right (Wp.6 88M) marked by a large cairn, I hope - I certainly built one, anyway.

To return by the same route
If you intend returning by the same route, stay on the main path and descend to the **Río Culo Perro** (Wp.7 95M) next to a rough wooden bridge, beyond which the path climbs to the **Cortijo de las Vacas**.

To link up with the Río Trevélez
To link up with the **Río Trevélez**, we take the cow path at Wp.6. Beware though, you need good route finding skills. What follows is a lot of detail for a very short distance, but there's only one way down that doesn't involve blundering through brambles or pitching over five metre drops, so hopefully every word is justified. Look down to the junction of the **Ríos Culo Perro** and **Trevélez**. On the left bank of the **Río Culo Perro**, there's a large, intensely green meadow. On the right bank, an escarpment climbs away from the

meadow, culminating fifty metres above the river in an outcrop of rock, just to the right of which, you should be able to pick out a threshing circle. This is our first objective.

From the cairn, we follow the cow path along the flank of the valley (SE), crossing a shallow depression, after which the path descends slightly towards a grassy platform in front of the white-fronted **Cortijo Encinilla** on the other side of the river. The cow path then heads in a more easterly direction, dividing just above the grassy platform. We can't see the threshing circle from here, but stick to the higher traces of the path as it swings back to the right (SE), after which the threshing circle comes into view again.

Just before it bears round onto a rocky ridge, we abandon the cow path at a point marked by a second cairn (Wp.8 104M - all subsequent times exclude the time between Wps. 6&7) and zigzag down the scrubby/scree slope towards the threshing circle, taking care to keep above the taller scrub running up from the river. There's an old barbed-wire fence just above the threshing circle with a gate in the middle, beyond which a very faint path descends directly to the threshing circle, about five metres from the cow path. Bearing round to the right of the threshing circle, we come to the remains of an old cabin built into the rock. We then descend between the ruined cabin wall and another outcrop of rock (NE) down to a solitary holm oak and a broken barbed-wire fence above the junction of the rivers.

Crossing the barbed-wire fence, we maintain a north-easterly direction toward the river junction and another large cairn (Wp.9 116M) thirty metres below the barbed-wire fence. We bear left here and follow a <u>very</u> faint trail (NW) until we see another cairn, still on the right bank of the **Río Culo Perro**, on a small grassy knoll below a large poplar. Don't be tempted by any previous 'shortcuts' down to the river - they all end up in brambles. The 'trail' bears right then zigzags down to the cairn (Wp.10 126M).

Wp.11 from the south-east

After fording the **Río Culo Perro** (you may have to take your boots off in Spring), we descend through the meadow seen from Wp.6, passing in front of a semi-abandoned *cortijo* and crossing a marshy dell to a ford over the **Río Trevélez** fifteen metres upriver. After the ford, a rough gate in a barbed wire fence (Wp.11 134M) leads onto a heavily waterlogged stretch of the **Camino Al Horcajo** (see Walk 25).

Turning right, we cross a rough bridge ten minutes later (Wp.12), after which we simply follow the right bank of the river all the way back to **Trevélez**, passing an inverted Y junction a couple of kilometres after the bridge (Wp.13) before joining a dirt track (Wp.14) just under a kilometre from **Trevélez** church (Wp.15) and **Plaza de la Iglesia**.

A straightforward walk, following the **Río Trevélez** from the domestic landscape near the village up to the wilder area below **El Horcajo**, a traditional pasture where, according to Gerald Brenan, shepherds were once wont to set upon unwary travellers and relieve them of anything relievable.

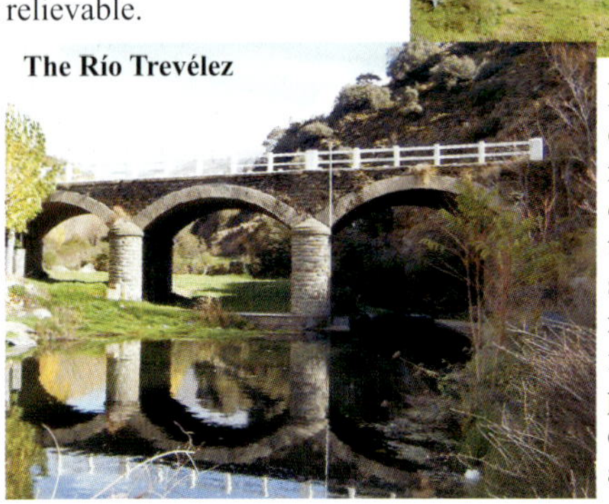

The Río Trevélez valley

The Río Trevélez

Fortunately, times have changed but the landscape remains the same. The only drawback is that, even though the river may be dry in summer between Wps. 3&6, much of the path is often flooded; not enough to impede progress, but sufficient to qualify as a river itself anywhere else.

Access by car:
Motorists should park in the **Plaza de la Iglesia** in **Trevélez's Barrio Bajo**.

* to **Hoya del Chordí** 2 : to the headwaters 3   ** in **Trevélez**

From the **Plaza de la Iglesia** in **Trevélez' Barrío Bajo**, we take the **Calle Cuesta** and turn right immediately behind the church (Wp.1 0M) onto the broad dirt track down to the river. One hundred metres after the track crosses a watercourse, we bear left onto a narrow dirt path (Wp.2 5M) that descends to the river twenty minutes later.

Bearing left at a Y-junction (Wp.3 28M), we climb briefly before rejoining the river above a series of small, improvised dams.

After fording a shallow affluent (Wp.4 40M) and splashing along a section resembling an *acequia* (Wp.5 45M) (it *is* still the path), we

Near Wp.3

Expect to get your feet wet!

bear right on a bank of raised earth by-passing a meadow. The path then climbs briefly to follow the **Acequia Nueva** before crossing a rough bridge (Wp.6 **55M**) shortly after which we have to cross the *acequia* again and take a larger bridge onto the river's left bank.

For the second crossing of the *acequia*, there's usually a couple of logs lying around to fashion a makeshift ford or bridge, but if they've disappeared and you don't have long legs, you may have to take your boots off and wade across.

We then climb the left bank of the river, passing the ford (Wp.7 **69M**) just above the junction of the **Ríos Trevélez** and **Culo Perro** (see Walk 24), shortly after which another deep *acequia* crossing marks the start of the more substantial climb towards the **Hoya de Chordí** (identifiable by a *cortijo* on the right bank), where the mountains become wilder and rockier.

Sticking to the left bank and ignoring all branches away from the river, we descend into the **Hoya de**

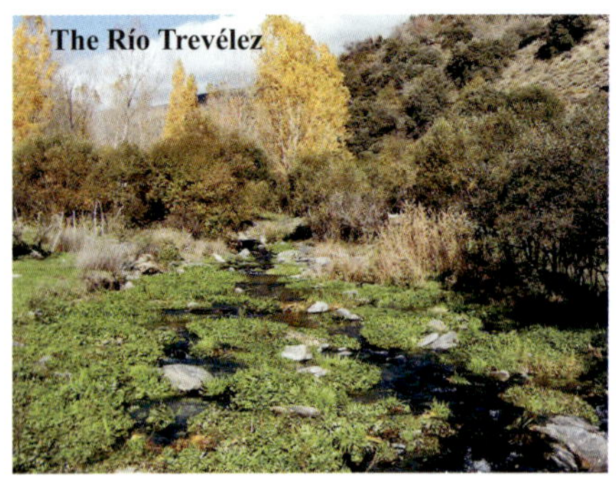

Chordí along a water-logged path.

The path loses definition in a meadow beneath a large shady ash with a cow's skull hanging halfway up its trunk (Wp.8 101M), but maintaining direction we soon pick up a badly eroded rock-laid stretch running alongside the river below the meadow.

After splashing through another flooded stretch, we cross another small *acequia* and descend on a drier stretch to the river below the **Tajos de Peña Cabrera**.

From here, if you look up towards the **Horcajo** at the end of the valley, you can see a small white building, which is about a hundred metres above our destination. The path continues along alternately dry and waterlogged sections till it crosses a very rudimentary wood and slate bridge (**Puente de los Aguiluchos**, Wp.9 127M) and, five minutes later, crosses back onto the left bank by a smaller slightly sturdier bridge.

After the second bridge, a succession of steady climbs leads up to the junction of the **Ríos Juntillas** and **Puerto de Jeres** that form the **Río Trevélez**. En route, there's a junction of paths marked with cairns (Wp.10 151M). We ignore the path on the right (the way to **Jeres de Marquesado**) and bear left on the main path to reach the junction of the rivers five minutes later (Wp.11 155M).

Our return by the same route takes two hours.

The **Camino de las Chorreras** or 'Trail of Gullies' (and there are plenty of them en route) is a grand little path that provides us with a pretext for this fabulous itinerary, counterpart to the classic **Culo Perro** loop (Walk 24).

In this case though, rather than climbing the popular paths directly above the village, we explore the little-known and less frequented eastern flank of the **Río Trevélez** valley, passing some superbly located *cortijos*, most of them abandoned, before returning via the evergreen, ever enjoyable **Camino al Horcajo** running alongside the river itself.

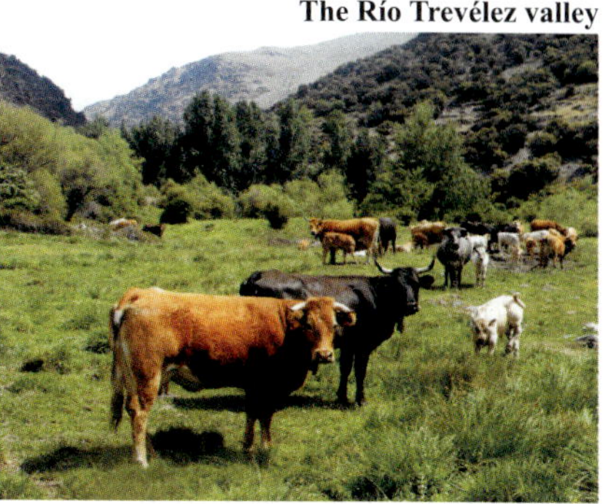
The Río Trevélez valley

My gratitude to Fernando Perez, whose useful pamphlet alerted me to the possibilities on this side of the valley. Pathfinding is not difficult, but calls for some attention between **Cortijo Guahi** and the river (Wps.10-15).

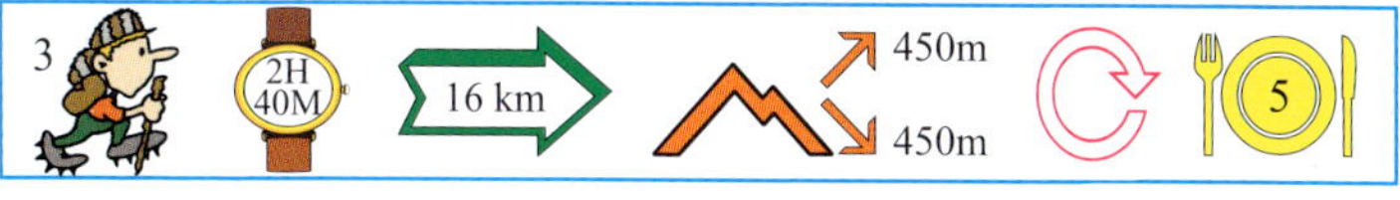

Access by car:
Park in the **Plaza de la Iglesia** in **Trevélez**'s **Barrio Bajo**.

Like so many good things in **Trevélez**, we begin with a stroll down to the river, taking **Calle Cuesta** out of **Plaza de la Iglesia** to reach the **Camino al Horcajo** dirt track behind the church (Wp.1 0M). We follow the track all the way down to the bridge over the river (Wp.2 15M), on the far side of which we pass a mapboard for the **SL78** (Walk 27) and climb past the ruins of **Molino Altero** to a corral.

Bearing left on the SL wayposted path above the corral (Wp.3 21M), we pass directly behind a new house and climb gently to cross the **Acequia de Cástaras**. 50 metres above the *acequia*, the wayposted **SL78** climbs to the right while we carry straight on, sticking with the unmarked **Camino de las Chorreras** (Wp.4 29M).

Following a lovely path snaking along the hillside overlooking the river, we pass behind the threshing circle of the ruined **Cortijo de la Jambre** (Wp.5 37M), so named either for the hunger (hambre) that until very recently plagued so many in this poverty stricken region, or for a particularly aggressive swarm (*enjambre*) of bees.

After dipping down to cross the **Barranco del Castillo**, we pass behind the partially maintained **Cortijo de la Solana Marina** (Wp.6 45M), and embark on a beautiful balcony path high above the river, within sight of two more *cortijos*, the uppermost of which is **Cortijo Guahi**.

Forking right at a Y junction (Wp.7 55M), we climb to and then cross the **Acequia de Orquialillo**, after which we pass the ruins of the **Cortijo de Cueva Negra** (Wp.8 60M).

After crossing the **Barranco de Guahi**, we stick with the main traces of the path (there's a lot of ruminating goes on up here, which isn't very helpful when it comes to maintaining coherent trodden ways) zigzagging up to a second Y junction (Wp.9 67M).

Forking left on the broader traces, we contour round the hillside before climbing to the inhabited **Cortijo de Guahi**, occupied by a very friendly couple and a pack of equally welcoming mongrels (Wp.10 69M).

Some care is required here as the clear path descending to the left returns us to the **Acequia de Cástaras** at a point where the aquifer wall is far too fragile to accommodate leisure walkers. We climb directly to the left of the *cortijo* (off path for the first few metres), behind which we pick up a clear path climbing toward a prominent rocky outcrop to the northeast.

The view north after Wp.10

After a steady, stony ascent amid holm oak, we approach the crest of a rise, just before which we can briefly see the bridge across the **Río Trevélez**, which we will use once we descend to the river. 50 metres after our glimpse of the bridge, some 600 metres from the **Cortijo Guahi**, the path levels out at a Y junction (Wp.11 85M), from where we have fine views up to the head of the valley and across to the **Culo Perro** affluent. We can also see, 300 metres ahead of us on our side of the valley, our next objective, the **Cortijo de Haza del Sabuco**.

Forking right toward the **Cortijo de Haza del Sabuco**, we cross a pasture, graced with a stand of magnificent cherry trees shading a rough stone bench. We then bear round to the left to reach the *cortijo* itself. In front of the *cortijo*, we pick up the faint traces of a path (Wp.12 91M) that heads northwest then abruptly disappears. However, if we maintain direction (NW) and pass to the right of an enormous threshing circle, we soon pick up clear traces again, which (after a second brief hiatus) swing round to the left (SW) to another Y

junction (Wp.13 95M). Forking right, we continue descending, now on an unmistakable path, well trodden by hooves if not boots, that zigzags down to the **Acequia de Cástaras**, 800 metres from **Cortijo de Haza del Sabuco** (Wp.14 102M).

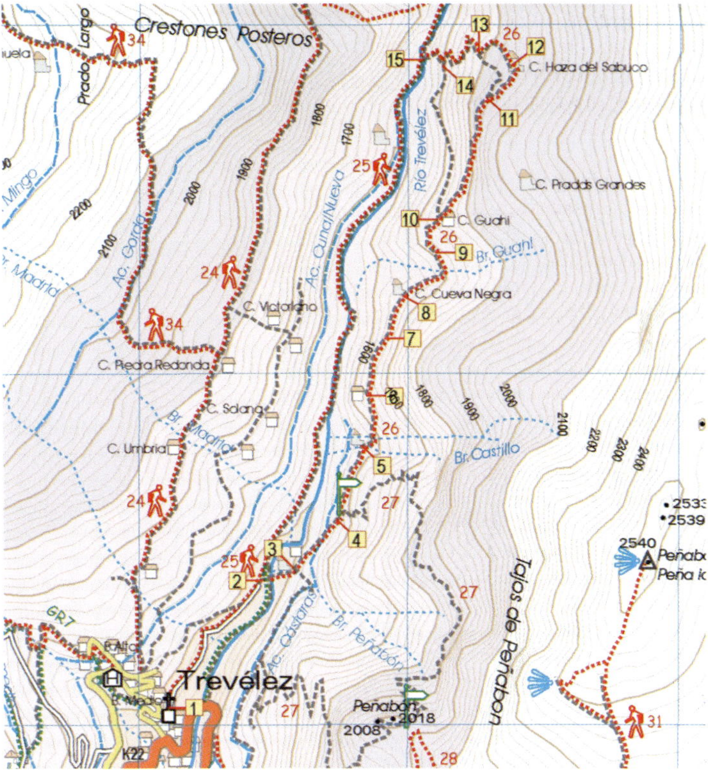

Crossing the acequia, we bear right before doubling back to the left 75 metres later on a waterlogged path, then descend directly toward the river to join the main **Camino al Horcajo** trail (Wp.15 106M) at a point where one might be forgiven for thinking the path is actually a stream itself.

Camino al Hocajo (Wp.15)

We now simply turn left to cross the bridge 75 metres later and follow the right bank all the way back to **Trevélez**, crossing the *parque nacional* boundary thirty-five minutes later, after which the trail, which is partially cobbled at this stage, climbs above the river before rejoining our outward route at Wp.2.

Glance up at the little outcrop of **Peñabón** from **Trevélez** and it looks nice enough, but it's not exactly one of those rocks that calls out to be climbed. This is a pity, since if any bit of rock around **Trevélez** deserves to be climbed, this is it.

It's a glorious little eyrie, offering spectacular views and even more spectacular paths, and it is well served by this brilliantly conceived *sendero local*, which provides maximum impact for modest effort. There's that many zigs and zags en route one starts to feel like the Artful Dodger making off down a busy street with a silk handkerchief, though in our case what's evaded is not the law but any sense of an arduous climb, the back of which is broken before we really notice it.

The exertion rating is exclusively for the last brief stretch of the climb. The paths are clear throughout and peppered with a superfluity of wayposts, so there is no possibility of getting lost.

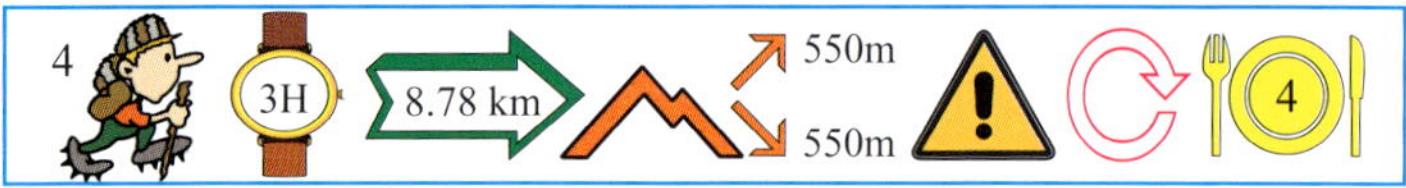

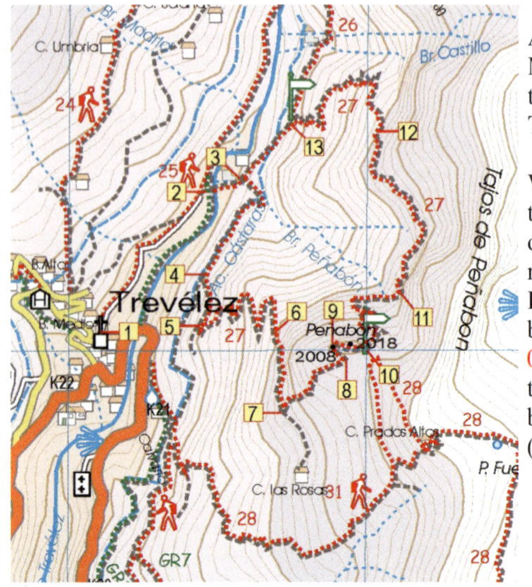

Access by car:
Motorists should park in the **Plaza de la Iglesia** in **Trevelez**'s **Barrio Bajo**.

We start as per Walk 26, taking **Calle Cuesta** out of **Plaza de la Iglesia** to reach the **Camino al Horcajo** dirt track behind the church (Wp.1 0M), which we follow all the way down to the bridge over the river (Wp.2 15M).

Crossing the bridge, we pass a mapboard of our itinerary and climb past the ruins of **Molino Altero** to a corral, behind which there's a signposted junction where we turn right for 'Penabon por el Monte', 'el Monte' being the familiar term among locals for the western face of **Peñabón** (Wp.3 21M).

Following a broad trail, we briefly climb alongside the **Barranco de Peñabón** watercourse before bearing right, crossing the watercourse and the **Acequia de Cástaras**. Our path then shadows this exceptionally broad and beautiful *acequia* for 400 metres to a Y junction (Wp.4 31M), where we fork left and begin climbing steadily amid the thick cloak of holm oak mantling **El Monte**. Forking left again at a second Y junction (Wp.5 36M), we zigzag up long, easy traverses amid more closely planted oak, passing below the lower crags of **Peñabón**. After enough zigs and zags to populate the creche of a 1970s commune, we go through (possibly under, it's very tightly tied) an improvised gateway in a fence (Wp.6 63M), then cross a small rockslide and pass a two metre stretch that is very slightly vertiginous.

When our path levels out on a spur (Wp.7 70M) a few hundred metres short of **Cortijo de las Rosas** (screened by trees at this stage), we leave the clearer path that carries straight on toward the *cortijo* and instead turn left on a slightly less well defined but clearly waymarked path climbing more steeply to the northeast, briefly bringing the *cortijo* into view off to our right.

Approaching the summit

A steady climb takes us straight up to the long sloping back of the **Peñabón**, where the path virtually levels out (Wp.8 86M) and we turn left to climb (off- path but on easy terrain) for 75 metres to reach the summit itself (Wp.9).

The views are quite exceptional, incorporating the entire **Trevélez** valley, **Mulhacén** (Walk 32), **Siete Lagunas** (Walks 33 & 34) and, immediately to the north, the superficially daunting terrain traversed in the course of our descent, which is in fact as immaculately plotted as our ascent.

After enjoying the views (this may take some time), we head east to the signpost directly behind the summit (Wp.10 91M). Ignoring a waypost 75 metres further to the east (part of the unofficial PR waymarked **Piedra Ventana** route), we turn left, initially on a faint path, but promptly recovering a clear path that resumes the zigzagging

The view north from the top

business with a vengeance, descending a steep escarpment in easy stages, soon bringing into view the line of the ongoing path cutting across the umbria or shady side of the mountain.

After crossing the head of the **Barranco de Peñabón** below daunting crags (Wp.11 110M), our path, which is never in doubt and never less than spectacular (frequently considerably more than that) snakes along the umbria, crossing a massive rockslide and **Barranco de Roaero**, an affluent of the **Peñabón**.

Trevélez seen from Barranco de Roaero

Thereafter, we continue contouring round the hillside to the north on a broader, better made path before descending to go through a second, more readily opened gate (Wp.12 134M). Continuing our steady descent, we traverse a dense pine wood before emerging amid pasture awash with yellow broom and buttercups, below which we cross a final stretch of woodland to join the **Camino de las Chorreras** (Wp.13 154M) (see Walk 26) where we turn left to rejoin our outward route at Wp.3 just under 400 metres later.

The climb to **Peña de los Papos** (sometimes also called 'Peñabón', but not to be confused with the summit visited in Walk 27) is conventionally done as a straight up slog from **Trevélez**, but after a lot of hard staring at the **Loma de Juviles**, it seemed to me that there had to be an easier way up to the highlands to the east of **Trevélez**, so I set off early one morning on the off chance. This is always a risky thing to do and frequently ends up with me cursing my folly and wondering why I wanted to waste a perfectly good day trailblazing a route that, for manifest and insurmountable reasons, nobody else had bothered attempting. In this case though, the attempt was a triumphant success, revealing a great ridge route that is highly recommended.

In essence, we follow the **GRs7** and **240** for a little under four kilometres then the **GR240** for another couple of kilometres, all of which is clearly sign and wayposted. Thereafter, if you're not using GPS, you need to be a confident and experienced pathfinder, as

Peña de los Papos

A bird's eye view of Trevélez

though we are rarely without a path of any description at all, much of the walking can be deemed off-path - worth the effort, though. It's wonderful, wild terrain, the views are superb throughout, and there's a real sense of satisfaction to completing what proved such a natural loop.

It's also a good walk for wildlife. I saw four large male *cabra montes*, five fox cubs romping at the mouth of their den, and dozens of brilliantly coloured bee-catchers. The final ascent from **Fuente Fria** to **Peña de los Papos** is given as an extension rather than an integral part of the itinerary as it was recorded during a different walk.

Access by car:
Our walk starts just east of **Trevélez**, where the **GR7** to **Juviles** (no longer signposted) and **GR240** leave the A4132. Motorists can park in the lay by on the right immediately after the bridge over the **Rio Trevélez**.

75 metres after the **Rio Trevélez** bridge, at the **Trevélez** city limits sign where there is also a sign indicating the end of the 50km speed limit, we take the broad trail climbing SE (Wp.1 0M). Climbing steadily, we quickly leave the road behind and pass a minor fork on the left (Wp.2) 100 metres before crossing the **Acequia de Cástaras**, immediately after which we fork right (Wp.3 9M). After passing a branch doubling back to the left (Wp.4 12M), the path levels off for a while and runs parallel to the *acequia* as we cross the shallow **Calvario** gully.

A gentle climb amid pine and holm oak brings us onto a spur where we fork right at a Y junction (Wp.5 24M). Enjoying fine views to the south and west, we traverse desiccated pasture above the deserted **Cortijo de los Castaños**, then dip down to cross a footbridge over the **Castaños** watercourse, immediately after which we climb to the left (Wp.6 34M). Threading its way through attractive woodland, our path eventually joins the end of an old logging track (Wp.7 58M), which we follow for 800 metres, passing en route a branch doubling back to the left (Wp.8 65M).

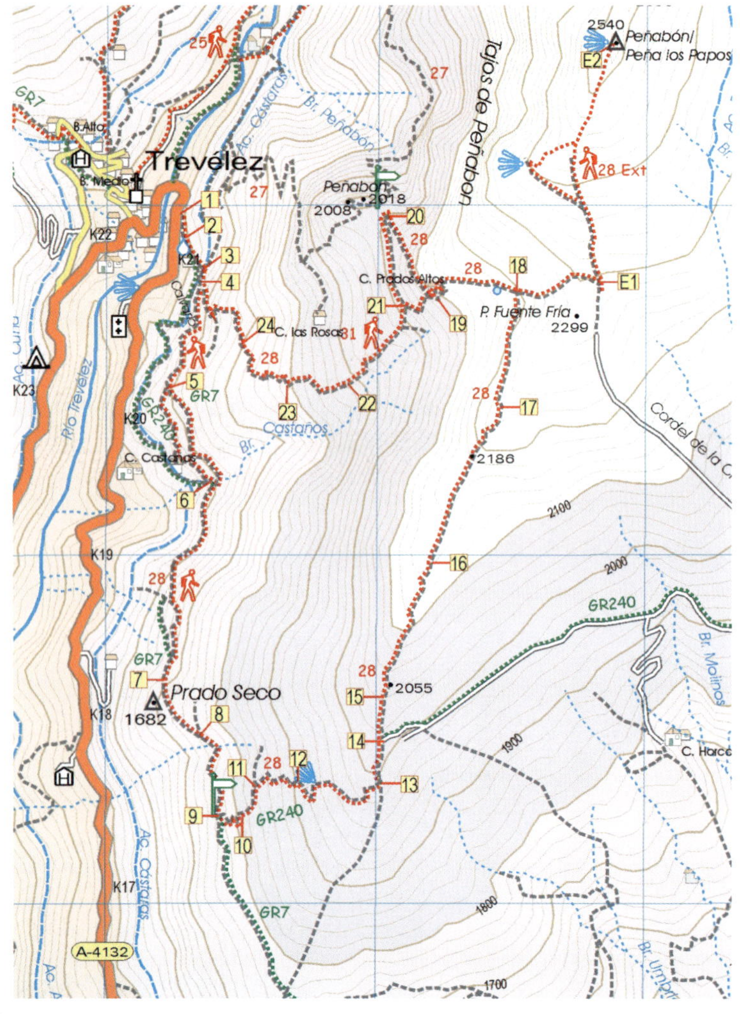

A little over 500 metres after the branch track, we come to a clearly sign and wayposted intersection where the two GRs diverge, the GR7 carrying straight on along the track for 'Juviles', while we fork left with the GR240 on a narrow path signposted 'Loma de Lastonar' (Wp.9 70M).

Climbing steadily through the woods, we turn left when the path joins a broad trail (Wp.10 80M) then fork right 125 metres later (Wp.11), once again on a path. Zigzagging up between the trees beside a broad firebreak, we cross a dirt track (Wp12 90M), 200 metres after which we pass a natural *mirador* overlooking the **Trevélez** valley.

After traversing a patch of open ground and crossing a final sparse band of pine, the **Sendero Sulayr** joins another broad firebreak (Wp.13 103M). Turning left, we climb between the twin **Portichuelo** trig points, 100 metres after which, the **GR240** turns right on a dirt track (Wp.14 105M). This is where we leave the wayposted itinerary, instead carrying straight on to reach the end of the firebreak (Wp.15 110M), which is where off-pathish bit begins.

Forking right, we follow a faint cow path (NE), passing to the right of the two immediately visible outcrops of rock and to the left of a stand of pine.

The dirt track at Wp.14

The chimney stack rock at Wp.16

The path disappears occasionally, but maintaining a northeasterly direction and staying on the high ground, we soon pick up new traces, passing fifty metres to the right of a distinct chimney stack rock (Wp.16 123M).

Enjoying superb views towards the slopes of **Mulhacén** and **Alcazaba**, we approach **Pico Fuente Fria**, essentially two bands of jagged rock backed by the smooth slope of **Peña de los Papos** and **Trevélez** comes into view.

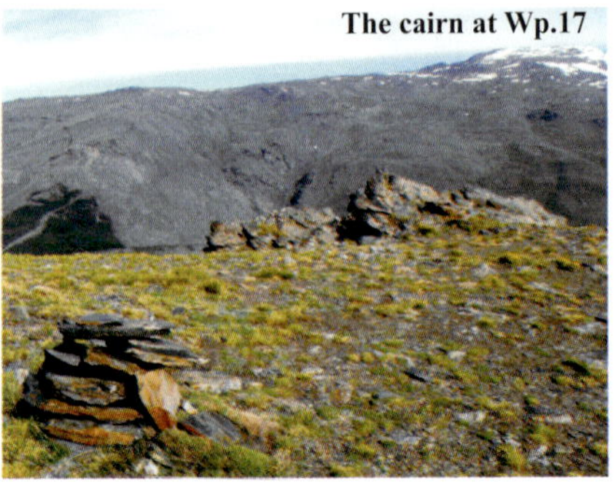
The cairn at Wp.17

The path, which is reasonably clear at this stage, climbs across the centre of the first band of jagged rocks, behind which, halfway to the second band, a large cairn off to our left indicates a clear, well trodden path skirting the western flank of **Pico Fuente Fria** (Wp.17 136M).

Taking the clear, cairn marked path, we head due north to a rough gateway in a wire fence, beyond which we descend gently toward the erosion channels below a large hanger of pine at the head of **Barranco de los Castaños**, which we cross fifty metres below the pine (Wp.18 146M). This is where the extension and main loop diverge. Peak baggers who want to add **Peña de los Papos** to their tally should turn right here and climb (E then NE) alongside the erosion scar (see below for a description of the extension). To return to **Trevélez**, we bear left (NW), passing a small, weedy reservoir 175 metres later.

The path becomes narrower after the reservoir, gradually bearing round to a westerly direction as we start descending on the northern side of **Barranco de los Castaños**, the folds of which down below provide a constantly shifting diaporama. It's worth pausing every once in a while to enjoy the spectacle, since we need to keep a sharp eye out to follow the increasingly faint path as it descends to pass above two roofless, ruined cabins (Wp.19 158M).

It's possible (and more logical in ascent) to head directly to Wp.21 from these cabins, but for an easier descent we take the clearest path to the NW, which follows a contour line before descending gently toward **Mulhacén**, the **Alcazaba**, and the stand of pine behind **Peñabón** (Walk 27). The path peters out in the woods (Wp.20 167M) five metres short of another clear path on which we turn left (SSE) following a contour line back towards the *barranco*.

500 metres later, at the uppermost corner of another pine wood (Wp.21 175M), cairns mark where we resume our descent (SW) along the southerly limit of the wood. The path is very faint to begin with, but the cairns and the line of pine which we keep on our right, define the way as we descend gently then steadily on an increasingly clear path that brings us down to a Y junction above a second, larger reservoir behind the fenced **Cortjo de las Rosas**, the buildings of which are visible down to our right (Wp.22 184M). This is the last point at which pathfinding is a little problematic.

Descending off path across the pasture to the left of the *cortijo*, we follow the lower fence round toward the main farm building.

Below the *cortijo*, down to our left, we can see another pine wood, directly above which there is a large outcrop of rock splashed with prominent red and white boundary markers. We descend across the pasture in front of the *cortijo* to this outcrop of rock (Wp.23 194M).

To the right of the outcrop of rock, there is a faint path that promptly becomes a cairn marked way descending through the woods, confirmed by white arrows (painted for those climbing, but useful for the descent as well).

Emerging on a patch of grass above a muddy swale at the lower end of the wood (Wp.24 203M), we bear right and follow the clearly cairn and waymarked path down to rejoin our outward route at Wp.4.

Extension to Peña de los Papos
5 walker, 1h40-2h, 4km, ascents & descents 450 metres
All data from Wp.18. Distances and the return time are estimates.

At Wp.18 of the main itinerary, we turn right and climb (E) alongside the erosion channel on a faint path. The path becomes increasingly faint and soon disappears, at which point cairns guide us away from the erosion channel (NE) up to a flat ridge where, some 500 metres from Wp.18, we join the traces of an old track (Wp.E1 18M). Bearing left, we follow the remains of this track to the north, ignoring a branch to the left. When, the track eventually peters out, we simply carry on along the ridge (NE) for about a kilometre, passing three discrete outcrops of rock before reaching the trig point on the main summit (Wp.E2 59M). We return to Wp.18 via the same route.

The **Bérchules** valley is a perfect example of that protean aspect of the Alpujarras I was banging on about in the introduction, its high pasture dotted with *cortijos* that bear a distinct resemblance to the cabins of the transhumance hamlets of the Atlas mountains, while the paths traversing the wooded slopes below **Cerro Gordo** are straight out of the Pyrenees. Our old version of the classic walk to the Junta de los **Ríos Chico** and **Grande** above **Bérchules** used to follow the lovely **Acequia Nueva**. Unfortunately, the **Acequia Nueva** is no longer quite so lovely, having been abandoned, bejewelled with rubbish, and blocked half way along.

Happily, the newly wayposted **PR28** neatly replaces both our **Junta de los Ríos** itinerary and the old **Cerro Gordo** route, exploiting the best of what is still feasible in the former and providing something comparable to the latter, but with a better path in the middle. Congratulations to whoever invented the itinerary. It's a beautifully conceived walk, marred only by a mildly monotonous descent and a heartbreaking little climb at the end. The wayposting and waymarking are reliable except at Wps.4 and 11.

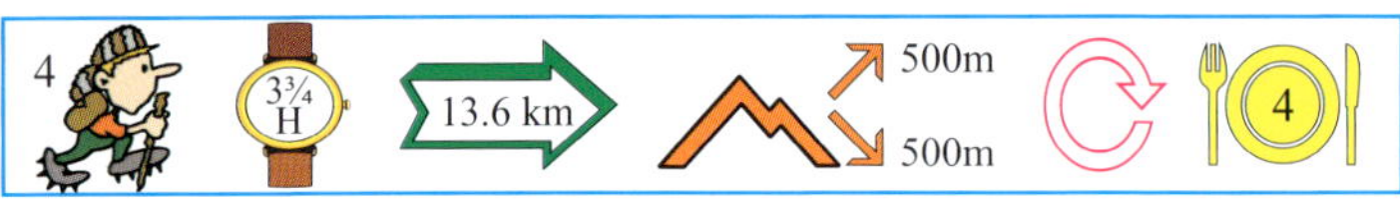

Access by car:
We start from the parking area on the right beside **Bar Duende** at the entrance to **Bérchules** village, where there is generally plenty of room, the space reserved for the bus stop notwithstanding.

From the entrance to the parking area (Wp.1 0M), we head into the centre of **Bérchules** along **Calle Iglesia** then cross **Plaza Abastos** into **Calle Real**.

Following the arrow signs guiding motorized traffic through the village, we reach **Calle Garcia**, which leads into a concrete lane with black railings. At the end of this lane, we come to a *lavadero/fuente* (Wp.2 10M) where there's a mapboard of the new green and white waymarked **Junta de los Ríos** *sendero local* and a PR waymarked sign for **Junta de los Ríos**.

The *lavadero/fuent* at **Wp.2**

Continuing on a broad path, we briefly follow an *acequia* and pass above a couple of large threshing circles, after which the path runs parallel to then joins a dirt track (Wp.3 21M). Turning left, we follow this dirt track as it climbs amid market gardens, ignoring two forks on the right, the first after 30 metres, the second (the old **Acequia Nueva** route) after 200 metres (Wp.4

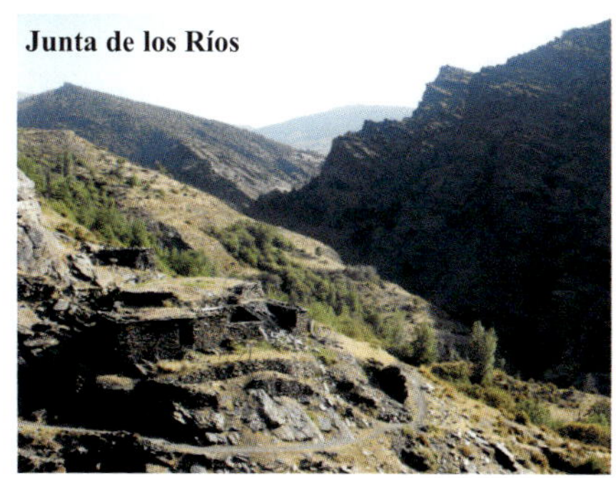

Junta de los Ríos

26M). Bearing right at a slanting T junction (Wp.5 29M), we stick with the track until it dwindles to a broad trail (Wp.6 32M). The trail snakes along the hillside in a northerly direction toward the obvious confluence of the **Ríos Chico** and **Grande** below the wild terrain of the **Tajos de Reyecillo**, last refuge of the leaders of the 1568 Moorish rebellion.

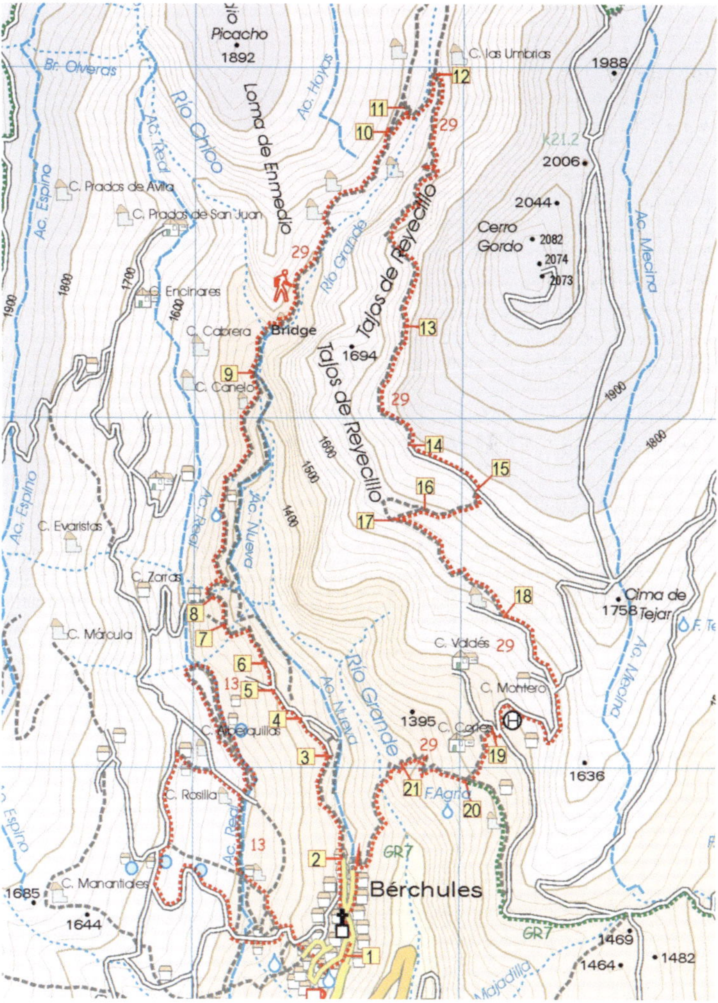

After crossing a dry stream bed, we pass a cluster of derelict cabins, ignoring en route two forks up to the left (Wp.7 37M & Wp.8 41M). As we approach the **Junta de los Ríos**, the **Acequia Nueva** path feeds in from the right (Wp.9 72M), immediately after which we see the **Fábrica de los Moros** ruins at the confluence of the two rivers.

Crossing the footbridge over the **Río Chico**, we climb behind the *fabrica* on a broad, partially paved trail, enjoying fine views over the **Reyecillo** cliffs, then follow a contour line high above the **Río Grande**.

After crossing a rockslide of thick slates and climbing gently, we pass in front of a ruin and traverse a stretch of holm oak and chestnut trees, beyond which the head of the valley comes into view, and we see two farmsteads off to our right above the left bank of the river. We cross the river below the lower of these, the **Cortijo de las Umbrias**, the *umbria* being the shady side of the valley as opposed to the southern facing *solana*. At a clearly waypoasted Y junction (Wp.10 94M), we leave the *sendero local* and fork right, following the PR, immediately bringing into view the line of our return path climbing above the left bank of the river.

140 metres later (Wp.11 96M), we again fork right, this time on a cairn marked path (confirmed lower down by waypoasts) that zigzags down toward the river then follows the right bank upstream toward the **Cortijo de las Umbrias**, just short of which we reach an idyllic ford with a rather fragile looking footbridge (Wp.12 103M).

Crossing the river and bearing right, we follow an exceedingly pretty path climbing gently to steadily amid pine and jagged outcrops of rock. There's nowhere to go wrong here, so stow the book and enjoy, both the cool of the shade and the spectacular views up and down the valley. Passing directly behind the **Tajos de Reyecillo** (Wp.13 135M), we descend 50 metres, then follow a contour and climb briefly before a final balcony path brings us onto the end of a logging track, from where we can see **Bérchules** (Wp.14 146M).

400 metres later, at a leftward bend beside a 'Parque Nacional' perimeter sign (Wp.15 151M), we bear right on a rough track descending to a wire mesh gate in a fence, beyond which a waypost confirms our route.

Following traces of a rough track, initially heading toward a distant helipad and reservoir (S) before bearing round to a more westerly direction, we descend steeply to a corner of the fence on our right. Bearing right, we follow the fence for 100 metres toward a stand of pine, where we turn left on a steep shortcut track (Wp.16 157M).

Bérchules visible on our descent

At the bottom of the shortcut (Wp.17 160M), we again turn left, back toward the helipad and reservoir. Joining a broader, better stabilized track leading to the **Corrales de Valdes** (Wp.18 168M), we bear left and follow the track as it meanders down to pass below the helipad and reservoir to reach the **Cortijo de Valdes**.

15 metres after the U bend in front of the *cortijo* (Wp.19 183M), we fork right on a broad trail that descends steadily to join the clearly wayposted **GR7** (Wp.20 188M).

Bearing right, we simply follow the GR for a steady to steep descent down to a footbridge over the river (Wp.21 205M), from where a brief, but mildly heartbreaking climb brings us back into **Bérchules** at the end of **Calle Agua**. Bearing left then forking right at the fountain fifty metres later, we rejoin our outward route just short of the bar in **Plaza Abastos**.

If you only have time for one 3000 metre peak, this is the one to do. It's wilder than the **Mulhacén**, less tiring, more interesting, and quite as 'unique', being the westernmost 3000 metre peak of the chain. However, pathfinding may be a problem in winter and there are frequently strong winds in the summer. The terrain is rough, so don't attempt it in poor conditions.

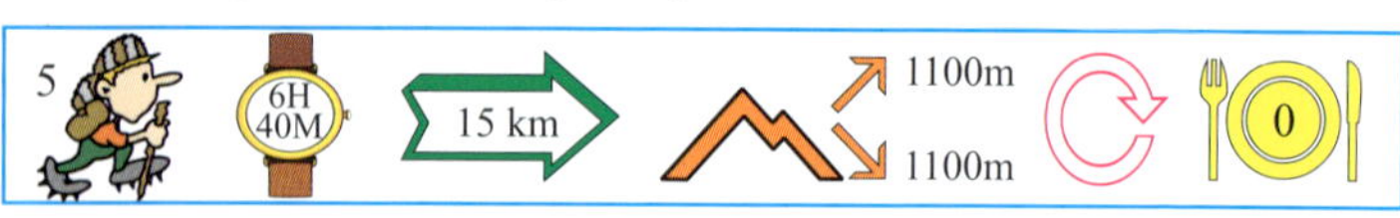

Access by car:
The walk starts from km16.7 of **Pista Forestal 1** (see Appendix A), where there is ample trackside parking. The start corresponds with Wps. 2-6 of Walk 16. For ease of cross referencing, the present itinerary does not have a Wp.1. The relevant waypoints have been appended to the waypoint file for the present itinerary.

The view south from near the start

First sighting of Caballo shortly after Wp.2

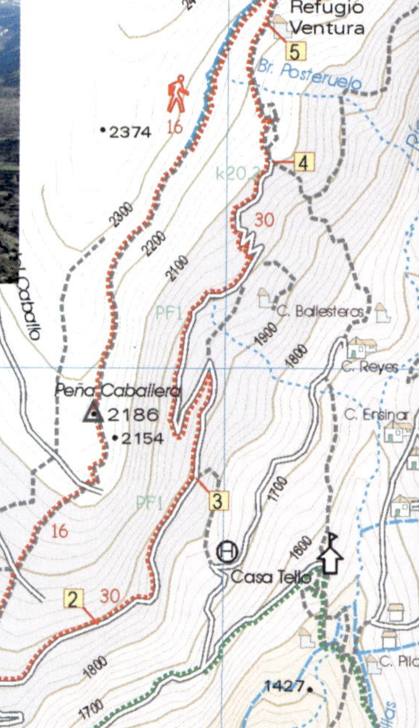

From km16.7 of **Pista Forestal 1** (Wp.2 0M), we follow Wps. 2-6 of Walk 16, climbing past the **Ventura** refuge to the Y-junction just short of a dense hanger of pine (Wp.6 77M). Forking left on the less well defined path, we climb to the *acequia*, but instead of turning left, we cross the *acequia* and continue climbing (NNE) for 50 metres.

Our path then levels out and follows a contour line, crossing the **Barranco de Hiniestral** watercourse and joining a firebreak circling a plantation of pine (Wp.7 105M). We cross the firebreak and take the path through the woods to their northernmost tip, where the path crosses the firebreak again and heads NE in a clearly visible line across the last stretch of scrub to the first rock slides.

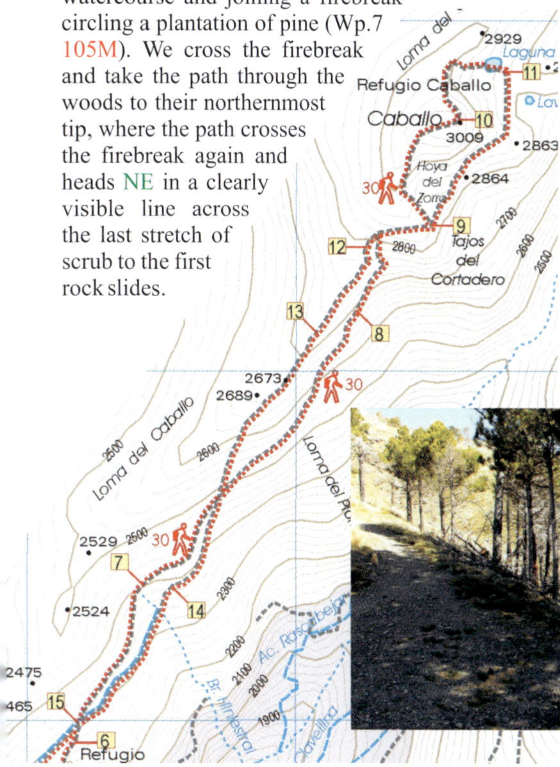

Here the landscape changes character. To the south we see something akin to the pasture-rich Pyrenees; to the north is a facsimile of the stony wilderness found in the High Atlas. The path becomes fainter, rougher and narrower as it climbs (NNE) towards the jagged crags of the **Tajos del Cortadero**, zigzagging through two steep sections and passing a small cairn (Wp.8 159M) before it loses definition beside a green-flanked rivulet just before the **Tajos**. The main path climbs to the left 15 metres <u>before</u> this rivulet, but it's difficult to see from below and you might find it easier to bear left <u>at</u> the rivulet, climbing off-path and aiming slightly to the right of the large rock, to reach a shallow col and a clearer path 50 metres later.

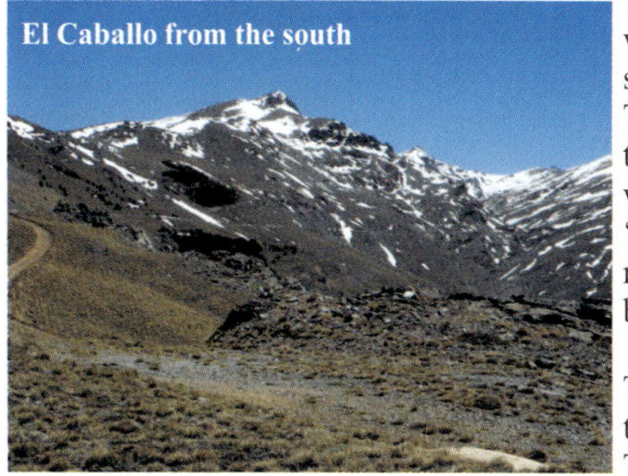

El Caballo from the south

Turning right on the clear path, we follow it up to the low stone walls behind the *tajos*. The walls (Wp.9 176M) are all that exist of what some maps, with infinite optimism, call the 'Refugio de Lanjarón', a refuge that was in fact never built.

The main path continuing past the 'refuge' is our return route. To climb **El Caballo**, we head

north-west (NW) from the 'refuge' (off-path but marked by a cairn) gradually bearing north, then north-east, then east, maintaining throughout a discrete distance from the drop into the **Hoya del Zorro**. We eventually join a faintly trodden path up to the peak (Wp.10 194M), from where we can see all the way along to the **Alcazaba** (just to the left of the **Mulhacén**) and can even pick out the main path climbing the **Mulhacén** from **Caldera**.

A clear path descends NW to the **Laguna & Refugio de Caballo** (Wp.11 209M) where a bathe is strongly recommended (always supposing your heart's up to it!) (N.B. bathing in the lagoons is prohibited by the park authorities, a prohibition like most Spanish prohibitions, more often neglected than respected).

The return path heads south from the refuge, passing the eastern face of the **Caballo** and the so-called 'Refugio de Lanjarón' to join the top of the path (clearly visible from above) (Wp.12 229M) down to the rivulet. From here you can return to the firebreak/pine-wood by the same route or take a more adventurous, pathless route along the crest (good visibility preferable).

The off-path route follows the line of the ridge, staying just to the east of the rocky outcrops along the crest, until it reaches an outcrop (Wp.13 244M) from where we can see the length of the ridge and, off to the left, the firebreak/pine-wood. We maintain a southerly (S) direction after Wp.13 until we <u>see</u> a large cairn topping another outcrop of rock in the distance. Bearing left to pass below a long, sloping crag, we aim for the northernmost tip of the firebreak/pine-wood, a twenty to thirty minute descent through broom and furze. Alternatively, cut straight down to the outward path from the firebreak/pine-wood.

Ignoring the path taken through the pine on the way up, we follow the firebreak round the lower part of the wood. When it starts climbing on the southern side of the wood (Wp.14 309M), we take the narrow path on the left down to the *acequia*. We then follow the *acequia* back to the point at which we first crossed it (Wp.15 319M), from where we follow our outward route back to the start..

The first time we tried this route, we turned back, defeated by our failure to find what a rather sketchy Spanish description dubbed a 'trail'. It was only when we later realized no 'trail' existed and the description was sketchy because its authors hadn't actually done the walk, that we were emboldened to go back and have another bash. Take that as a warning. Despite beginning and ending on dirt tracks, this is a largely pathless walk and is only suitable for those who positively enjoy getting well off the beaten track.

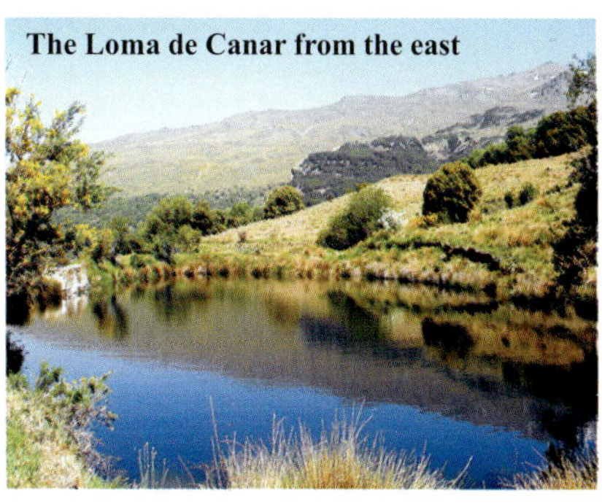
The Loma de Canar from the east

That said, the rewards are remarkable, with great views, a real sense of high mountain adventure, and a degree of isolation that is likely to be complete save for the local shepherd and the odd Spanish hiker doing a traverse of the entire *sierra*. It's very dry and exposed though, and is not recommended in hot weather or when visibility is poor.

Access by car:
The walk starts from the **Puente Palo Área Recreativa** at km11.2 of **Pista Forestal 2** (see Appendix A).

From the western end of **Puente Palo Área Recreativa**, we take the chained track climbing to the north (Wp.1 0M). Sticking to the main track and ignoring all branches, including (Wp.2 31M) the cairn marked turning on the right for **Pico Alegas**, we climb steadily across the pine covered slopes of **Prado Quinto**.

Toward the top of the woods, the track describes a long level southerly arc before doubling back at a junction distinguished by faint blue waymarks (Wp.3 47M), after which we resume our steady ascent. Climbing clear of the more closely planted trees, we see what appears to be a stone cabin with a green door, in fact one wing of the shepherd's corral that marks the start of our off-path antics. Fine views open out behind us over the **Guadalfeo** valley and the **Contraviessa** as we continue zigzagging up the track till we reach the corral. Directly behind the building, a shallow watershed points toward a distinct, bare conical summit, pricked with a nipple-like cairn. This is the smaller of the two summits on the **Loma de Cáñar** that go by the name of **Cerillo Redondo** and is the culminating point of the present itinerary.

To reach the top, we turn left behind the corral, leaving the remains of the track in order to climb along the right bank (left hand side as we ascend) of the shallow watershed (Wp.4 75M). Goat pellets and the odd better-trodden patches of bare earth suggest this is the way taken by the local shepherd, but as

Grazing, above Wp.5

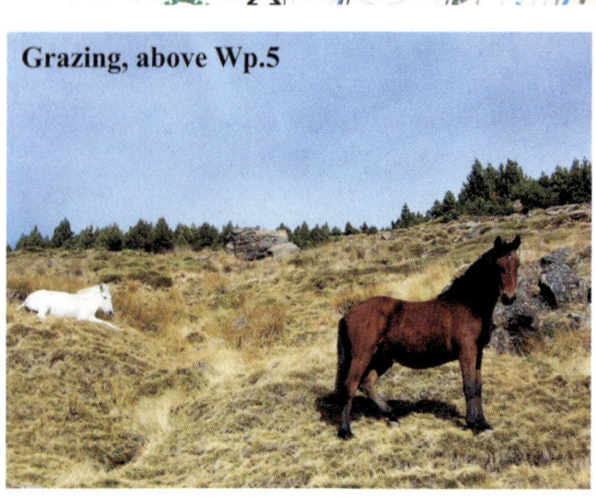

usual, the goats go every-which-way so take this as already being off-path. For the sake of descriptive convenience (the walking could as well be done either side), we stick to the right bank of the watershed, climbing steeply to its 'source' where it bifurcates on a shallow grassy platform (Wp.5 92M).

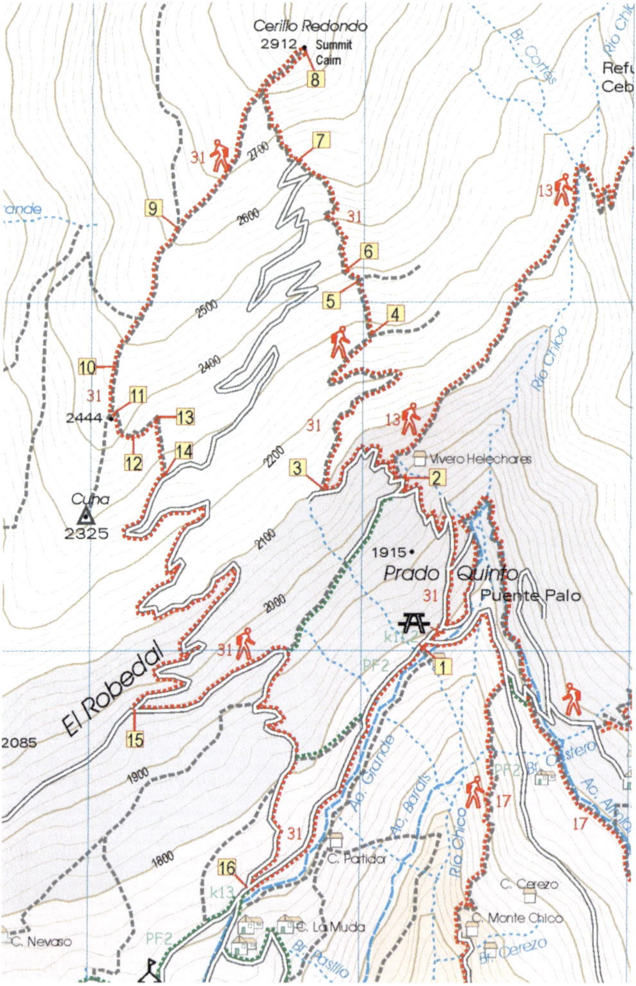

We follow the fork to the left and continue climbing (N), passing a cairn on a large rock 100 metres later (Wp.6). Bearing slightly right toward the line of crags on our right, we climb across very rough, natural terracing, bringing

Cerillo Redondo back into view as we weave our way through a wall of stubby pine.

On the far side of the pine, looking up toward **Cerillo Redondo** and the head of the crags on our right, we can see a patch of clear path and, to it's left, the last zigzags of a dirt track that climbs from **El Robledal**, the oak forest south of **Puente Palo**. Roughly following the course of a dry watershed, we climb steeply (NNW) to follow the patch of 'clear' path (not so obvious once you're on it), until it joins the end of the dirt track (Wp.7 129M). If you've got this far and suddenly concluded 'off-path' is not your thing, this track is your escape route, rejoining the described itinerary at Wp.14.

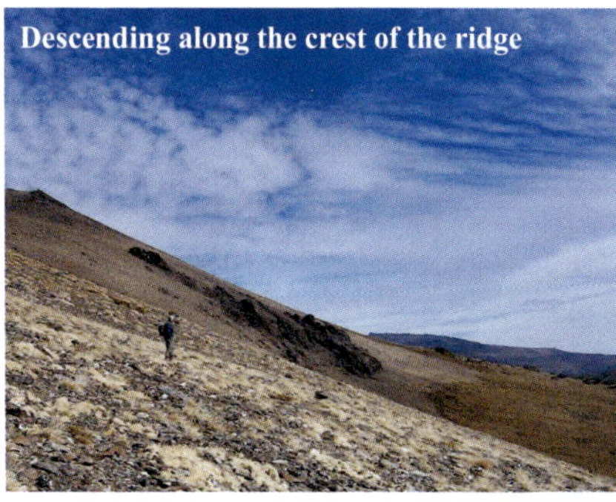
Descending along the crest of the ridge

Crossing the end of the track, we climb toward the lower crag immediately south of **Cerillo Redondo**, picking our way across the debris-strewn slopes, taking advantage of the more path-like patches of grit between the bulkier debris. This is hard going and toward the end you maybe wondering whether it's worth the effort, but I assure you it is.

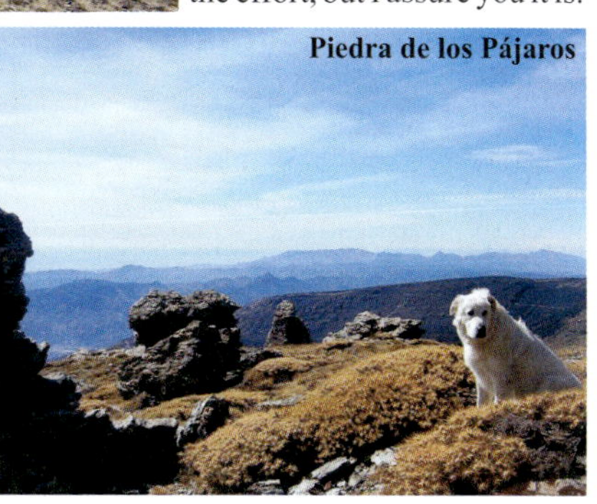
Piedra de los Pájaros

As we pass to the right of the lower crag, a significant lump of rock itself from close up, **Caballo** comes into view and, on the final stretch up to the pillar cairn on **Cerillo Redondo** (Wp.8 162M), a fabulous vista opens out including **Tajo de los Machos**, **Veleta** and **Mulhacén**.

Retracing our steps to the lower crag, we pick our way along the ridge, still off-path, bringing into view the clear line of a narrow path about a kilometre to the south. How you reach this path rather depends on which views you favour, west or east, but either way, it's a relatively easy descent as we make our way along one flank of the ridge or the other avoiding the more obtrusive central crags. The views are superb, particularly over the **Contraviessa** and, to the west, the **Axarquía**.

Aiming for the little cluster of rocks at what appears to be the lip of the ridge, we join the clear, narrow path seen from above (Wp.9 184M 2622m). If you need a windbreak, the cluster of rocks 300 metres later is probably your best bet on this route. In an emergency, 200 metres SE of these rocks there is a shelter built into the rock, though I haven't actually visited it, so I don't know what state this is in.

The path peters out as we descend from the first cluster of rocks, but soon becomes clear again as we approach the next cluster, **Piedra de los Pájaros**, and the line of scorched earth (Wp.10 200M) marking the fire damage that moved us to replace the ascent to the **Casa Forestal de Tello** with the present itinerary.

The original path descended along the western flank of the ridge past the **Cuna** rocks, but as this is now such a desolate landscape, I recommend one final off-path stretch.

225 metres into the patchy scorched scrub, we turn left behind **Piedra de los Pájaros** (Wp.11 205M), descending off the ridge and off-path toward a clear dirt track above **El Robledal**, the same track crossed at Wp.7.

After passing between a gateway of red and grey rock (Wp.12 210M), we swing left (NE) traversing rough, rocky ground to join the end of a new firebreak branching off the track we saw from above (Wp.13 213M). From hereon, the walking is considerably easier.

Following the firebreak down to the dirt track (Wp.14 218M), we turn right and embark on an infinitely gentle descent, snaking down the hillside, each switchback offering an alternative outlook. Shortcuts are possible, but probably not terribly desirable at this stage, so I recommend staying on the track. Eventually, after more hairpins than an upmarket salon, we pass a row of beehives and reach a junction (Wp.15 270M), where we turn left to continue on the main track as it runs parallel to the upper limit of **El Robledal**.

We stick to this track as it drops down to descend through the oak forest, eventually reaching the **Puente Palo** track at a major junction (Wp.16 305M), where we have a choice of routes. To return directly to the start, simply turn left and follow the track back to the *área recreativa*. Alternatively and more attractively, 150 metres down the branch track you will find on your left the path along the very lovely **Acequia Grande**, which climbs past two driveways before joining a third that leads to a denuded platform just south of the *área recreativa*.

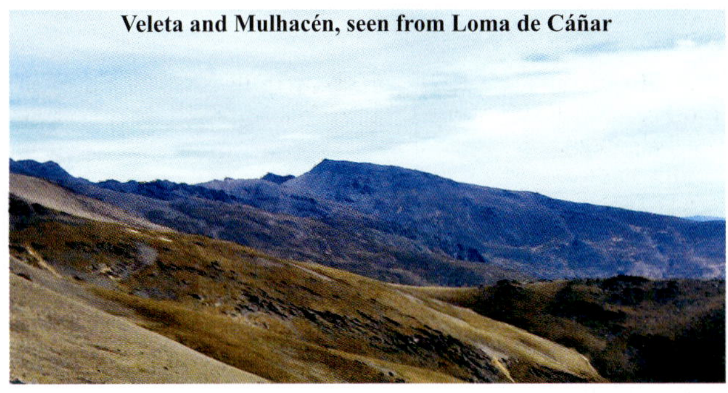

Veleta and Mulhacén, seen from Loma de Cáñar

The **Mulhacén** is the highest mountain on the Iberian Peninsula and therefore a must for many visitors. This circuit is intermittently waymarked and poses no serious orientation problems. It's not the most interesting ascent, but it is the most practical day trip. For the most part it's an easy walk along clear dirt tracks, however it is very, very long and the final climb to the peak is very steep. The park leaflet claims it takes seven hours, I timed it at eight-and-a-half, but given the length and height climbed, you should allow up to twelve hours counting rest-stops.

This route is included as the most practical single-day circuit to the top. But the descent is a bit boring! If you have the option of being picked up at the end of the day and have good pathfinding skills, or have already done Walks 18 & 21, I recommend taking the bus from **Capileira** to the **Mirador de Trevélez**, following either of the Short Versions to the top, then descending via the **Caldera** and **Poqueira refuges** and the **Río Naute** to **La Cebadilla**. Beware though: the link path crossing the headwaters of the **Naute** from **Cortijo de las Tomas** is a little vertiginous and involves crawling on hands and knees for a couple of metres.

We do not recommend this route in Winter
Just to emphasize the seriousness of this recommendation, three British climbers died of hypothermia on the summit in 2006.

Walking the route in summer
In summer, late July, early August are the best times, before the electric storms begin. The most likely problem you'll have with the weather is wind, though snow can stay on the peak as late as August. The problem with a summer ascent is that, by the time you get to the top, heat will have hazed the views for which the peak is so justly renowned. The only way round this is to camp out at the **Refuge Caldera** and climb early in the morning. Summer temperatures are pleasant at this altitude, but the UV is very intense: sun-hat, sunglasses, sun-cream are ESSENTIAL; long sleeves/trousers recommended. Water is available at the **Refuge Poqueira**, but has such a vile taste it's best to bring your own.

Several dirt tracks are used here. I use the local name for the main one, the **Carretera de Veleta** (**PF3** after the chain).

The walk starts from the **Hoya del Portillo** car park at km10.4 of **Pista Forestal 3** (see Appendix A). For access details to the short version, which is detailed at the end of the main itinerary, see Walk 33.

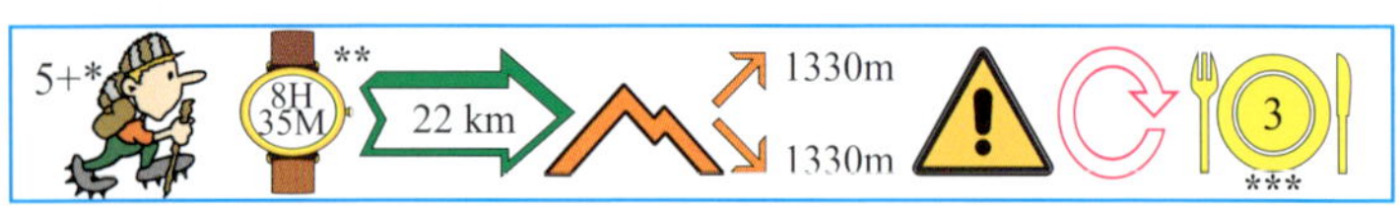

 * 5+ for the full walk, though to be honest, length and altitude send it off the scale. It's not difficult but you need a lot of stamina.

** Given the sheer length of this walk, I've broken times up for easier reference:
Hoya del Portillo - Poqueira Refuge 2 hours 10 mins
Poqueira Refuge - Caldera Refuge 2 hours 10 mins
Caldera Refuge - Mulhacén 1 hour 10 mins
Mulhacén - Hoya del Portillo 3 hours 5 mins

*** at the **Poqueira Refuge** - a lower rating than in Walk 21 as it comes too soon in this itinerary to be really useful.

HOYA DEL PORTILLO - POQUEIRA REFUGE (2 hours 10 minutes)

From the traffic control barrier at **Hoya del Portillo** (Wp.1 0M), we take the path to the left of the control hut and follow the waymarked route through the woods for 1.3 kilometres, passing a shortcut doubling back to the right after 600 metres (Wp.2), to reach a firebreak below **Puerto Molina** (Wp.3 25M). Crossing the firebreak, we take a broad track to the north-west.

The track descends slightly before bearing right and levelling out. Ignoring a minor branch on the left (Wp.4 50M), we stick to the main track climbing gently towards the **Cascar Negro** quarries. At the first quarry, when the track bears right, we turn left onto a broad, wayposted path (Wp.5 60M) that soon widens to a dirt track climbing past another extraction site.

This track levels out for a long rather dull haul to the junction with the dirt track to the **Poqueira Refuge**.

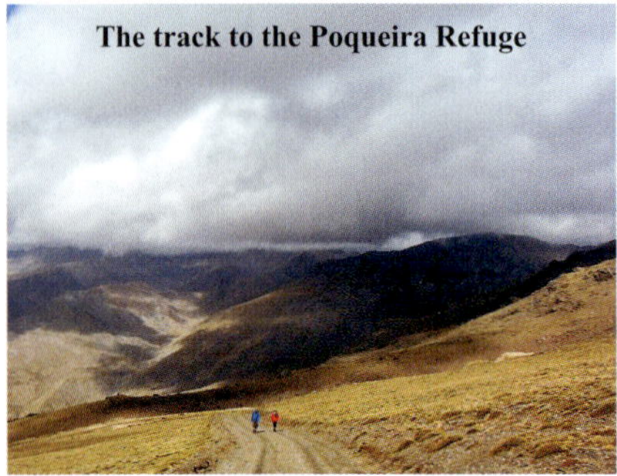

The track to the Poqueira Refuge

Four hundred metres before the two tracks join, we take the wayposted shortcut on the left to the **Poqueira** track (Wp.6 100M).

We bear left on this track then right behind a rocky outcrop and stone byre to descend to the **Poqueira Refuge** (Wp.7 130M).

Taking the well-trodden path from the refuge (NW), we gradually bear right (N) to join the **Río Mulhacén** ten minutes later. We then follow the left bank of the river (N) till the river runs dry, where we cross onto the right bank beside a cairn (Wp.8 35M).

The remainder of the climb to the **Refuge/Laguna de Caldereta** is a little confusing. Most maps place the route (there's no path) on the left bank of the *río*, but most of the cairns favour a route with fewer obstacles on the right bank.

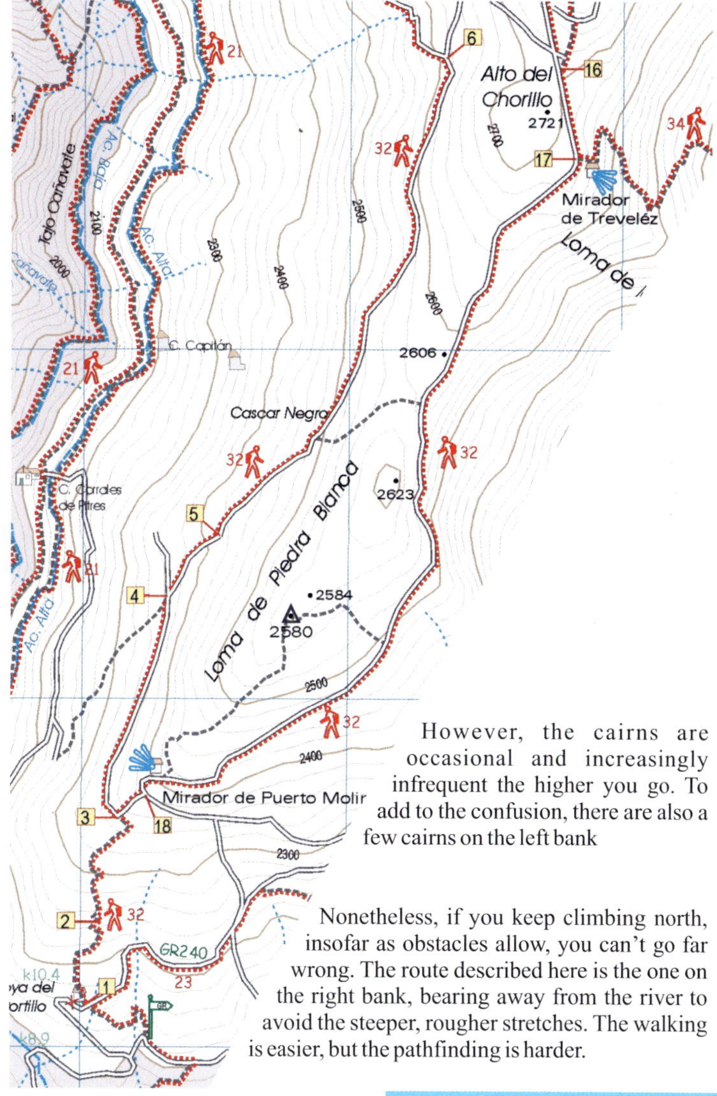

However, the cairns are occasional and increasingly infrequent the higher you go. To add to the confusion, there are also a few cairns on the left bank

Nonetheless, if you keep climbing north, insofar as obstacles allow, you can't go far wrong. The route described here is the one on the right bank, bearing away from the river to avoid the steeper, rougher stretches. The walking is easier, but the pathfinding is harder.

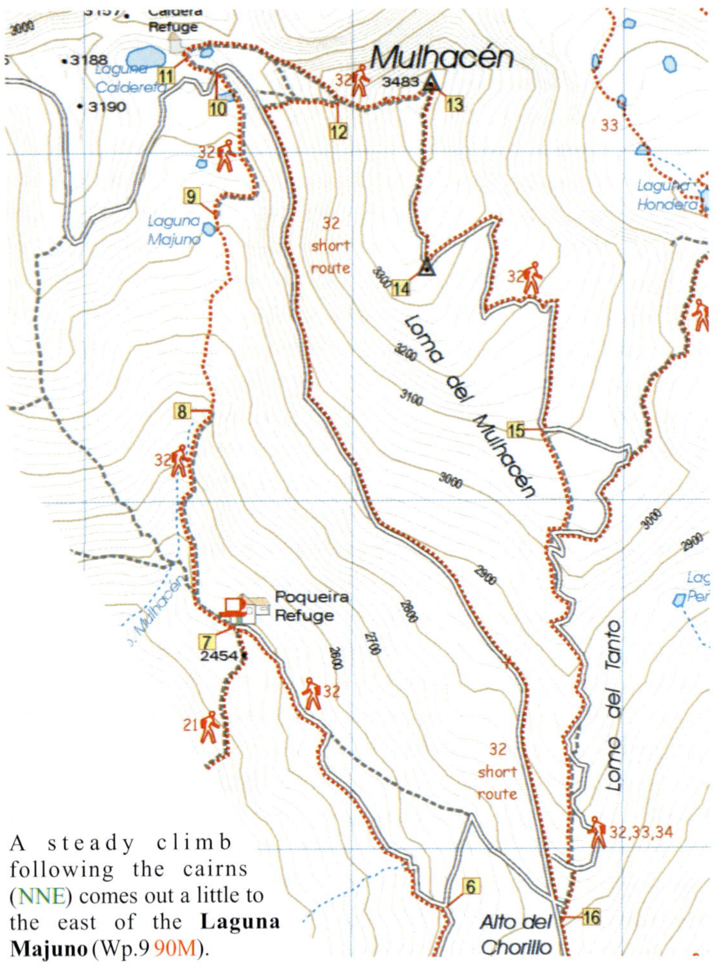

A steady climb following the cairns (NNE) comes out a little to the east of the **Laguna Majuno** (Wp.9 90M).

After bearing right alongside the marshy area feeding the lagoon, we climb a shallow stony depression (N) between a rocky outcrop and the **Carretera de Veleta**, which is clearly visible 100 metres above.

This depression leads into a grassy swale which we follow towards the centre of the *cirque* defined by the **Mulhacén** and the **Puntal de la Caldera**, crossing another (probably dry) lagoon onto the *carretera* (Wp.10 125M). Crossing the *carretera*, we maintain direction to reach the unmanned but well-maintained **Caldera Refuge** (Wp.11 130M).

CALDERA REFUGE - MULHACÉN (1 hour 10 minutes)

East of the refuge, the main path up to the peak is clearly visible. About halfway up, another narrower path comes in from the left. This is the path to take for a slightly gentler start to the ascent.

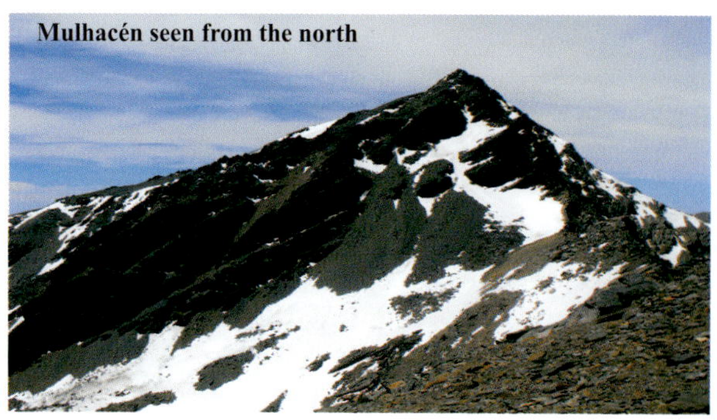

Mulhacén seen from the north

Following the faint path east from the refuge, we cross a brief pathless stretch over rocks before recovering the trodden way above the splendid jagged cliffs on the northern face of the **Mulhacén**.

After the two paths join (Wp.12 30M), comes the really testing bit - straight up through the most modestly sketched zigzags to the peak (Wp.13 70M), which will probably be relatively crowded, both with Spanish hikers and *cabra montés* so blasé about human beings, they're almost domestic.

On a clear day, you can see as far as Algeria (the ruins on the top are left over from a geodesic triangulation survey of North Africa at the end of the nineteenth century) though the likelihood is, you'll not see much further than a great expanse of white to the south-east, the *Mar de Plastico* or 'Plastic Sea', covering the Dalías Plain near Almería and responsible for all those chemical tomatoes littering supermarket shelves in England in the winter. However, even on the haziest of days, the views are breathtaking and there's a certain dizzying pleasure to be had from peering over the cliffs to the north, down to the **Laguna de la Mosca**, 500 metres below, a climb some demented enthusiasts undertake in winter when it's a wall of ice - not always with ropes either!

MULHACÉN - HOYA DEL PORTILLO (3 hours 5 minutes)

The descent is easy, but dull and very, very long. We start along the ridge to the south, along a clearly trodden path that soon joins a stony dirt track laid at the time of geodesic survey and currently neatly covered with blocks of rock in an attempt to regenerate the natural landscape. The track bears left just before a

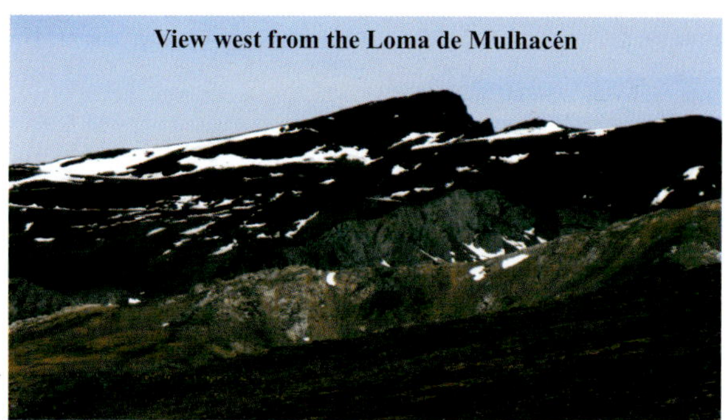

View west from the Loma de Mulhacén

cluster of rock-shelters/windbreaks and another triangulation post (Wp.14 15M) sometimes known as **Mulhacén II**, from where we have clear views of the way back to the **Hoya del Portillo**.

Whether you follow the track all the way down to **Alto de Chorillo** or take the shortcuts (notably Wp.15 45M marked by a cairn), is a matter for you and your knees to come to an arrangement over, but as a general rule, the lower we go the easier and more inevitable the shortcuts seem. Taking the shortcuts, we join the **Carretera de Veleta** a few hundred metres south of the end of the track from **Mulhacén**.

We now follow the *carretera* to the south, passing the junction with the **Poqueira** track, a signposted turning onto the 'Alto del Chorillo' (Wp.16 95M), and the **Mirador de Trevélez** bus stop (Wp.17 105M). We stick with this track for nearly five kilometres until, at length (very great length!), it passes the **Mirador de Puerto Molina**, below which we turn right on the firebreak (Wp.18 160M) descending back to Wp.3.

SHORT VERSION

via Caldera: 5 walker, 4 hours, ascents and descents 783 metres
via the Loma de Mulhacen: 4 walker

From the **Mirador de Trevélez** bus stop (Wp.S1 0M), we simply follow the **Carretera de Veleta** to the north, passing a signposted path on the left up to the **Alto del Chorillo** (Wp.S2). 175 metres later, a signposted track forks left for the **Poqueira** refuge (Wp.S3 6M).

At this point we have a choice of routes. The main itinerary carries straight on along the **Carretera de Veleta**. However, for an easier ascent or if the summit is still under snow, we can take the unmarked path forking right to climb via the **Loma de Mulhacén**.

For the main itinerary, we simply continue along the *carretera* for almost five kilometres, passing a traffic barrier 1500 metres from Wp.3 (Wp.S4 26M). A few hundred metres before the **Caldera Refuge**, we take a clearly trodden path on the right (Wp.S5 76M), climbing steeply to join the main **Caldera** path (Wp.S6 84M) then pass the junction with the path used in the long version of the walk (Wp.S7), from where we climb straight up to the summit in a little under 40 minutes (Wp.S8 146M).

The descent via the **Loma de Mulhacén** takes us back to Wp.3 via **Mulhacen II** (Wp.S09 161M) and numerous shortcuts, notably at Wp.S10 191M and, 600 metres later, Wp.S11.

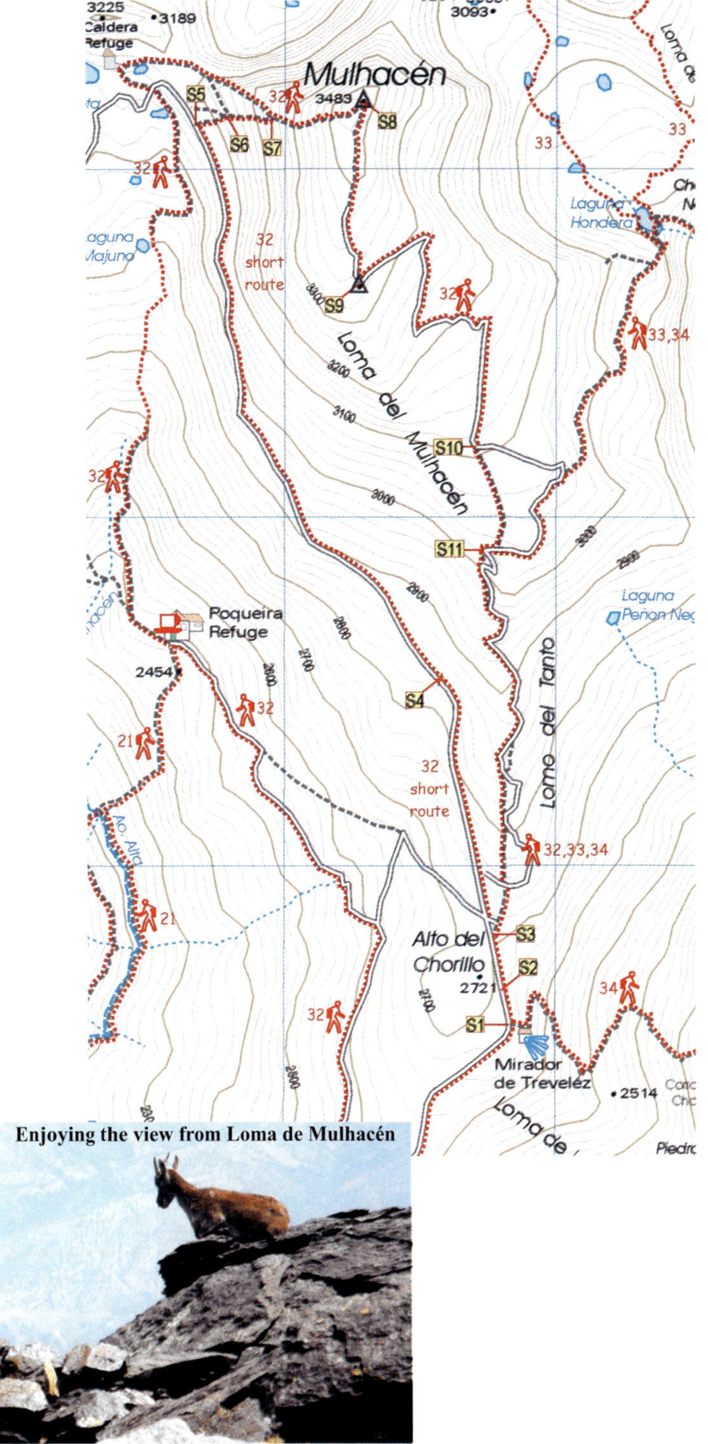

Enjoying the view from Loma de Mulhacén

Although this is essentially one walk devised as a way up the Sierra Nevada's third highest peak, the **Alcazaba**, I have split it in two because I did not want what is indisputably a tough outing in its entirety to discourage those of you of a more promenading bent from doing the easy bit to **Siete Lagunas**. This cluster of small lakes enjoys almost cult status amongst local hikers, largely I suspect because the place is so difficult to reach. I know experienced walkers who embarked on the classic ascent from **Trevélez** (Walk 34), only to give up at the foot of the last climb. And often as not, those who do get to the top are too knackered to properly appreciate the fabled spot. But catch the early bus from **Capileira** to the **Mirador de Trevélez/Alto del Chorillo** and suddenly **Siete Lagunas** becomes a lot more accessible. Indeed, it is so very accessible that when I got there, I thought, "Hang on, this can't be it, it's got to be further than this". Thereafter, if you're catching the evening bus back, you've got at least five hours for exploring the lakes, picnicking, and lounging about looking nonchalant as red-faced ramblers labour up the **Chorreras Negras** waterfall.

The main loop up to the **Alcazaba** is something else. It is by far the wildest walk in the book and is really only for dedicated peak-baggers and people who like to get off the beaten track - right off, there aren't any! There are patches of trodden path (possibly more than I saw since when I went up there I was knee deep in snow much of the time), but it would be irresponsible to recommend the route to anyone without experience of walking in wild places at high altitudes. Treat it as an off-path itinerary and you may be agreeably surprised by moments of easy walking. Set off expecting a neatly tailored trail and you'll be in trouble.

There are two ways up the **Alcazaba** from **Siete Lagunas**. We opted for the tough way up via what locals call the **Peñon del Globo** 'Colaero' (which I take to be an elision of *coladero*, a narrow path or pass) and the easy way down via the **Loma de Culo Perro**, though 'tough' and 'easy' are very relative terms in such wild terrain. There is no point at which we flirt with manifestly dangerous drops or anything like that, but it's very rough throughout, and there are long spells without any cairns let alone waymarks to guide us. Good visibility is essential. Don't even think about it if the forecast is a bit dubious. Thoroughly discouraged? If not, it's probably the sort of walk you'd appreciate, because, of course, all I've said above about rough, tough, pathless terrain constitutes the principal appeal of this itinerary. There's every chance that you'll find yourself alone up there (another reason not to take risks with the weather), which is rarely the case on **Mulhacén**.

By way of comparison with **Mulhacén**, the views are as good if not better, and the walking is infinitely rougher but less exhausting as the very steep bit is briefer. It's also a less monotonous climb. In fact some might wish it were a little more monotonous as we are so busy concentrating on the walking and the pathfinding throughout that we have to take time to stop and enjoy the views. If you're debating which to do for your first 3000 metre summit, opt for the **Mulhacén** as being tamer and less isolated. If all those discouraging adjectives above encourage you, well, the sky's the limit!

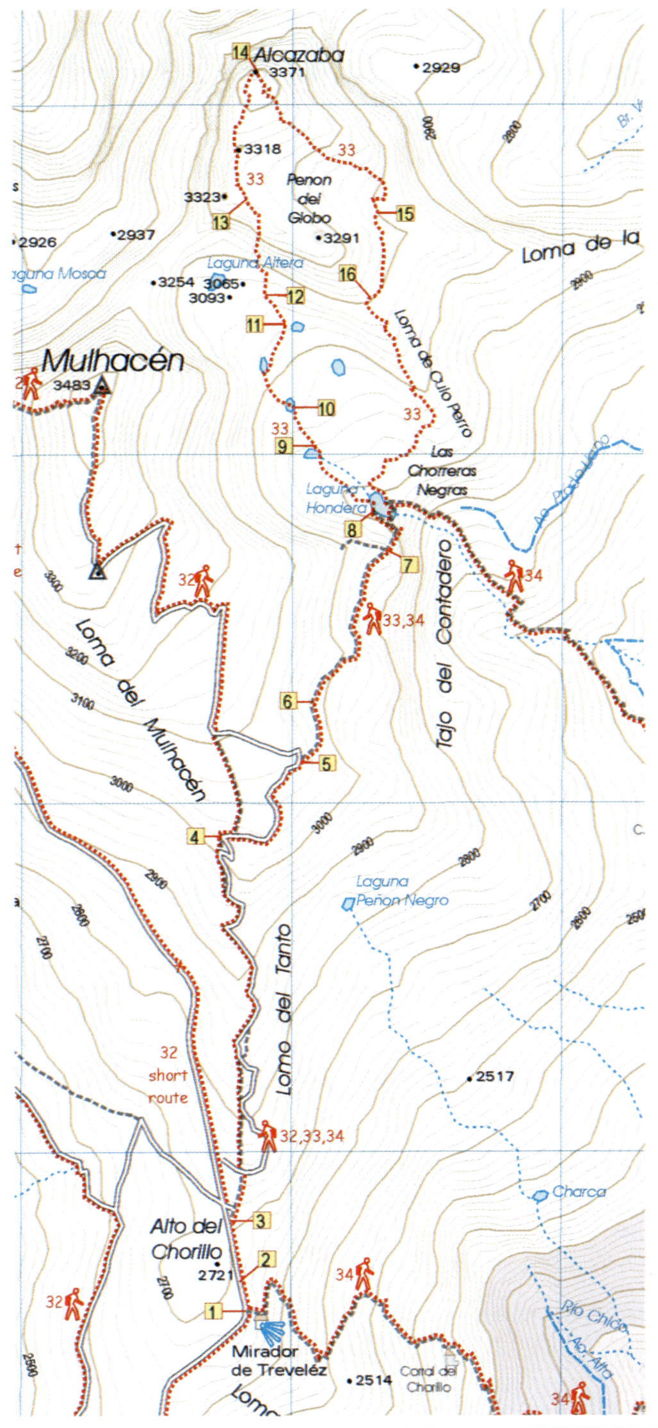

14 Alcazaba
3371
2929
3318
33
33
Penon del Globo
3323
13
15
2926
2937
3291
Loma de la
Laguna Altera
16
3254 3065
12
3093
11
Laguna Mosca
Mulhacén
3483
Loma de Culo Perro
10
33
33
9
Las Chorreras Negras
Laguna Hondera
8
7
34
Loma del Mulhacén
32
33,34
Tajo del Contadero
6
5
4
3000
2900
Laguna Peñon Negro
3000
Loma del Tanto
2517
32
short route
2800
2700
2600
Charca
32,33,34
3
Alto del Chorillo
2
2721
34
Río Chico
1
32
34
Mirador de Treveléz
2514
Corral del Chorillo
Loma
34

    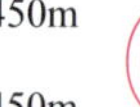  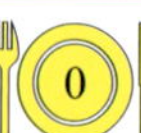

Ticket office and bus stop, Capileira

Access by bus:
This is a summer and autumn walk since it relies upon the seasonal **Mirador de Trevélez/Alto del Chorillo** bus from **Capileira** (10 euros return, 6 one way). Only the first bus in the morning and the last in the evening go beyond **Hoya del Portillo** or the **Mirador de Puerto Molina**

It's essential that you book in advance, either by phone (671 564 406 or 958 763 090) (best enlist a Spanish speaker for this task) or in person at the **Servicio de Interpretacion de Altas Cumbres** office on the A4129 in **Capileira** (open Wednesday to Sunday 10am-2pm and 5pm-7pm, though the mobile phone number is still valid for Monday and Tuesday). This office can also tell you about snow conditions and weather forecasts. The morning bus leaves at 8, 8.30, or 9 depending on the day of the week and whether a large group has booked it for a particular time. If the bus is not fully booked, those who have booked may be asked to pay the difference, usually only one or two euros a head.

Access by car/bus:
If, as is sometimes the case, there is no return bus in the evening, or you prefer not to be tied to somebody else's timetable, it's possible to buy your tickets in **Capileira**, drive up to **Hoya del Portillo** (see **Pista Forestal 3**, Appendix A), then pick up the bus at the barrier and return at your leisure on foot. I've done this three times over the years. It's a practical option, but not one I'd recommend wholeheartedly, as it is a dull walk down from the **Alto del Chorrillo**.

For both itineraries, I'd recommend taking it easy at the start. When you've just been plonked down at 2700 metres, the thin air can make even a modest climb seem uncommonly arduous.

The route between Wps. 1-3

From the bus drop off point (Wp.1 0M), we continue along the **Carretera de Veleta**, passing a sign and wayposted *sendero local* that climbs to the left onto the heights of 'Alto del Chorillo' (Wp.2). 175 metres later, at a junction with a signposted track that forks left to the **Poqueira** refuge, we leave the **Carretera de Veleta** and fork right (Wp.3 6M) on an unmarked path climbing to the north, which crosses the faint remains of a dirt track 300 metres later.

This old dirt track (laid by surveyors working on **Mulhacén** in the nineteenth century) and its shortcut paths are fairly vital for us. If we stick to the shortcuts we'll end up on **Mulhacén** rather than the **Alcazaba**, but you feel a bit foolish ignoring them altogether. In theory, one could just count the shortcuts until the point at which we leave the path and stay on the track, but since at least one of the shortcut paths is obscure and easily missed, I prefer to identify the key spot by describing it in detail. Depending on which you notice and which you count, we depart from the **Mulhacén** path at the third, fourth or fifth shortcut, around 40 minutes and nearly three kilometres from our starting point.

The key features to look out for are a steep scree covered escarpment up to our left and, down to our left, the continuation of the **Carretera de Veleta** track, which has been obscured from view hitherto. When you see the escarpment and the track below, the next shortcut cuts across two bends in quick succession as it climbs towards a small outcrop of rock with a short blade like protrusion at its western end. We can take the shortcut across the bends, but when the path leaves the track to climb to the outcrop of rock (Wp.4 44M), we stay on the track, which is much wider and smoother at this point. Heading east, then following the track as it curves round to the north, we reach a waist high, cone shaped cairn with a red plastic post stuck in the middle of it (Wp.5 54M). This cairn is unmistakable as there's nothing else like it around here.

At this point, we leave the track and fork right, initially off path but on easy, stony ground heading northeast along a line of knee high cairns, promptly bringing into view off to our left the rocky outcrop of the **Peñon del Globo** and, immediately behind it though almost indistinguishable from this perspective, the **Alcazaba**.

Laguna Hondera

Following an increasingly clear path, we descend into the first of two broad basin-like coombs in the flank of the **Loma de Mulhacén**, from where we already have fabulous views toward the head of the **Trevélez** valley. After a gentle descent, the path peters out in debris at the top of a meltwater channel (Wp.6 62M), but resumes 75 metres to the northeast. A slightly steeper descent brings us into the second basin for an easy traverse to its northern rim, from where **Laguna Hondera** is visible (Wp.7) and we have a clearer view of the looming

7 Lagunas & Peñon del Globo from Wp.7

cliffs of **Peñon del Globo** to the north.

A steady, slightly skittery descent brings us down to a large windbreak (dozens of which are scattered about the lagoons) on the southern side of **Laguna Hondera** (Wp.8 85M).

If this is your final objective, it's now simply a question of footling about and enjoying yourselves, exploring the lakes as far as taste and time dictate. For the rest of us, it is the occasion for a bit of the old girding up of loins, because this is where the real walking begins.

(b) **Alcazaba** (summary data includes **Alto del Chorrillo** to **Siete Lagunas**)

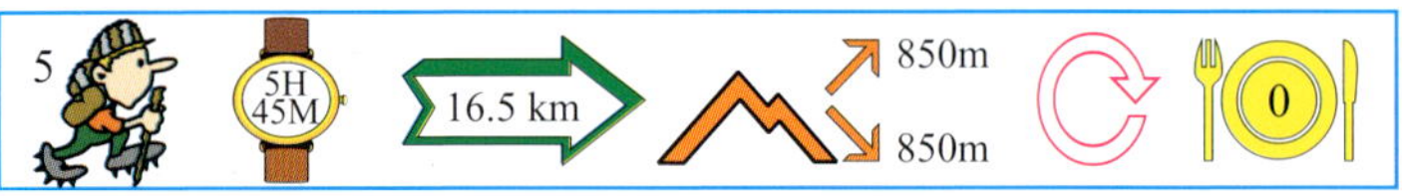

From the **Laguna Hondera** windbreak (Wp.8 85M), we head northwest across the tufty turf and marshy ground behind the lake, then climb gently across scree, following the watercourse feeding the *laguna* and aiming for the obvious dip between the tail end of **Mulhacén** and the bulky swell of **Peñon del Globo**. We cross the watercourse at a second area of marshy land (Wp.9 93M) then climb more steeply on a faint trodden way (more readily discernible from a distance than when you're actually on it) to a second lake (Wp.10 101M).

The temptation here is to leave the lake on our right and climb straight up the waterspill channel behind it. At least, that was the temptation I succumbed to (as anyone using a GPS will see from the trackfile) and it is one to be resisted. Instead, bear right below the lake and head north, toward the **Peñon del Globo**, skirting the rocks dividing this *laguna* from the next, which is invisible from this perspective. A little under 500 metres away, you will find a nine foot green, orange and white post. From the post (Wp.11 113M), we proceed to the northwest, following yet another of the myriad watercourses feeding the *lagunas*, at which point you should start to see the regular cairns that guide us up the **Colaero**, a steep corridor of scree and debris to the west of **Peñon del Globo**.

At the top of the watercourse (Wp.12 120M), we bear right, heading in a more northerly direction toward the **Peñon del Globo**, possibly on a faint trodden way (though I can't vouch for it as this was where the snow kicked in), soon bringing the diminutive **Laguna Altera** into view down to our left.

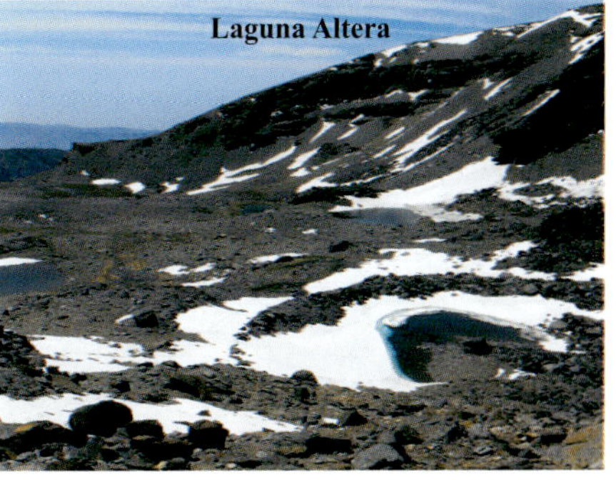
Laguna Altera

Once we are directly above **Laguna Altera**, cairns and intermittent patches of trodden way take us up through a maze of scree and rubble, directly to the west of the **Peñon del Globo**.

Climbing steeply, but never precariously, we reach the foot of the **Peñon del Globo** crags, where the gradient steepens appreciably, though you might not appreciate it, despite the fact that we are now following a clear trodden way, zigzagging up the remaining 100 metres of the **Colaero**.

At length, very great length, with great sighs of relief all round, and possibly a few gasps, too, we pass below the overhanging rocks at the top of the **Colaero** and emerge at the head of the **Meseta de las Borregas** (Wp.13 156M), which isn't really a *meseta* at all, but rather another broad coomb, from where the summit of the **Alcazaba** is clearly visible.

The view north from the top

We now contour round the head of the *meseta* (you may do this quicker than me - knee deep in snow again) for a final easy climb (N) across rough scree onto the summit (Wp.14 178M).

The peak itself is a slightly scruffy affair of jagged rock topped with a small cairn. There's nothing majestic, monolithic or monumental about it. But the views! It's one of those jobs where anymore birdseye and you'd be a fish finger.

I mentioned in the introduction that we take the easy way back to **Siete Lagunas**. It's easy in that the walking is never arduous. Pathfinding is not really a problem, either, though there are no paths. The difficulty I found is that local maps and descriptions imply there is a single, coherent and straightforward route over the **Loma del Culo Perro**. There ain't. There are at least four of them as far as I could work out, all haphazardly marked with cairns in their later stages. I make no claims therefore for this being the best route. But given that it's the one I found, I suspect it's the most obvious.

The initial descent is unmarked, but relatively straightforward, as we simply head southeast, descending into the **Meseta de las Borregas**, aiming for the lip where the coomb appears to drop off a cliff, our crossing point over the **Loma de Culo Perro** being just to the east of the main rise of the **Peñon del**

Globo. Picking our way across the scree and rocks and taking advantage of the occasional patches of gravel, we cross increasingly commodious terrain. At the bottom of the *meseta*, where there's a little patch of pasture, we bear round to the right, climbing (S) toward a pass at the eastern end of **Peñon del Globo**, where we find the first cairns of our return route (Wp.15 221M).

Following the cairns and steering clear of the high ground, we contour round the base of the **Peñon** for nearly 600 metres until **Laguna Hondera** comes into view again (Wp.16 233M). Shadowing a line of tall cairns that lie off to our left, we head southeast, descending gently along the **Loma de Culo Perro** toward a point where it looks like we're going to tip off a cliff. In fact, as we descend, the *loma* tapers rather than tips, allowing us to gradually curve round to the south, back toward the lagoon, eventually crossing the watercourse just east of the lagoon to rejoin our outward route near the windbreak (253M). We now follow our outward route back to the start, taking care at Wp.7 not to stray onto the path that climbs on the right to the **Mulhacén**.

Optional return to **Hoya del Portillo** from the **Mirador de Trevélez/Alto del Chorillo**
(1 walker, 1¼ hours, 6.2km, descents 500 metres)

If you're returning to **Hoya del Portillo** on foot, the next several thousand steps could not be more straightforward, nor a lot more wearisome, as we simply carry on along the **Carretera de Veleta** for nearly five kilometres, the route abbreviated by a single shortcut a little under a kilometre from Wp.1, doing our best to enjoy the easy walking, airy feel, and some decent views over the **Trevélez** and **Poqueira** valleys. At the head of a firebreak below the **Mirador de Puerto Molina** (Wp.17 55M), we turn right and descend along the firebreak for 100 metres toward the **Rules** dam. We then turn left on a PR wayposted path (Wp.18 58M) that descends through the woods to a Y junction (Wp.19 69M), where we bear right, sticking with the main waymarked path rather than the shortcut, a pattern that is repeated twice in the next 600 metres before we emerge in the **Hoya del Portillo** car park (Wp.20 75M).

Bit of a marathon this one, but amply rewarded by a real sense of wilderness above **Campiñuela** and access to one the Alpujarras' most celebrated sites, the **Seven Lagoons**. Needless to say, the views are stunning throughout. So's the climbing! The upper reaches of the **Río Culo Perro** (Wp.5) are worth visiting even if you don't do the final climb to the lagoons.

For an easier approach to **Siete Lagunas**, see Walk 33.

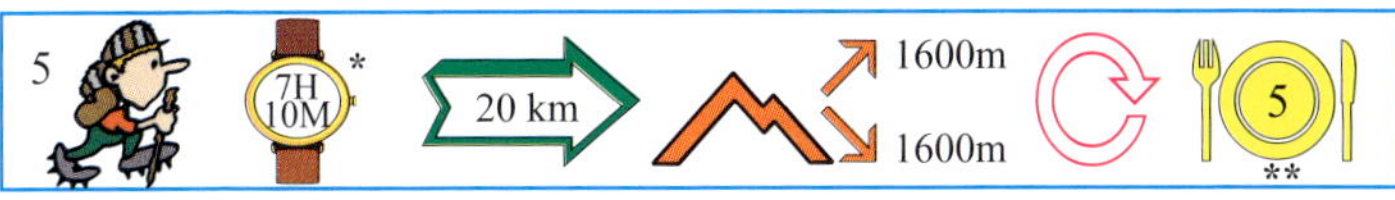

* 7 hours 10 mins for the full circuit, but given the distance and climbing involved, allow 10 hours

** in **Trevélez**

Laguna Hondera:
7 hours 10 mins, but likewise, allow 8 hours

The start is the same as for Walk 24, but since we don't return via the **Río Trevélez**, we start from the **Plaza Barrío Medio**. Parking is limited in the square itself, but there's usually plenty of room further back on the road down towards the **Barrío Bajo**.

Taking the narrow street past the excellent **Panadería Federico**, we turn left at the 'comidas/camas/jamones' sign, right on **Calle Horno**, left at the *lavadero*, then take the first path on the left (Wp.1 0M). We then follow Walk 24 to Wp.3 (42M) and bear left at the 'Campiñuela/7 Lagunas' signpost to climb a clear path marked with cairns, wayposts and red/green waymarks.

Climbing steadily for fifteen minutes, we cross two gated fences, after which the path bears north, going through another gate and crossing a marshy area before climbing to the **Acequia Gorda** (Wp.4 86M). We follow the *acequia* for 150 metres then bear left at a waypost to climb steadily through recently planted pine to the scattering of rocks and boulders at **Los Posteros**.

Bearing right at the upper limit of **Los Posteros**, we cross another replanted area, then bear left to climb steadily up **Prado Largo**, gradually coming in sight of the **Lomas de Mulhacén** and **Alcazaba**, and the **Chorreras Negras** waterfall feeding the **Río Culo Perro**. We then bear right above **Prado Largo** for a gentler climb to the small cabin and large threshing circle at **Cortijo de la Campiñuela** (Wp.5 133M).

The path continues past the ruined walls of the **Campiñuela** byre (NW), crossing a tiny rivulet above a small reservoir.

The signpost after Wp.3

Looking south, near the start of the walk

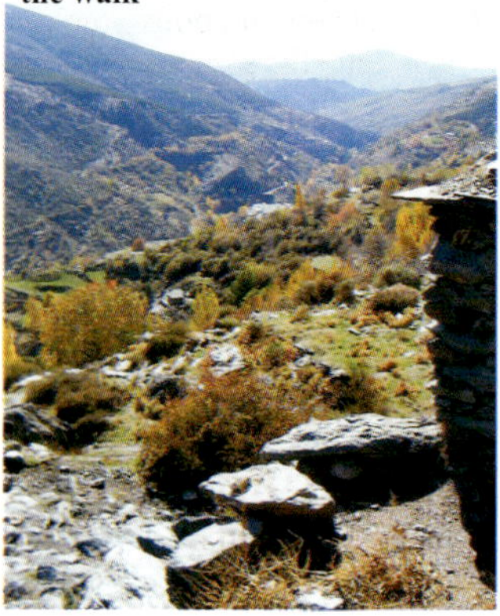

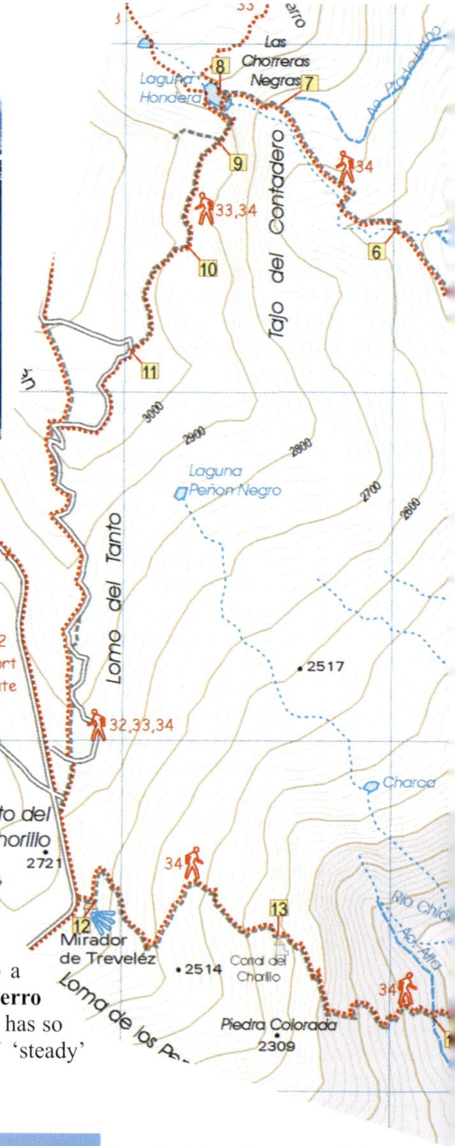

It then climbs (at first steadily then more gently) to cross a narrow torrent, after which another steady climb leads to the **Río Culo Perro** just above a narrow dike (Wp.6 165M), sometimes called **El Vertedero**. We can either follow the path till it crosses the river fifty metres later or (as mapped) cross the dyke and head upriver toward the **Tajo del Contadero** cliffs to pick up a fainter stony path climbing away from the river toward the **Chorreras**.

Now we follow the cairns up to a minor affluent of the **Culo Perro** (Wp.7 197M) where a climb that has so far been at the upper limit of 'steady' suddenly turns 'steep' - and nasty!

Trevélez, and the Loma de Mulhacén

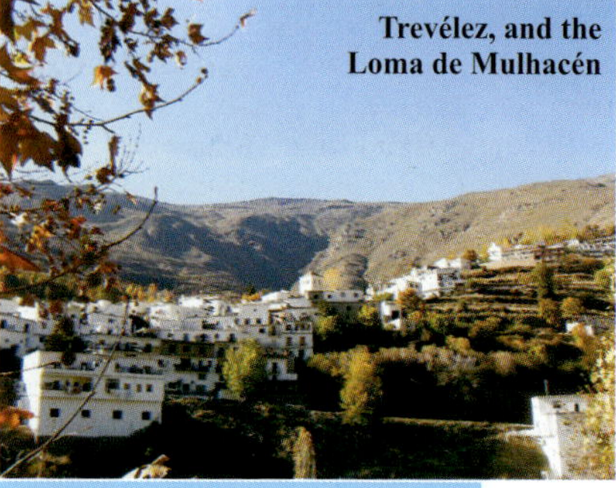

But don't be discouraged; it's tough, but not as tough as it looks. Crossing the affluent, we climb alongside the cascade, looking out for the cairns where the path disappears under rockfalls, and soon (certainly sooner than seems possible from Wp.7) come to **Laguna Hondera** (Wp.8 216M), the

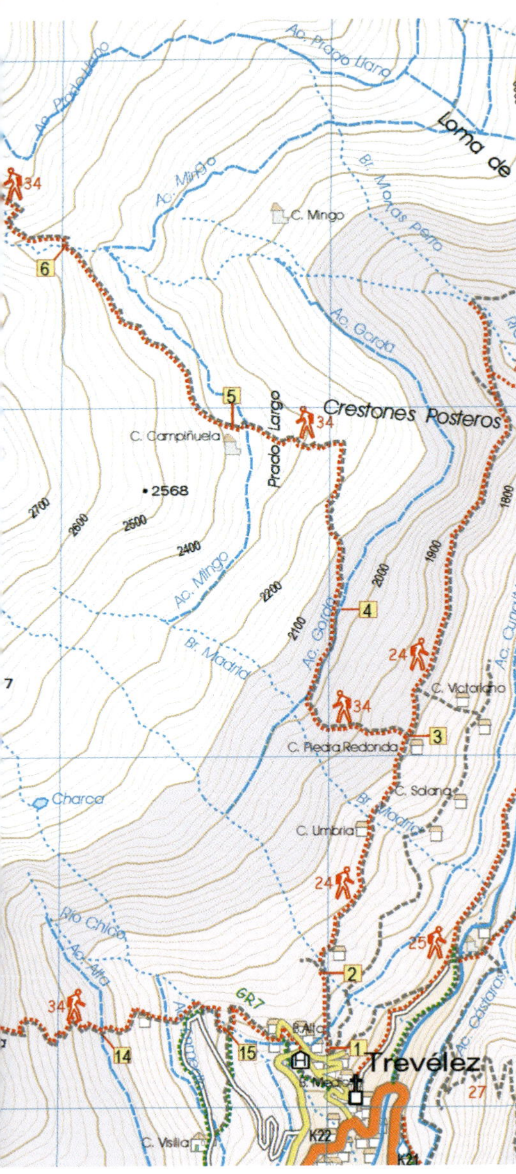

largest and lowest of the seven lagoons tucked into the glaciation cirque defined by the **Lomas de Mulhacén** and **Alcazaba**.

We can either return by the same route or, if you can face climbing another 200 metres, make a loop via the **Loma de Mulhacén** and the **Mirador de Trevélez**.

LOMA DE MULHACÉN & MIRADOR DE TRVÉLEZ LOOP

On the south-east tip of the ridge round the cirque, there's a tall thin cairn. At first glance there's no way up to this, but in fact to the south-east of the **Laguna Hondera**, behind a large rock and a small windbreak (commonly known, a tad rosily to my mind, as the **Refugio Natural de Siete Lagunas**), a very faint 'way' that gradually becomes something approximating a path, does wind up past the tall thin cairn to another fatter cairn built on a large rock (Wp.9 227M).

Ignoring the clear path climbing to the right along the **Cuesta** or **Cuerda de Resuello**, we head south-west from the fat cairn to cross the first of two shallow depressions or *hoyas* that lead to the **Llanos del Mulhacén**. There's neither path nor cairns to begin with, so you'll have to take my word for this, but after a couple of hundred metres you'll come to the first of a series of cairns marking the way and a slightly clearer path. You'll also probably see plenty of *cabras montés*.

Bear right as you cross this first *hoya*, staying near its upper/western limit to traverse the higher patches of grass just below the shallow cliffs, where you should find the first cairns. Maintaining a south-westerly direction, we cross a

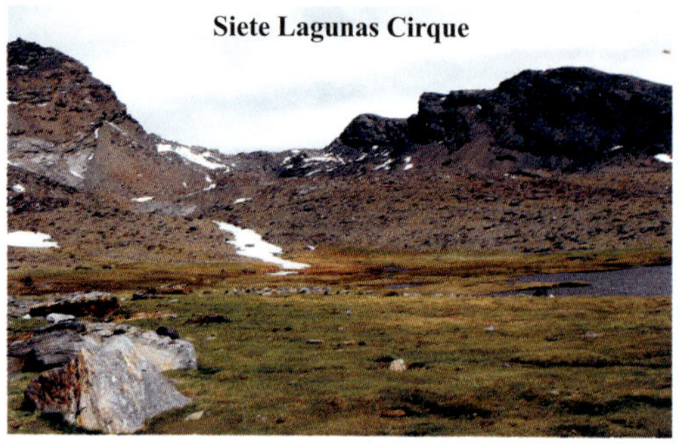

broad grassy stretch on the far side of the *hoya* to pass two cairns marking a reasonably clear trail which climbs slightly before bearing left up to a large cone-shaped cairn.

The path virtually disappears again here, but faint traces and a series of tall cairns indicate the way out of the first *hoya* onto a ridge overlooking the second shallower and stonier *hoya* (Wp.10 243M).

The stones are smaller here, so the trodden way is slightly clearer, and is also well marked with cairns. Again we circle round the head of the *hoya*, climbing gently to its highest recess, where a steeper path, just discernible from Wp.8, climbs out of the *hoya* in a SSE direction onto a scree slope where it disappears. We bear right here and follow the cairns off-path (W) as the slope gradually levels out and leads up to the **Mulhacén** branch of the **Carretera de Veleta** (Wp.11 260M). We then follow this track (see Walk 32 for a generic description) to the **Mirador de Trevélez** (Walk 32 Wp.17).

At the *mirador*, which is identifiable by the lay-by where the Capileira bus pulls over, we leave the *carretera*, turning left to reach the top of the path (Wp.12 320M) down to **Trevélez** which is visible below us.

We then follow this path, ignoring both the tracks over the rocky ridge to the south (the **Loma de los Penoncillos**) AND, if you care for your knees, the various shortcuts (a 1300 metre descent in 3km really doesn't need shortcuts, as well).

The path is well wayposted, passing the abandoned *cortijo* and threshing circle of the **Corral del Chorillo** (Wp.13 370M), and crossing first an *acequia* (Wp.14 400M) then, a hundred metres below, a dirt track. It then descends to a restored *cortijo*, below which it crosses private land, passing three gates before emerging on another dirt track at a bend above two threshing circles. We take the wayposted path between the threshing circles for a final descent to the **GR7** (Wp.15 425M) five minutes from **Barrío Alto** in **Trevélez**.

a

abandonado	abandoned, in poor repair
abierto	open
acampamiento	camping
acantilado	cliff
acequia	water channel
agua	water
agua no potable	water (not drinkable)
agua potable	drinking water
alto	high
aparcamiento	parking
área recreativa	designated picnic spot; may have tables, water
arroyo	stream
autopista	main road, motorway
ayuntamiento	town hall

b

bajo	low
barranco	ravine
bocadillo	bread roll
bodegón	inn
bosque	wood

c

cabezo	peak, summit
cabra montés	mountain goat
calle	street
camino	trail, path, track
camino real	old donkey trail (lit. royal road)
camino cortado	road closed/blocked
carretera	main road
casa	house
casa rural	country house accommodation to let
cascada	waterfall
caserío	hamlet, village
cementario	cemetery
cerrado	closed
cerro	hill, mountain without a real peak
cerveza	beer
choza	shelter
clinica	clinic, hospital
colmena	bee hive
comida	food
cordillera	mountain range
correos	post office
cortijo	farmstead
costa	coast
coto privado de caza	private hunting area
Cruz Roja	Red Cross (medical aid)
cuesta	slope
cueva	cave
cumbre	summit

d

degollado	pass
derecha	right (direction)
desprendimiento	landslide

e

embalse	reservoir
ermita	chapel

f

farmacia	chemist
fiesta	holiday, celebration
finca	farm, country house
fuente	spring

g

gasolinera	petrol station
guagua	bus
Guardia Civil	police
guia	guide

h

hostal	hostel, accommodation
hoya	depression (geological)

i

iglesia	church
información	information
isla	island
izquierda	left (direction)

l

lago	lake
lavadero	laundry area (usually communal)
librería	bookshop
llano	plain
lluvioso	rainy
lomo	broad-backed ridge

m

mapa	map
mercado	market
mirador	lookout/viewing point
montaña	mountain

n

nublado	cloudy

o

oficina de turismo	tourist office

p

particular	private
peligroso	dangerous
pensión	guesthouse
pico	peak
pista	dirt road/track
pista forestal	forest road/track
playa	beach
plaza	square
policia	police
pozo	well
prohibido el paso	no entry

| *puente* | bridge |
| *puerto* | port, mountain pass |

r

rambla	dry watercourse/riverbed
refugio	refuge, shelter
retama	broom-like shrub
río	river, stream
robledal	oak woods
roque	rock
ruta	route

s

salida	exit
senda	path, track
sendero	foot path
sierra	mountain range
sin salida	no through road/route

t

tajo	cliff, escarpment
tapas	bar snacks
tienda	shop
tinao	typical Alpujarran balcony/terrace
tipico	traditional bar/eating place
tormentoso	stormy
torre	tower
torrente	stream
tubería	water pipe

v

valle	valley
vega	meadow
ventoso	windy
vereda	path, lane
vivero	plant nursery, aboretum

z

| *zona recreativa* | recreation area |

APPENDICES

APPENDIX A

DIRT TRACK ACCESSING THE GR240 SENDERO SULAYR & WALKS IN THE HIGH MOUNTAINS

Having got through two clutches, a gear box, several universal joints, something vital and un-nameable related to the tie rod, and numerous sets of tyres in the last ten years, I've become a bit more circumspect about recommending off road driving, especially since our clients have told us hire cars aren't insured for dirt tracks.

But one of the principal appeals of mountains is that they don't readily accommodate themselves to the convenience of people and occasionally it's worth putting aside worries about your wallet in order to reach spectacular places. The following dirt tracks have been drivable for decades, were all driven in the course of updating this book, and SHOULD remain drivable for the foreseeable future. However, it's still worth making enquiries on the spot, either in tourist information offices, or from the Medio Ambiente workers (look out for their four wheel drive vehicles with a green blazon) who maintain the park and drive up the tracks every day.

(a) Pista Forestal 1 Lanjarón to Tello and Ventura - Walks 16 & 30

The track starts just before km6 of the A348 at the western end of **Lanjarón**, between the **Hotel Balneario** and **Restaurant El Frenazo**. Follow the signs for 'Tello' (until km13) and the 'Sendero Sulayr'. The first stretch is concreted, but it soon gives way to dirt, which is frequently very rough in the lower stages, but improves higher up.

- km 1 End of concrete, continue on dirt track for 'Tello'

- km 4.3 **Mirador Pallarin**

- km 6.4 **GR7** forks left, we fork right, passing **Fuente Pedro Calvo**

- km 13 Ignore 'Tello' branch on right and continue to left on main track for 'Ventura'

- km 14.4 Join **GR240 Sendero Sulayr**

- km 14.6 **GR240 Sendero Sulayr** branches left on minor track

- km 16.1 Chained branch to left at right hand hairpin bend, START OF WALK 16

- km 16.7 Last broad stretch before the track narrows and descends into the **Río Lanjarón Valley**, identifiable by two metal chain support posts beside a solitary pine tree, START OF WALK 30

(b) **Pista Forestal 2 Ermita de Padre Eterno** to **Puente Palo** - Walks 17 & 31

The track starts opposite the **Ermita del Padre Eterno**, which is 0.9km east of the **Soportújar** turning on the A4132. Until recently the first four kilometres were surfaced. At the time of writing, this is no longer the case, though the local authorities claim this stretch is due to be resurfaced. The signs indicating that the surface is in poor condition ('Firme en mal estado') refer to this first stretch. Follow the signs for the **Puente Palo Área Recreativa**.

- km 0.5 Cross the **GR7**

- km 2.4 Access on right to the **O.Sel.Ling Buddhist Centre**

- km 4.3 End of asphalt? Park authority *casa forestal* on right, minor branch on left to a horse riding centre.

- km 4.7 U bend, major branch on left, mapboard for the PR22, START OF WALK 17

- km 6.9 Turning on right into private property, Wp.2 of Walk 17

- km 10.6 Minor branch on right, Wp.13 of Walk 17

- km 10.8 **Puente Palo**

- km 11.2 *área recreativa*, START OF WALK 31

(c) **Pista Forestal 3 The Carretera de Veleta** from **Capileira to Hoya del Portillo** - Walks 19, 20, 21, 23, 32, & 33

Though never fully surfaced, this was once the highest road in Europe, and was open to vehicles until the 1990s. Happily, this is no longer the case, but the stretch up to **Hoya del Portillo**, which is still open to the public, remains extremely useful for accessing the Sierra Nevada's highest summits. The dirt track after km5 is much smoother than the asphalt that precedes it. The Carretera is the continuation of the A4129 above **Capileira**. Distances are counted from the coach park ('P Autocares') on the right directly above **Capileira**.

- km 1.5 Branch on the right for 'Cortijo Prado Toro'

- km 2.7 Branch on the left to **La Cebadilla**, ACCESS TO WALKS 19 & 20

- km 3.8 Branch on right signposted 'Área Recreativa 3km', ALTERNATIVE ACCESS TO WALK 23

- km 5 End of asphalt

- km 7.1 Branch on left, ACCESS TO WALK 21

- km 10.4 **Hoya del Portillo** car park, START OF WALK 32 AND ALTERNATIVE ACCESS TO WALK 33

ADDITIONAL STROLLS

A few extras that didn't really fit in with any of the walks or *pistas forestales* but seemed too good to ignore!

The Río Chico above Bayacas

From **Bayacas** bridge follow the left bank of the **Río Chico** (N). Pass under the main road bridge and climb to the left of the silt-dam for a pleasant picnic spot and some small plunge pools. If you're feeling more adventurous and energetic, continue up the right bank along rough goat trails littered with fallen trees to a high waterfall and a wilder glade. If you really want to get the blood moving, cross the glade to join a broader path winding up to a junction. Carry straight on for a vertiginous *acequia* path to source, <u>or</u> turn right for a threshing circle with fine views south over the valley and the **Sierra Lújar** and, north, up to **Puente Palo** and the **Loma de Cáñar**.

The Mirador de Poqueira

Hundreds of people stop here everyday, but few realise the views from the little watchtower along the ridge are even more dramatic. To be honest, few even notice the watchtower! 400 metres after the **Pampaneira** Fina station (in the direction of **Pitres**) take the rough path from the *mirador* along the ridge to the outcrop of rocks for giddying views of the gorge.

The Acequia de Cuna

A stroll that's also a paddle - providing there's water in the *acequia*; if there isn't the fun is dramatically diminished. We often walk alongside *acequia*s, here we walk <u>in</u> one. Take your plastic sandals. 10 metres south of the km23 sign on the **Trevélez-Busquístar** road, directly opposite the metal sign for the **Trevélez** campsite, a tiny path between two young plane trees climbs very steeply for about 15 metres to the *acequia*. For an easier access, take the path 75 metres further south where the road bears right. Follow the *acequia* south to the second large outcrop of rock, beyond which it has been abandoned, becoming increasingly overgrown, eventually petering out after a fence in the **Barranco de la Bina**. Return the same way, taking the alternative access path for an easier descent.

The best swimming pool in the Alpujarras

Two kilometres from the **Trevélez** bridge (in the direction of **Juviles**), park in the lay-by just after the **Barranco de los Castaños**. Take the path below the crash barriers before the next bend to descend to the river. At the Y-junction, bear left for a pleasant picnic/bathing spot under immense poplars, right for a deep swimming pool below the metal footbridge. **N.B.** Don't swim too near the waterfall on the off-chance that some debris might be pitched over.

THE ALPUJARRAS ON LINE

Times have changed since we first went to the Alpujarras and there is now a plethora of information on the internet about the region. Better still, it is not all posted by estate agents. The following sites have proved useful:

Ben and Rebecca at are doing sterling work in their efforts to put people like me out of business, offering free walks and a wealth of background material about itineraries throughout Andalusia:-

http://www.treksierranevada.com

Another distressingly good source of free **walks** both within and beyond our area is to be found at:-

http://www.topwalks.net

For local **bus timetables**, see:-

http://www.alsa.es

For **accommodation** with a broad range of customer-rated options:-

http://www.booking.com

For articles, trip reports, up to date information, and packages, see:-

http://www.sierra-nevada-news.com/

For a similar service including **weather** conditions, see:-

http://www.spanishhighs.co.uk

They also have a useful page describing the unmanned **refuges** of the Sierra Nevada:-

http://www.spanishhighs.co.uk/mountain-huts-refuges-sierra-nevada.php

The **Poqueira Refuge** has its own (Spanish) site featuring useful information on routes, services, and conditions (both for reaching the refuge and the high peaks), including webcam images of the area:-

http://refugiopoqueira.com

For detailed **forecasts** about conditions on the high peaks, see:-

http://www.mountain-forecast.com

For statistics about **seasonal norms** in the high places, see:-

http://www.yr.no/place/Spain/Andaluc%C3%ADa/Mulhac%C3%A9n/statistics.html

For a decent **general** site about the Alpujarras that doesn't appear to be set up with the express intention of flogging you stuff, see:-

http://www.alpujarras.eu

Twitchers should have a look at:-

http://www.birdwatchalpujarras.com

It's a commercial site promoting birdwatching tours, but it does what it says on the tin, too, and will give you an idea of what to expect even if you don't want to pay someone to show it to you.

If you're interested in the **GR240 Sendero Sulayr** touring the entire Sierra Nevada park, details are available on the regional government's website:-

www.juntadeandalucia.es/medioambiente/sulayr

The step-by-step description is only in Spanish, but since the itinerary is waymarked and signposted and follows dirt tracks for the most part, a simple list of toponyms and times should be more than adequate for following the route.

The following sites promoting individual accommodation options have gone out of their way to establish their rambler-friendly credentials:_

Bérchules   http://www.hotelberchules.com
http://casa-rural-el-paraje.blogspot.fr/

(The Bérchules Paraje blog is particularly recommended, full of background information, updates on weather damage to paths, and walk itineraries.)

Bubíon   http://www.aplaceinbubion.com
Busquístar   http://www.cortijosreyfini.com/
Nr. **Cádiar**   http://www.alqueriamorayma.com/en/
Capileira   http://www.mountaincortijo.com
Mecina   http://www.hoteldemecina.com.es
Pórtugos   http://www.cortijoopazo.com

BUSES & TAXIS

Alsina Graells,   www.alsinagraells.es   958 185 480
the main bus company

La Tahá Bus, the local company   950 510 800

Getting a taxi can be a challenge. If the harvest needs bringing in, something more lucrative turns up, or the driver's simply busy in a bar, service may be suspended. At the same time, restaurant owners and complete strangers have been known to offer lifts to stranded tourists, and hitching is always an option.

Juan Funes 958 785 331/619 957 817. Local & landrover taxi based in **Órgiva**. No English, but says he can be contacted through his English speaking friend Eladio at the Hotel Taray (958 784 525). By Alpujarran standards a model of reliability, though sometimes absent in Granada.

The best way of finding transport is to ask on the spot. That said, other taxi numbers you might try, are as follows:

Bérchules   958 753 061 & 958 764 047
Bubíon   958 763 148
Busquístar   958 766 036
Cadíar   958 768 703
Capileira   958 763 125
Cástaras   958 753 035
Lanjarón   608 849 585 & 958 770 097 & 958 770 703 & 659 849 768
Órgiva   958 785 331 & 619 957 817 & 958 785 487
Pampaneira 958 763 002
Pitres   659 111 745 & 958 766 196 & 654 520 140 & 958 766 005

Pórtugos   958 766 006
Trevélez   609 911 657 & 958 858 727

Nevedensis   www.nevednesis.com   958 763 127
 - local information about the Alpujarras

Tourist Offices
Lanjarón   958 770 282
Pampaneira   958 763 301

Turismo Alpujarra   958 784 495   958 784 484
c/Lora Ramayo 17/18400 Órgiva   alta-alpujarra@asociacion-tierra.org

National Meteorological Institute   906 365 365
Local long-range forecasts are posted outside the Nevedensis office in
Pampaneira.

Emergencies
Emergency co-ordination centre Andalucía   112
Emergency Civil Guard   062
Red Cross   913 354 545
Casa de Socorro   958 770 002
(local medical emergencies)

Sierra Nevada Administrative Centre
   958 026 310   958 026 300
National Park Visitors' Centres
(weekends)   958 340 625 / 958 763 127
Spain's national parks website   www.mma.es/parques

A pamphlet of local addresses, telephone numbers and festival dates for the
Alpujarras is available from:
Tursimo Andaluz SA   952 836 369   952 838 785
Centro Internacional de Turismo de Andalucia
Crta. Nac. 340 – Cádiz-Málaga km 189.6
29600 Marbella.

For detailed information/updates about the GR142 - Paco   958 784 340

… about the GR7 - Jesus Espinosa   659 109 662
(if you can't get through, contact him at the Nevedensis office)

Lanjarón Spa (balneario):   958 771 070   958 770 137
   www.aguadelanjaron.es

Horse-riding from Trevélez
Rutas a Caballo   958 858 601

For a small but carefully chosen selection of books in English, try Atenea on Calle Lora Tamayo (behind the bus stop) in **Órgiva**. Below is a selection of currently available publications available from bookshops or from amazon.co.uk :-

MAPS

Alpujarras Tour & Trail Super-Durable Map (3rd edition)
Discovery Walking Guides Ltd November 2012
ISBN 9781904946885
£8.99

BOOKS

South From Granada (pub. Penguin Modern Classics 2008)
Gerald Brenan (Author), Chris Stewart (Introduction)
Paperback: 336 pages
ISBN 9780141189321
£6.99 paperback and kindle

Walking in Andalucia (includes 6 routes in the Alpujarras)
Guy HunterWatts (Author)
Paperback: 288 pages
Publisher: Santana Books; 7th Revised edition edition (9 Jan 2012)
ISBN 9788489954922
£23.99

Hiking in Spain (Lonely Planet Walking Guides 4th ed 2010)
(includes 3 routes in the Alpujarras)
Stuart Butler (Author)
Paperback: 396 pages
ISBN 9781741044706
£15.99

Lionel Aggett's Andalucia and Las Alpujarras: An Artist in Lemon Country (Halsgrove 2002)
Lionel Aggett (Author)
Hardcover: 144 pages
ISBN 9781841141954
£24.95

Driving Over Lemons: An Optimist in Andalucia (Sort Of Books 2009)
Chris Stewart (Author)
Paperback: 304 pages
ISBN 9780956003805
£8.99 paperback, £4.79 kindle edition